continued . . .

"*The Courage to Be Rich* combines practical financial advice with an understanding of the fears a lot of people face when confronted with the bottom line."   —*Good Morning America*

"[Suze Orman] knows how to work a crowd as she preaches the gospel of abundance. . . . Her enthusiasm is infectious."
—*The Cleveland Plain Dealer*

"Her chapter on the newest savings perk, the Roth IRA, is one of the clearest explanations around. . . . Read *The Courage to Be Rich*."
—*Fort Worth Star-Telegram*

"Orman, a self-proclaimed financial therapist who eschews extravagant clothes and expensive jewelry, has now devoted her career to making sure middle America doesn't get taken advantage of the same way she did. She advises people never to pay commissioned brokers or financial planners and encourages them to get smart and take control of their own money."   —**The Associated Press**

"Well-organized and easy to understand."
—*Austin American-Statesman*

ALSO BY SUZE ORMAN

You've Earned It, Don't Lose It

The 9 Steps to Financial Freedom

The Road to Wealth

THE COURAGE TO BE RICH

CREATING A LIFE
OF MATERIAL AND
SPIRITUAL ABUNDANCE

SUZE ORMAN

RIVERHEAD BOOKS

NEW YORK

Riverhead Books
Published by The Berkley Publishing Group
A division of Penguin Putnam Inc.
375 Hudson Street
New York, New York 10014

This publication is designed to provide accurate and authoritative information in regard to the subject matter covered. It is published with the understanding that the publisher and author are not engaged in rendering legal, accounting, or other professional services. If legal advice or other professional advice, including financial, is required, the services of a competent professional person should be sought.

Certified Financial Planner® is a federally registered mark owned by the Certified Financial Planner Board of Standards, Inc.

The term Realtor® is a collective membership mark owned by the National Association of Realtors® and refers to a real estate agent who is a member thereof.

Copyright © 1999, 2002 by Suze Orman
Book design by Deborah Kerner
Cover design by Kiley Thompson
Photograph of the author © Dana Fineman/Sygma

Published simultaneously in Canada.

First Riverhead hardcover edition: March 1999
First revised Riverhead trade paperback edition: January 2002
Riverhead trade paperback ISBN: 1-57322-906-7

Visit our website at www.penguinputnam.com

The Library of Congress has catalogued the Riverhead hardcover edition as follows:
Orman, Suze.
The courage to be rich : creating a life of material and spiritual
abundance / by Suze Orman
p. cm.
Includes index.
ISBN 1-57322-125-2
1. Finance, Personal—Psychological aspects. 2. Finance,
Personal—Moral and ethical aspects. 3. Wealth—Psychological
aspects. 4. Wealth—Moral and ethical aspects. I. Title.
HG179.O756   1999   98-55935 CIP
332.024'001'9—dc21

Printed in the United States of America

10 9 8 7 6 5 4 3 2 1

This book is dedicated to my most precious mama,

who has inspired me with her acts of courage

and richness. All that I am I owe to you.

ACKNOWLEDGMENTS

♦

After this, my third book, I now know without a shadow of a doubt that no one writes a book in a vacuum, that the process itself is a rich and courageous one, one that involves more people than one can ever count. I would like to thank all those whose names I know, and also all those who, behind the scenes, believed in and participated in the writing of this book.

First, I would like to thank my dear friend and collaborator Cheryl Merser, who brought more to this project than she ever imagined she could and stayed the course from beginning to end. Her family, Michael and Jenna Shnayerson, were, in their way, very much a part of the process, and I thank them as well. May we be friends forever, and collaborators just as long.

Also first—my thanks to my editor, Julie Grau, who has the most extraordinary mind, heart, and stamina of almost anyone I have ever met. This book really is our book, my friend, and I so hope you are proud of it. You are the best, and I feel blessed to work with you.

To my agent and mentor, Binky Urban, who has guided me impeccably on this journey—what an inspiring ride it has been. I love and respect you so very much. I knew for sure God loved me when I was sent to you.

To Sandi Mendelson. Stop the presses for this lady. Sandi, my publicist and buddy, stood behind me from the start, and she is still standing right there, and, boy, do I love it. There are no better than you, my dear, and I hope that you always remember that.

To the people at Riverhead, my total love and thanks for your caring, your attention to detail, and your commitment—all of which has totally overwhelmed me. To Phyllis Grann, Susan Petersen, Marilyn Ducksworth, Cathy Fox, Barbara O'Shea, and all the people from sales and marketing who were involved in getting the word out. To the dedicated and tireless Hanya Yanagihara, Elizabeth Wagner, Kim Seidman, Tricia Martin, Catharine Lynch, Ann Spinelli, Kiley Thompson, Lisa Amoroso, Claire Vaccaro, Bill Peabody, Rachel Krieger, and all the other talented, hardworking people in design and production who were involved in getting the book out.

How can I ever thank the team at Harpo enough for sending my message into millions of homes? To the most creative and courageous production talent in the world, Dianne Atkinson Hudson, Katy Murphy Davis, Kelly Groves-Olson, Ray "Bug" Dotch, Garrett Moehring, and Suzanne Hayward, and most important, to Oprah herself, who has truly changed my life forever.

Incredible thanks and gratitude go right from my heart to the hearts of my QVC family—all the hosts and everyone at QVC and Q Direct who has supported me from the very beginning, especially Karen Fonner, my dear, dear friend who always, always believed, long before anyone else did.

I would also like to thank my PBS team: Alan Foster, Gerry Richman, Larkin McPhee, Tedd Tramaloni, Erika Herrmann, and everyone at KTCA who backed my PBS specials and helped to bring the words of my books to television. Hasn't it been the best?

To Carol Bruckner at ICM Lecture, one of my favorite people in life. We're just starting to cook, my dear. And to Jenna Lamond at ICM, who never misses a trick.

To Anne Heller, my editor and friend at *Self* magazine, who brings my words and thoughts to life every month. Anne, you have such a golden mind; always let it shine, my dear.

A very special thank-you to those who read this book in manuscript and added the wisdom of their hearts and minds: Janet Dobrovolny, Gail Mitchell, Barry Pickers, Frederick Hertz, and John Claghorn;

Ann C. Diamond, Esq., of Bronstein, Van Veen & Bronstein, P.C. (NY), for her careful reading of the section "For Love *and* Money"; Kenneth Grau, Esq., and Edward T. Braverman, Esq., of Braverman & Associates, P.C. (NY), and Howard Grossman, Esq., of Goldstick, Weinberger, Feldman & Grossman, P.C. (NY), for lending their expertise to "Buying a Home"; and Ira G. Bogner, Esq., of Proskauer Rose LLP (NY), for his insights into "Thinking Ahead."

My many thanks to the people who shared or inspired the case studies in this book, and with these thanks goes the hope that I was able to help.

My gratitude to the wonderful people at The Literary Guild, Doubleday Book Club, and Bantam Audio for showing their courage in supporting this book.

Thanks again to Esther Margolis of Newmarket Press, who started the ball rolling, and to Chip Gibson and everyone at Crown, who took the ball and ran with it.

To my brothers, who mean so very, very much to me. As I think about both of you, all I can do is say thank you for your love and support. Please know that I can feel it all the time.

To Melissa Howden, who stuck by my side and who over the years has helped me to find my own courage and stay focused on the real goal. What a gift you are to this world. And to Mary Bourn, whose infectious laughter and heart of gold have touched all those lucky enough to know her, especially me. May the three of us always have golden minds and golden lives.

Finally, I would like to thank my friends who have always been there and always will be there—Noni Colhoun, Suhasini, Laurie and Jim Nayder, Woody Simmons, Kai Ekhammer, Karen McNeil, Ruth Carnovsky, Catherine, Bill, and Suzanne Parrish, Pat Holt, Marilyn Golden, Liz Brown, Bobbie Birleffi, Beverly Kopf, Gloria Weiner, Arina Isaacson, Linda Gottlieb and Rob Tessler, Caryn Dickman, Peggy Kiss, Carol Nockold, Connie Palmore, Kimi Beaven, and my dear Laura Duggan.

CONTENTS

◆

PART IV

BUYING A HOME

PART V

THINKING AHEAD

PART VI

THE COURAGE TO BE RICH

INTRODUCTION:
THE SOUL OF COURAGE

What would it take for you to change course in your life? For you to feel rich in every way possible, both in the way your bottom-line numbers read and in your heart, your soul, and the way you live each day? What would it take for you to say aloud to yourself in the mirror, "Things are going to be different, starting now"? What would it take for you to believe it? To live it? To make it true?

The single most important quality you need in order to change the course of your life is courage. A great deal of courage.

Can you remember the courage it took to endure a setback or overcome an obstacle in your own life—the unexpected loss of a job, the illness of a loved one, a devastating rejection from someone you cared about? That feeling of waking up in the morning with pain in the pit of your stomach, pain that stayed with you as you went through the day in a fog, wondering how you could possibly cope, how you could go on, let alone rebuild your life. But you did. What enabled you to go on was your courage.

It takes courage to live with financial hardship, and, unbelievable as it may seem, it takes courage to be rich. Why? Because choosing wealth as a goal requires facing everything about your money bravely, honestly, with courage—which is a very, very hard thing for most of us to do. But it can be done.

WHAT WOULD YOU HAVE LEFT IF YOU LOST EVERYTHING?

SUZE'S STORY

After working as a waitress for seven years after college, I applied for—and, amazingly, got—a job as a stockbroker at Merrill Lynch in northern California. To this day I believe they hired me just to fill a women's quota, but who cares? I got the job. My mom was very excited for me, and a little scared, too, I think. To celebrate, she gave me a necklace she treasured, made out of little chips of diamonds from her engagement ring, so I would look as if I belonged. She even went out and got me a proper watch so that people would think I had money and maybe even do business with me.

From my first day, I was in a world very different from anything I'd known before. It felt like a dream to me, working in such a fast-paced office, where the other brokers seemed so self-assured, as if it were a given that they'd make money, lots of it. But I did well, too, and I remember how proud my mom was when, years later, I was able to buy my first luxury car and another watch, this one made of heavy gold. I wore designer clothes and vacationed on private islands. And I kept on doing well, later accepting a position as a vice-president of investments at Prudential-Bache.

Not long after, I decided to start my own business. The doors to the Suze Orman Financial Group opened for the first time on May 1, 1987. I had brought in as a partner a close friend who was a brilliant expert in estate planning, and from the beginning, the office had a wonderful aura around it, one of strength and hope, and was nothing like the tense, pressured offices of the highly structured Wall Street firms I had grown accustomed to. Until the morning of June 22, 1987, that is, when we discovered our office had been robbed, in a very intimate way. A woman working for me had come in after midnight the night before and cleaned out every-thing—my files, my Rolodex, all my computer programs and records, everything. I'll never know why. I spent the next few days stunned and in shock, trying to find my clients to warn them. I remember thinking at the time that it might take a month or two to sort things out, but I soon learned that reconstructing paper trails and seeking justice are time-consuming matters indeed. In the end, it took me three years and many, many days in court to resume my life and my practice. During those three desperate years, I lost all my courage.

At first, I burned through a range of emotions—rage, self-pity, terror. Sometimes I doubted I would ever re-enter the financial world, thinking instead that I would go back to being a waitress. Maybe that kind of life, which I knew so well, was my destiny. Maybe I had been wrong to ask for more.

I hid my fears and the truth of what had happened from my friends, and was still quick to treat them to dinners, the movies, whatever. Even with no money coming in, I deprived myself of nothing. I used up my savings and retirement money. When I had nothing left, I refinanced my house and began living off that money and my credit cards (debt it sub-sequently took me several years to clear). I had once been poor, yet had lived with spirit, courageously. Now I was living with the trappings of wealth, but had no money. I was living a lie. I no longer had even the courage to be poor.

But somehow over those years, I found the strength to begin asking myself some hard questions. Why did this really happen to me? Who was I, now that I had lost all my money? Who had I been before, when I thought I had it all? How could I stop the downward spiral, emotionally, spiritually, finan-cially?

I began looking at myself in a new way, too, and didn't much like what I was seeing. I had started to believe that because I made a lot of money I was better than others. I had started looking down on the world, even as my money ebbed away from me. For me, the turning point came when I was sitting in a Denny's restaurant one day, thinking about everything that had happened. Suddenly I looked closely at the woman waiting on me, and it dawned on me that she surely had more money than I did. I might have looked richer, wearing my designer clothes and with my fancy car parked outside. But I knew that the only wealth that I had at this point was a negative, drawn in red ink. Looking again, I could see clearly that this waitress was also happier than I was, and more honest. I was the poor one, inside and out. Where would I find the courage I needed, the courage to change?

I drew strength from a spiritual quest I had begun earlier, which now began to occupy a bigger place in my life and thoughts. I meditated and contemplated the teachings of the masters with a hunger I hadn't felt before. Slowly, I began to consider all that was happening to me in terms of what God might want to teach me. If I could view these years as a gift to be unwrapped, I thought, I might find a way to feel enhanced rather than diminished, grateful rather than bitter. I thought, too, about my parents, the strength—and, yes, courage—they had exhibited through their many hardships, and of a motto I once learned that reminded me of the way my parents lived every day: Be a warrior. Don't turn your back on the battlefield. *I decided I wouldn't.*

At last, after years in the court system, the case was resolved. Finally, I was free to move on. In retrospect, however, the inner battle to restore my courage was the battle harder won. The lesson I learned was that my attitude toward money had made me poor and that with that attitude, no amount of money could have made me rich—the wealth had to come from somewhere else, from inside. Money doesn't bring courage, I learned. It's the other way around. Once I took that lesson to heart, I began to rebuild my life.

In all realms of life it takes courage to stretch your limits, express your power, and fulfill your potential; it's no different in the financial realm. In a buy-now, consume-now culture like ours, it takes courage to make the decisions today that may make us rich tomorrow. It takes courage to face up to the facts of old age and mortality and to prepare for them. It also takes courage to live generously, regardless of your financial state of affairs. I've seen many times in my own life, as well as in my readers' and clients' lives, how easy it is to live within the familiar limits of poverty, however you define it, and within the limits imposed upon you—by yourself or others. It takes courage to ask for what you want. And it takes courage to live honestly, wisely, true to yourself—and true to your desire for more.

DWELLING ON THE HIGHEST, RICHEST PLANE THERE IS

What's keeping you from being rich? In most cases it is simply a lack of belief. In order to become rich, you must believe that you can do it, and you must take the actions necessary to achieve your goal. There is nothing wrong with wanting more. You do not need to feel guilty for wanting more. If, however, you deny the possibility that you can have more, you'll be making yourself a victim of today's circumstances, and the cost will be your tomorrow.

Let me ask you a question: How do you feel about your money? Most of us, when asked, regardless of how much money we actually have, feel afraid. We worry that there isn't enough today and that there won't be enough tomorrow. We worry about what we haven't done with our money, and we worry about what we have done. Try as we might to push the fears away, to deny them, they keep coming back into our thoughts, uninvited, and we must push them away again. If you spend a lifetime pushing your fears away, I can promise you that ultimately you're pushing money away as well. The courage to be rich lies in the opposite stance, when you can give yourself the gift of believing in more.

I wrote my first book, *You've Earned It, Don't Lose It,* to address what I saw as a growing—and legitimate—fear people had about not having enough money to make it through their retirement years. I felt an urgency in alerting people to the dangerous mistakes that could rob them of the financial security they had worked so hard for their whole lives—lessons I'd learned from my aging clients, many of whom faced real hardship because of poor choices, bad planning, or insufficient or incorrect information.

The publication of that book brought me into contact with hundreds of people whose stories I heard when they would approach me at appearances or speaking engagements, or read in the letters they would write. I listened to their concerns and their problems, and believed that it was important not only to provide them with the practical means to right the financial wrongs in their lives but also to help them truly to understand the relationship between their emotional lives and their financial ones. That was what led me to write *The 9 Steps to Financial Freedom.*

In *The 9 Steps* I hoped to help people come to terms with their past as a way of coping with their present. I firmly believe in the lessons of that book and the path it lays out, but in time I began to feel the need for a new message, a lesson we could take with us into the next millennium. Because it's my belief that the past always holds truths for the future, I looked back a hundred years and thought about the attitude and outlook our grandparents and great-grandparents took with them as they entered the twentieth century. In the strength of their hope and their dreams of a better future, I saw the perfect embodiment of courage and an inspiring example to draw upon as we face the century before us. I wrote *The Courage to Be Rich* not to retread information covered in my earlier books (though a certain amount of overlap in the finite realm of finance is inevitable; in those instances, I cross-reference the earlier books or other reliable sources), but to build upon their foundation a new way for each and every one of us to seize the future. With faith, determination, and courage.

You know, I know, it takes tremendous courage just to keep going, to work hard to pay the bills every month, to meet the next financial or emotional challenge that comes along. The courage to be rich, however, goes beyond the chains and limitations of our minds and present-day circumstances, and it brings tomorrow—when yesterday's defeat will be long past us—into every today. This kind of courage is vision, and it refuses to let today's defeat block our path into the future. This kind of courage is not about just getting by or simply accepting the cards that have been dealt to us. Instead, it is about excelling beyond our own seemingly endless limitations, even in the darkest of financial times—and we all have dark financial times. The courage to be rich gives us the material and spiritual tools to see our way out of the darkness and into the light. For when the light of courage illuminates our way, we always find true richness at the end of the path. Courage is faith. Faith in a higher being, perhaps, or faith in the essential rightness of the world, that correct actions and beliefs are not only their own reward but also qualities that themselves will be rewarded. Is there a grand scheme to the world? I'm not equipped to say. However, if we live each day of our life as if there is, and with courage, we are living on the highest, richest plane of this earth, regardless of the answer.

PART I

ACTS
OF
COURAGE

CHAPTER 1

THE COURAGE
TO LOOK WITHIN

Over the many years I've worked with people and their money, I have tried to answer what to me is the most puzzling financial question of all: Why is it that some people have money while others do not? It's almost mystical, really. Day after day I see people who have grown up in similar circumstances, had basically the same opportunities, and earn more or less the same salaries, yet how very differently their bottom-line numbers can read. I'm sure you've seen this yourself. Haven't you known really good, hardworking people who end up with very little? Haven't you met people who should have had less but have more? Or people who, time after time, almost seem to make it and then, boom, something happens and they have to start all over again?

Is it that some higher being looks down on all of us and chooses who among us is going to win life's financial lottery? I doubt it. Is it simply that those who have all the money they could ever need wanted it more than others? Not from what I've seen.

In my twenty-one years as a financial planner, never once have I come across a client who didn't have the desire to have more, or the intelligence and the ability to achieve the desire. Not once. So what was stopping them? The same thing that no doubt is stopping you: financial obstacles.

And what are those financial obstacles? Some of the obstacles that are placed in front of us are external and easy to recognize—lack of cash or opportunity, the family we are born into, lack of financial knowledge, or maybe just laziness. Legitimate obstacles, some of these, but after all these years working with people richer and, yes, poorer than you are today, I've seen people overcome each of them countless times. These are the easy obstacles, for what you can pinpoint you can overcome.

Harder to recognize, and much harder to overcome, are the internal obstacles, the emotional obstacles, that keep us from having what we want and enjoying what we have.

I have come to believe that the way each of us thinks and feels about our money is the key factor in determining how much we ultimately have. The main underlying reason that some of us don't have money is that our thoughts and feelings about money have become internal obstacles that prevent us from having or keeping what we want. In the same vein, the reason that others do have money is that, with their thoughts and feelings, they have created the means to achieve and hold on to what they desire. In other words, our thoughts and feelings about money are, to me, fundamental factors in determining how much money each of us will, in this lifetime, be able to create and keep.

LESSONS MY CLIENTS TAUGHT ME

Years into my practice, once I began to understand the powerful hold our thoughts and emotions have on our money, I started to ask my clients different kinds of questions—questions about "how" and "why" rather than simply questions about "how much." I began trying to get to the heart of their financial emotions: "Why have you let all this money just sit in a bank account for ten years earning two percent interest?" I'd ask. Or "How did you begin to get into all this debt?" Or "What are the money issues you and your spouse fight over?" Or "Why, when you have so much more money than most people, do you feel so poor?"

The answers were remarkably similar, regardless of how much money was actually at stake: "I'm afraid to invest. I feel safe leaving my money alone." "Suze, I'm so ashamed of my debt, I can't even tell my husband." "I'm just so angry at the way he spends our money." "I am afraid. What if I lose it all?"

I listened carefully to the words that my clients were using, over and over, to answer my questions or simply to talk about their financial situations. I noticed that whenever people had financial difficulties, whether they were in debt, had nothing to show for their years of work, had no idea where the next dollar was going to come from, or felt like they never had enough, they seemed to have one thing in common. They all used the same words to answer my questions. Regardless of their particular financial dilemma, their answers all contained at least one of the following words: *Shame. Fear. Anger.*

Let's say a client came in to see me because she found herself in terrible debt and needed help to find her way out. If I asked her, "How do you feel about having so much debt?" her answer would likely reflect one or more of three emotional variations: "I'm so ashamed; I don't want anyone to know about my debt." "I'm so afraid; I have no idea how I will ever get out of debt." "I'm so angry at myself for allowing myself to get into this situation." *Shame. Fear. Anger.* The emotional obstacles to wealth.

Perhaps it's easy to see how staggering debt could incite these emotions, but it's less apparent in situations where there seems to be enough money, or at least no immediate threat to one's security. And yet I can cite countless examples of clients whose deep-seated emotions kept them from achieving greater wealth—be it in the form of emotional or financial security. Fear, loss, shame about the past. Anger at the circumstances over which you have to prevail.

UNLOCKING THE EMOTIONS

You may be thinking, How is this possible? Just because I'm afraid, how does that relate to the fact that I have no money? Isn't it the other way around? Isn't it that I'm afraid because I don't have any money?

That's the way most people think. Especially people who do not have money—or the courage to be rich. It's easy to blame your emotional state of affairs on your financial state. But from what I've learned, the opposite is true. Your emotional state ultimately determines your financial state.

I have found that when negative emotions control the purse strings, money will not flow purely and evenly. When it comes to money, emotions can speak louder than reason or necessity. Your emotions, expressed through your financial actions, have gotten you to where you are now and will continue to shape your financial future if you let them. If shame, fear, or anger is at the wheel, then I can promise you, you are not on a course toward richness. By having the courage to face and overcome your inner obstacles, however, you will change the outer trappings of your financial life forever.

YOUR EXERCISE, PART ONE

I want you to take a few minutes to consider how you feel about your financial situation today. Don't think in terms of numbers, the bills, how much you owe, or how much you've saved. Think instead about how you truly feel about your finances. Is money—the money you've spent, the money you have, the money you need—a constant worry for you? Do you feel that you're not good enough to get what you want or that you don't deserve what you have? Are you embarrassed by how much you have? Envious of what others have, angry that you don't have such things? I want you to address your emotions honestly and commit your thoughts and feelings to paper. If you don't have the money to pay your bills, write down how it feels not to have enough money. If you're in debt, write down how that feels. If you have far more money than your friends, write down how that feels as well. On the other hand, if you think you remain emotionally unattached to your money, I still want you to try to complete this exercise, because you might surprise yourself by uncovering emotions that have been long buried. I want you to close your eyes and look deep within yourself until all that exists in your consciousness is a clear sense of yourself and your feelings about your financial life.

After you have spent some time contemplating your situation, please write a few more sentences describing how you feel about it as precisely as you can.

A sample paragraph might read:

"It's terrifying how much debt we've managed to build up in just five years of marriage, with having the children and everything else. I'd be so embarrassed if my parents knew. I'm worried about how we'll make it until the children go to college, let alone college itself."

Now take a good look at the words you have written and see them not as words but as your *current truths*—statements that not only describe your state of mind but also have the power and veracity to determine your outlook and, subsequently, your actions. Underline or highlight any words that have to do with an emotion. In the case above, for example, the writer would highlight *terrifying,* a word describing fear; *embarrassed,* a word describing shame; and *worried,* another word describing fear.

Without having seen what you wrote, I can guarantee that you've used words describing shame, fear, or anger. This is not a financial planner's party trick; rather, it demonstrates the universality of our impoverished feelings about money.

MONEY, POWER, RESPECT

Strange as it may sound to you, money is attracted to people who are strong and powerful, respectful of it, and open to receiving it. I want you to think about this—it is something I firmly believe and have said time and again: Money behaves and responds just like a person—nurture it, treat it well, and it will grow and flourish; treat it carelessly, or with disrespect, and it will dwindle away to nothing. Quite simply, if you respect money and give it the attention it needs, it will respect you back.

Conversely, the emotions of shame, fear, and anger cloud your financial judgment, take away your power over your money. When these emotions determine your spending patterns or force you to deny or defy the truth about your money, they not only wreak havoc on your finances, they actually repel money from you. This is not to say that there aren't people with a lot of money who feel shame, fear, or anger—there are plenty of such people. Although they may have a good amount of money, they're not rich in the sense of living a full, expansive, and contented life. And often such people are unable to hold on to their money. How frequently do we read in the tabloids of wealthy people whose fortunes are destroyed by drugs, ugly divorces, unscrupulous business practices, or similar disgraceful causes? Why do you think this happens? I believe it happens because their underlying emotional states are powerful enough, and corrosive enough, to repel even vast fortunes. No matter how much money you have, power and respect—for yourself, for others, for your money—attract riches, and powerlessness and disrespect repel them.

The roots of these emotions take hold in childhood. So strong are they that they grow even if we try to ignore them, gaining the power to control our thoughts, words, actions, and fortunes. If we let them. We've all felt shame, fear, and anger—the emotions of poverty. And we all have the power to confront them and expel them—from our emotional lives, and from our financial lives as well. I have seen so many people change their financial lives after facing down these treacherous feelings. You can, too. For the sake of your dreams, I urge you to have the courage to do so now.

FINANCIAL SHAME

What does financial shame look like? Its posture is head down, eyes down. It's contained and hidden, but the effects of its presence are apparent even so. It's the most deeply rooted emotion of all, because it cuts to the core of who you are—telling you you're not good enough, not deserving of what you have, less than others, no matter how much you have. Experience the sensation of shame just once, and you're not likely to forget it.

M A R K ' S   S T O R Y

I must have been about nine or ten, and we were having this Sunday school outing. Everyone in my class was going hiking on the nature trail in the morning and then out for lunch afterward. Our minister was taking us, and we all liked him, so this was a pretty big deal. I can't remember anything about the nature trail, but I will never forget that lunch. There were about ten of us, and we got a big table at a soda fountain. Cokes for everybody, in a big glass with a straw. I had a grilled cheese sandwich and french fries, and we all had ice cream for dessert. Then, when the bill came, all the kids put five dollars on the table, and I just froze. I didn't have five dollars. I didn't have any money, my parents hadn't given me money. Not a cent. Ricky, who was sometimes my friend and sometimes my enemy, noticed and said, "Hey, why aren't you paying up?" I was mortified. Everyone was looking at me, real quiet. I remember getting hot, and I remember starting to cry in front of everybody, which made it worse. They all were staring. I felt so ashamed. I'll never forget it.

Powerful memory. And Mark has been paying to make up for it ever since. To this day, he's the one who always treats, the first to pick up the check, a big tipper and a big spender. His shame that day made such a powerful impact on him that he sees to it that everyone knows he has money to spend. What they don't know, however, is that he spends it all, leaving himself with nothing, ultimately as penniless and ashamed today as he was all those years ago at his Sunday school lunch.

Maybe you were ashamed growing up because your family had less than the other families you knew. Maybe you didn't have the right clothes or car or belong to the country club, or your mother was the only mother who worked, as mine was, which was a source of shame to me. Maybe you didn't have the money to attend or finish college, the way your friends did. In some cases, the shame is "Why me?" shame, because you might have had more than everyone else and didn't feel you deserved it. Your shame might have come from a specific incident, as Mark's did, or from a cluster of incidents you never forgot. In any case, shame has real staying power and can destroy your pride, self-respect, self-worth—and ultimately, net worth.

How does shame come into play in grown-up financial life? If you feel "less than," you'll spend more—possibly even more than you have—in order to feel like more. If you feel you don't deserve what you have, you'll neglect it, it will fail to grow, and eventually it will stagnate. If you feel undeserving, you will never take real pleasure in the money you have and what it can do. If you believe that you truly don't deserve the things you really want, then they'll never be yours. Defeat won't be a problem for you. But success will.

FINANCIAL FEAR

What does financial fear look like? Watch, sometime, when you see a line of people handing over money or a credit card to a clerk in a store. If there's fear, you'll be able to see it. Watch the way the other customers clutch their money too tightly, take just a second longer than they should to relinquish it, hold out their hand before the clerk is ready to give them the change, hold their breath until the credit card clears. Perhaps instead you might see them distance themselves from their money, hand it over too quickly, toss it, or push it. When it comes to money, fear is constantly constricting and debilitating, like a companion or a voice in your head, reminding you of all the bills you have to pay, intruding on times that should be pleasurable, keeping you up at night. It can express itself in one of two ways. Fear can prevent you from doing what you should with your money, or it can cause you to do what you shouldn't with your money.

PAM'S STORY

My mother wore her money dress my whole childhood. It was a royal blue shirtwaist, and the print was dark golden coins, coins scattered all over it. White collar. The belt was red patent leather, and the belt buckle and the buttons were coins, too. She wore it to church with gloves, and she wore it to take us to the first day of school, to the PTA, every time she wanted to look nice, I guess. We called it the money dress, and we knew that when she was wearing it, it was an occasion. I was always proud of her in the money dress. You could just feel how great she felt in it, and it was as if her pride was contagious. Then one day, when I was about eleven, we were going to my grandmother's house, because my cousins were coming to visit. We all were instructed to wear our best clothes, and after I got dressed, I went into my parents' room. There was my mother, sitting on the bed in her white slip, holding the money dress and crying. I had never seen her cry. It was then that I saw that the patent leather belt was cracked, and the "gold" was peeling off the coin buttons. Then my father came in and screamed at her that he couldn't afford to get her a new dress, just put the dress on and get ready. She cried harder, and he kept screaming. Then I understood. This wasn't about the money dress. It was about money, and we didn't have any. I was so afraid, I ran outside. But I could still hear the crying and the screaming.

The fear is still with Pam today. She and her husband both work, and they make more than enough, but they are anything but rich. Pam overspends, pure and simple, and her credit card debt is keeping pace with her salary. She has a closet overflowing with real money dresses, and her children have the absolute best of everything, at a cost far greater than Pam and her husband can afford. They live in the best neighborhood, drive showy cars, and live in terror, waiting for the moment when their financial lives are going to come crashing down on them.

If your parents quarreled about money when you were young, if you grew up feeling there wasn't enough, you almost certainly harbor some fear about money today. Fear has nothing to do, necessarily, with the financial facts of your life; you can certainly have money and still be afraid. Yet you cannot be rich, truly rich, if you're living with fear. Whether or not you have enough today, if you fear you don't, then one way or another you'll make sure that you don't. Or you may go the other way and become a miser, holding on to your money as desperately as you hold on to the fear, unable to take pleasure in spending a penny and unable to be generous, which will render you poor in every way.

FINANCIAL ANGER

What does financial anger look like? It looks clenched. Clenched fists, clenched mouth, creased forehead. It makes you look closed and unyielding. It is anything but welcoming, and it turns away money as readily as it turns away other people. Maybe you feel anger at yourself for what you've done or what you haven't done with your money, for a raise you didn't get, at your parents for the ways in which you still feel they let you down, at friends who have more than you, at a spouse who left you powerless and penniless, or simply at the unfairness of life—and the unfairness of money. If you do, this anger may be extremely well concealed but can still translate into debt and dishonesty with yourself about what you are doing (and aren't doing) with your money.

STEPHEN'S STORY

My family emigrated from Europe to the United States when I was eleven years old, and it was a really traumatic time for us all. For my mother, especially, because she had to leave her mother, who was ill, and her twin brother. There was this sad sense that we might never see them again. I remember we had to sell all our property before we left. For the most part, our furniture wasn't new or nice, so the neighbors just kind of came and paid what they could for everything—the beds, the kitchen table and chairs, the dishes. But about six months before we had known we were leaving, my mother had bought two comfortable cushioned armchairs. I can still see them. She was so proud of these chairs, and she hated to have to part with them, but when she knew she had to sell them, she at least wanted to get a good price. Nearly everything else was gone by then, so there were just these two flowered chairs in the little living room. A man came, some kind of a dealer, I

*guess, and he paid her only about half of what she expected
to get. She tried to negotiate with him—plead with him is
more like it—but he was very contemptuous. When he left
with the chairs, she cried and cried for hours in the empty
house. I was so angry at him—how dare he take such advantage of my mother? I remember thinking that when you have
something valuable, people will always try to take it from
you.*

Stephen is still angry, angry at the unfairness of the world, so angry
that to this day he really believes that he has to protect himself and
every single penny he has, or else someone will take advantage of him.
In effect, he's still buying high and selling low. He's left two jobs, thinking he might be fired. He thinks everyone, from the corner grocer to
the people who tabulate his phone bill, is probably out to get him. He
hoards his money. His anger has so convinced him that the world is a
financial minefield that he's virtually retreated from it.

An adult's anger is the same as a child's—anger at not getting what
you want. But as adults, we're in control (at least we're supposed to
be); we're the ones with the power to say yes or no. If you want something badly, something you can't afford, you're going to be angry if you
say yes to yourself and angry, too, if you say no. In this no-win situation, there's nowhere for the anger to go, and it can stay with you,
causing a good deal of damage, throughout your life. If you're angry at
being deprived, you might keep up the deprivation in order to sustain
the anger—or maybe you'll lash out at the anger with reckless spending. Perhaps you will feel suspicious that others are trying to short-
change you, and if you feel it, others will sense it. If anger is a recurring
theme in your life, your actions around money will be grudging and
pinched, to the point where the flow of your money will become con-
stricted, dwindling, in some cases, to a trickle.

When your outward appearance and way of living suggest to others that you have more money than you do, you're angry. When you've
invested more money in today than tomorrow, you're probably angry

as well. And no matter where you cast the blame for your anger, in the end the person you'll be the most angry with is yourself.

When emotional reflexes steer our financial actions, we are not acting in our best financial interests—anything but. As you can see from these stories, you are not going to get rich by feeling ashamed, afraid, or angry, but by purging these emotions from your financial life so that they no longer taint your actions, by making different choices, by expanding your financial worldview beyond today and into tomorrow.

If you've made mistakes, so what? We all make mistakes. If you trusted someone you shouldn't have trusted, you can learn to trust yourself. If you are in debt, you can get out of debt—millions of us have. If you face your finances truthfully, just the way they are now, you can begin to change them, a little today, perhaps a little more tomorrow.

But first you have to render those emotions of fear, shame, or anger powerless over you and your money.

YOUR EXERCISE, PART TWO

You can try saying to yourself, Okay, no more anger, but it won't get you very far. Because emotions have lives of their own, it is hard to pin them down, look them directly in the eye, and send them away. First you have to identify their source, then evaluate them with the adult perspective—and compassion—you have now. This begins the process of defusing their power.

I'm asking you to go somewhere quiet, taking with you a pen and the piece of paper on which you described how you feel about your money today. Look closely at the paragraph you wrote at the beginning of this chapter and ask yourself this question about the emotions you identified: Where do you think that feeling came from?

In essence I am asking you to go back in time. Go back to your childhood to find, if you can, the financial memory that planted the shame, the fear, the anger. Use the word that most prominently and accurately describes your present-day feelings toward your finances as a sort of password, a key to unlock painful episodes that still resonate, even subconsciously, in your life today. Was it that your neighbors once offered you hand-me-downs because they thought you were too poor to buy things of your own? Did that make you ashamed? Was it that your mom once took you grocery shopping, filled the whole cart, then discovered that she had forgotten her wallet and had no way to pay? Did that make you afraid? Was it that all your friends went to Europe one summer, while you had to take a part-time job? Did that make you angry? Was there enough, too much, or never enough? Was money a source of happiness or of despair?

For instance, let's say that you're so ashamed of the amount of debt you've incurred that you're keeping it a secret from those closest to you. Shame and secrecy are your passwords. Search your memory and see what those words call to mind. Perhaps they remind you of feelings of shame you had as a teenager, when you felt you weren't good enough and had to pretend to be something other than yourself to gain acceptance with the "in" crowd. But don't stop at the first recollection that suggests itself. If you go deeper, farther back, you might recall where you learned that lesson—maybe your mother told you as a child to keep the family's money problems a secret from your friends, because if they knew you were poor, they might not like you anymore.

Bingo. When you finally get to the heart of the matter, it will be as clear to you as if a flashbulb had gone off. I urge you not to give up, not to turn away until you've reached that moment of clarity. Incidentally, the process I took you through in the previous paragraph was the very one I myself went through to connect to the source of my shameful feelings about my debt. Those memories, those secrets, were my own.

When you've reached that moment of understanding, please write your memory down on the same piece of paper you used in the first part of the exercise.

Now let's go deeper. What are you doing today, as an adult, to keep that feeling alive, to allow it to control your financial life? For example, if you don't believe you deserve what you have or can achieve what you want, your feelings of unworthiness likely stem from the shame you've been harboring since your youth. If you believe that you could lose everything you have or will never feel financially secure, your present-day fear is fueling that childhood emotion. If it seems to you that everyone else has more and you'll never have enough, your feelings of inadequacy and hostility are nurturing youthful versions of those feelings into adulthood.

Add to the piece of paper what you are doing today in your actions, thoughts, or feelings about money to keep the emotions of shame, anger, or fear alive and in control of you and your money.

In Mark's case, for example, his flamboyant spending today is an attempt to make up for the shame of yesterday, but in fact it is keeping that emotion alive. With the weight of Pam's debt, she is trying, today, to dispel the pain of yesterday's poverty, but her actions leave her even more afraid of not having enough money to pay the bills. Stephen's financial demeanor, suspicious and tightfisted, is keeping his anger alive—and keeping the world at bay. Each is paying an emotional toll today, and a financial one as well.

Now it's time to cut off the power of the emotions holding you back, just as you would apply a tourniquet to an open wound. Think about these memories, the misguided actions you're taking today, and how they might be connected to your past. Think of the child you were when the memory was formed, and why you felt the way you did in the context of who you were then. You were powerless. You were a child and had a right to feel the way you did. Think of who you are now and the power you can summon to change.

You must release yourself from the hold these memories have over you. You can no longer afford to live in the past; make the present your point of reckoning. Today and tomorrow are all that matter. Take responsibility for your life, and for your money, from this moment on.

ALWAYS FORGIVE

The only way to get beyond the emotional obstacles standing between you and more money is to let them go, to forgive. Forgive the people who helped to etch those memories on your young soul. Forgive yourself for the way those emotions have played out in your financial life up until now. Forgive the past and present, in order to make the future a blank slate on which you can engrave different goals and different numbers.

We all know how hard it actually is to forgive—but we all know, too, the healing powers of forgiveness. For me, the shame, fear, and anger I felt from growing up, at least in my own mind, as poor little Suze Orman from the South Side of Chicago, daughter of a chicken plucker, defined me well into adulthood. No matter how well I did or how much money I made, I never felt good enough, smart enough, attractive enough. These feelings were all that my entire being could bear; there wasn't room for any other, more generous emotions. I didn't feel entitled to anything—love, friendship, and especially money. For the longest time, I can honestly say, these thoughts and feelings kept me from being rich.

I didn't realize the extent to which these emotions defined me, even as I grew unhappier, lonelier, and angrier over those years. One day, I was getting ready for work, utterly miserable and about to get into the shower. In the way we all invoke God when we're at rock bottom, I silently screamed out to Him: Why can't I have what everybody else in this world has? Is this all there is for me? I remember it so clearly—my distress and then a feeling of calm as my plea was answered with a prayer that I had learned as a child and which suddenly came back to me. I repeated it over and over as if it were my salvation, as perhaps it was. It went like this: *I ask to be forgiven and released by all those whom I have hurt and harmed, and I ask to forgive and release all those who have hurt and harmed me.*

Forgiveness, for me, was a process, one that took a long time to complete—to forgive my parents who had, after all, done the best they could, and to forgive myself enough to believe that I was fine just as I was, and entitled to whatever I could create and achieve. With my prayer, over time, I released myself from the bondage of those terribly destructive emotions and finally made room for more.

YOUR EXERCISE, PART THREE

Read what you've written from the earlier exercises again. Add to it if you feel the need—if you can recall more vivid details, if there's something you wish to express to another. You may think of this document as a letter to a higher power, a direct line of communication. Purge yourself of all aspects of the memory in the process of capturing it on paper. Read what you've written one last time.

Now I'd like you to take this paper and burn it. Watch it as it is transformed from paper to ashes. Think of the fire as representative of the fire of love that is burning in your heart; see the ashes as all that remains of your past hurts as your writings go up in smoke; release the hurt and pain; let the past go.

It's time to start over. It's time to forgive. To forgive Mom, Dad, the world, and, above all, yourself. Use my prayer or create one of your own. Find the words of forgiveness that bring you release. Articulate your feelings in some form—trust a friend with your story of forgiveness or contemplate forgiveness in a place of worship.

Do it now. Now is the time to forgive the child you were, the child who was ashamed, angry, or afraid. You were just a child. Forgive the shame. You reacted as any child would, and today you can see that whatever you were ashamed of then would pass, and ultimately it wouldn't matter. Forgive the fear. Where did the fear come from? Your parents, who were doing their best to make everything okay? They tried to shield you. They did the best they could. Forgive them. Let your anger go. Today you're no longer angry at whatever made you angry yesterday. Release it with forgiveness. You have what you have. This is your starting point.

Every day things happen that may put more obstacles in your path to wealth, that could create overwhelming hardships, that could leave terrible scars. Forgiveness is a never-ending process. It is not enough simply to forgive what happened in the past. You can learn from the setbacks that happen today, release them, and move on. Over time, with forgiveness, you will stop blaming your past for your present, and you will learn to take responsibility for your actions, financial and otherwise, today and forever. Take your financial destiny into your own hands and your own heart. See it as the act of courage it is.

CHAPTER 2

THE COURAGE TO HAVE MORE AND TO BE MORE

What do you think when you think about your money?

What do you say when you talk about your money?

What actions have you taken with your money?

When it comes to your money, what you think will direct what you say, what you say will direct what you do, and what you do will create your destiny. True richness begins with thoughts of true richness. True greatness begins with thoughts of true greatness, and the potential for greatness resides in all of us.

Over the years, I've heard from many people who think they don't have enough, that they will never have—or be—enough, that they can't: can't get out of debt, can't provide for their children, can't face the future. I have heard tales of sadness, hopelessness, and despair from people facing the facts of the financial lives they have created. There is a vast difference between facing reality, bad as your particular financial reality might be at this moment, and thinking that you can't do anything about that reality. Whether you're wealthy, whether you're poor, the constricting thoughts that tell you *you can't* are immensely powerful and terribly destructive; I have come to refer to them as thoughts of poverty, and thoughts of poverty can dwell in all of us, no matter how much or how little money we have. These thoughts of poverty are insidious; they lead to words of poverty or defeat, and ultimately to actions of poverty and a legacy of poverty that can be passed down for generations. We must learn to still those thoughts.

I learned this lesson from the life of my dad.

M Y   D A D ' S   A N D   M Y   S T O R Y

At first, children accept the world they're born into, and in my family, our world was my dad's chicken business, a series of small chicken stands, which sometimes did a little better but mostly did a little worse. I felt poor living in a family that calamity struck often—fire nearly killed my dad and left him with emphysema; powerful chain stores threatened our chicken stands; landlords more than once forced out my dad's business.

Growing up, I never once questioned that this was the way it was meant to be for us. It never occurred to me that our lives, my dad's life, might have been different. Then, at a family get-together not long after my father died, my cousin said casually, "I still think it's too bad that your dad never got around to finishing law school." What? It was as if an electric shock went through me. Law school? My dad went to law school? How was it possible that he had gone to law school and ended up plucking chickens? And why didn't he ever tell me?

As the story came out I learned that my father had, indeed, gone to law school, working at a flower shop between classes and selling produce from a cart on weekends to pay his tuition. He lived at home, in a one-bedroom apartment with his parents and brother, and contributed his share toward the family's household expenses. Just as he was about to start his last year of school, however, my grandfather asked him for money to help open a new chicken store. My dad gave up his dreams, gave his tuition money to my grandpa, joined him in the chicken business, and never became a lawyer. Why not? He got sidetracked. He settled. He lost heart. Perhaps he simply chose to think his father's thoughts. No one knows why, and the reason scarcely matters. Regardless of why, ultimately he convinced himself that this was his destiny, not the one he had dared, for a time, to imagine.

It was quite a shock for me to learn how different our lives might have been. My dad had played such a vital role in my life, and I had learned the lesson of my childhood well. This was the plan for us. Who was I to think I could have more, be more? In retrospect, I can see that for a long time I thought his destiny was mine as well, because the message he'd passed on to me was the lesson of less and the thoughts of I can't.

As I look back, and from conversations I've since had with other members of my family, I now realize that my dad's thoughts were always thoughts of poverty, that his internal voice told him you can't. It wasn't as if he didn't try, because he did try. He worked harder than anyone I've ever known, every day of his life. Three times he talked investors into investing in new chicken stands, and three times he started over from scratch. It was not that my father was without courage, for at least in my eyes, he had more than most; he had amazing courage. Despite this, my brothers and I also heard him say, more than once, "This is just the way it was meant to be, and there's nothing I can do about it."

Finally, as an adult thinking back on what I knew of my father's life, I got it. No matter how hard he tried, his schemes never worked out for him because he never thought, deep down inside, that they could, never thought that they would. He thought he was never going to make it, thought it and thought it until he believed it, said it, and made it happen. He *stilled the internal voice that said* I can't *once, by attending law school, but then let it resume its chant and never even got his degree. What a pivotal point in a man's life! He did everything he knew to try to make it, except to think that he could, say that he would, and then, from that position of strength and clarity, take the actions that would have led him to a rich and fulfilling life. With his thoughts he created his destiny, as do we all.*

THOUGHTS OF COURAGE

Day in, day out, your thoughts accompany you everywhere: to work, throughout meals, while socializing; you even drift off to sleep with your thoughts. Sometimes they're obsessive—after a fight with your partner, say, or if you've been unfairly reprimanded by your boss. Most other times, they free-float, reminding you that it's time to call your mother, that you're due at the dentist, that you're going to wear your new shoes to the party tonight. Happy thoughts, tedious thoughts, routine thoughts are with you all the time. And so are money thoughts, the thoughts that tell you how much you have, how much you need, and how much you want. Ultimately, these thoughts tell you more about yourself than your checkbook does—they tell you who you are and who you can become. If you can start to change the thoughts that tell you *you can't* into thoughts that tell you *you can,* you can begin to change your financial destiny.

The power of positive thinking is hardly a new idea, and it has helped many people in many ways—in their relationships, in their work, in coping with loss. Now imagine unleashing that power upon your money. Positive thinking is seldom talked about when it comes to our financial lives; it's not a slogan you'd be likely to see hanging in a financial planner's office. But I can tell you that most of the problems we're plagued by in day-to-day life have to do with money, and necessarily, they occupy our thoughts. If you really want to live a rich life, the process must begin in your head, with positive thoughts.

How do you turn your thoughts about money around? The same way you direct any of your other thoughts. Think of thoughts as actors inhabiting your mind, with you as director, in control of where they'll stand—at center stage, in the background—and when they'll speak. If you're on a diet and determined to do well, you'll be able, with firm stage direction, to still the thought of a hot fudge sundae. If anxious thoughts tell you to call the office and say you're sick, you can over-power those thoughts by reminding yourself that this is the day of your big presentation and you're not going to miss it because of cold feet. In the same way, every negative, harmful, or unproductive money thought can be replaced, redirected, banished from the stage. If your thoughts turn to your debt and how you'll never be able to pay it off, replace the thought: *Yes, I have debt, but there are ways to get out of debt; millions of people have, and I will, too.* If your thoughts turn to your elderly parents who are unwell, turn your thoughts again: *There are agencies that can help with this, and I am going to look into elder services and see where I can get help for them and for me.* If your thoughts turn to how in the world you'll ever pay for your children's education, redirect your thinking: *I wish I had saved more by now, but I will still do what I can and will look into loans, grants, and the best state schools, and find what's best for us.* Replace each thought of powerlessness with a powerful thought, a thought that says *I can,* and then move away from the thought. Think about something else. Replace a thought of powerlessness every time it comes into your mind, over and over again. This is not an invitation to live in denial. You're not pushing the problem away, you're simply meeting it in a new way, head-on, with the strength of your positive new thoughts.

Every day, people confront adversity—destructive acts of nature, tragic illnesses, bills that get out of control, houses that fall apart, lives that are shattered in ways that only money can fix. Why is it that some people triumph over adversity and others succumb to it? You can trace their actions to their thoughts. If they think they'll triumph, they will go on to say they will and to take the actions that lead them out of adversity. Still the thoughts that tell you *you can't,* because *you can.* Beginning today, look toward a brighter future; leave the past behind. The will to change begins with your thoughts, then gathers strength with your words.

THE FORCE OF LANGUAGE

Where there is a flow, any flow, of money, even a trickle, you have the power to increase it. Believe it or not, it almost doesn't matter how much or how little money you have coming in every month. All money has the power to grow or to dwindle, and when you unleash powerful thoughts over even small amounts of money, you are turning toward more. What will begin to make you richer is how you think about yourself, your circumstances, and all the possibilities that lie ahead.

Where do your thoughts take you? They take you to your words, the words you use—or don't use—when you talk about your money.

The connection between our words and our wealth is a subtle one, and one that hasn't been explored very much, but it's a connection that has fascinated me ever since I became a financial planner and began to hear, really hear, the words we use when we talk about money. In my practice, I have seen people who are clearly preoccupied with their debt but whose words try to obscure the damage. I have seen husbands and wives married many years who've never talked honestly about money. I've also seen thoughts and words intermingle in ways that make no financial sense: "But you told me everything was going to be okay." "Well, maybe I did and maybe I was wrong." Do our words always reflect our true thoughts about money? Not always. But if the overriding goal is to create more, then your thoughts and words must be in alignment—toward the truth, toward the goal, toward the means to the goal. When you talk about money, you have to be very careful of what you say, because just as your destiny begins with your thoughts, your words bring you closer to that destiny.

The way we talk about and handle our money is, for each of us, as distinctive as a fingerprint, and as intricate. If you can learn to listen very carefully to the words you use in relation to your money, you will uncover truly important clues as to why you aren't as rich as you would like to be or as rich as you could be.

When clients come into my office and tell me about their finances for the first time, the conversation is nearly always riddled with words of discouragement, limitation, and defeat—words that, in my opinion, drive away any hope of having money. "I'll never get that job, so I'm not even going to try." "I'll never get rich." "I'll be paying off this debt for the rest of my life." "We'll never be able to afford a house." "I'll probably lose everything." I cringe whenever I hear people talk like this, and I find myself spontaneously exclaiming aloud, "Please, God, don't listen to them. They don't mean what they're saying." Then I ask them to take back what they said, to apologize for their words. I've had more than one client look at me as if I'd gone loopy, but when it comes to money, I take words very, very seriously. After years of dealing with people who have it and people who don't, I have learned that words, all our words, hold the power to make us rich or to keep us poor. Your words are as important as your thoughts, because your words are the bridge from thoughts to actions.

Think thoughts of poverty, speak words you don't believe, and you will never take the actions necessary to achieve wealth. You'll never be rich, either, if you think grand thoughts and speak only of poverty. It takes rich thoughts to lead to rich words. It takes rich words to lead to rich actions. All our thoughts, all our words must be compelled in the same direction to inspire the actions that lead to wealth.

WORDS OF POVERTY, WORDS OF WEALTH

Whether you notice it or not, you talk about your money dozens of times a day, even if silence about the subject is your native financial language. *I can't . . . I'll never . . . I don't know how . . . I wish I had* . . . Used in connection with money, these words, regardless of how much or how little money you have, are words of poverty.

To have more, you have to begin by thinking you can have more, but then you have to say it: *I can* . . . *I always* . . . *I am learning how* . . . *I will have* . . . To have more, you must learn to speak in the language of wealth, a language that shows self-respect—and also respect for your money.

You must learn to listen to the language of money around you and the words you choose to express your thoughts. When you begin to do this—and it isn't very hard, it's like listening for a song, or a chord, or a word you just learned—you can read your financial future in the words you speak, hear, and exchange every day. Try to listen to yourself to learn what an astute financial planner might know about you after meeting you just once. Speak poor, and you'll be poor. Speak rich, true words, on the other hand, and you start to change your entire outlook.

LETTING YOUR THOUGHTS
EXCEED YOUR WORDS

Do you hear yourself in the words and phrases below? If so, you're speaking the language of poverty. Instead, I want you to learn to speak the language of wealth.

- *I'm broke.* The words "I'm broke" suggest, in fact, that you're broken, at rock bottom, unable to function, unable to meet your responsibilities. Is that the message you want to send to the world?
- *I know I should* . . . Anything that you "should" be doing is something you're clearly not doing. "Should" is another way of absolving yourself of responsibility. Any sentence that contains the word is not even close to a statement of intent.

♦ *It's only money.* There's nothing "only" about money. Money *matters,* plain and simple. If this is your attitude toward money, believe me, your money will take the same apathetic attitude toward you.

♦ *I need a new . . .* Do you really *need* it? Is "need" the right word? Elevating desires to needs is destructive—to ourselves and to those around us. Let's say you saw a new suit and you thought, I would like to own that—you were able to keep need out of it. Isn't that statement more accurate and therefore truer to the language of wealth?

♦ *Never.* Never say "never," when it comes to money. "Never" cuts off tomorrow, and tomorrow holds the possibility of always. "I'll never be rich." "I'll always be rich." One word makes a world of difference.

♦ *I could start investing if . . . When I get a raise, things will be different.* "If" and "when" take us away from the here and now to a place that exists only conditionally.

♦ *Oh God.* "Oh God, how am I going to pay these bills?" "Oh God, everything is so expensive!" "Oh God, I would love to come with you to the Caribbean if I just had the money." So often when it comes to our money we invoke God, which gives an unnecessary, desperate urgency to what we are trying to say. It's the language of longing, not the language of wealth.

♦ *Poor Bill,* or whoever. The words evoke someone who is bankrupt, not necessarily financially, perhaps, but certainly emotionally and spiritually. A pitiful case, a person who must be treated with extra sensitivity, a person who's weak. The words evoke poverty. They also enforce poverty. Either Bill, through his thoughts, words, and actions, is soliciting pity, or else poverty is being thrust upon him by what other people think and say about him. Either way, the poorer the thoughts, words, and actions are, the harder it is to rise above them.

WORDS AND POWER

It is not enough to push away thoughts and words of poverty. You must also use words of wealth, bounty, and abundance. Any words, repeated often enough, become true. Begin your process of change with thoughts and words that encompass richness, possibilities, dreams, openness, and hope: "I know there is a great job out there just for me." "I am going to invest and do a great job at it." "I have debt, and I am paying it off." "We will be able to afford a house one day soon." This is the language of more.

Here is an exercise I always practiced with my clients and still practice myself. It's a simple, one-step exercise to make sure your thoughts and words are in agreement. Before you say anything with respect to your money—your prospects, your goals, your financial worries—I want you to ask yourself the following question: Are your words stating what you wish to be true? For example, if you are about to say, "I will never get out of debt," I want you first to ask yourself: Is this what I want to be true? Of course it isn't, so don't say it. Rephrase what you're trying to express until it passes this test. In this case, "One day I will be out of debt" is likely what you want to say.

Every time you're about to speak about your money, ask yourself this essential question—*Do I want this to be true?*—and speak only when the answer is yes. For instance:

- "I'll never get around to investing."
  Do you want this to be true?
  Say instead, "I am finally beginning to learn about investing."
- "I just know the market's going to crash."
  Do you want this to be true?
  Say instead, "I believe that the stock market is a good investment over time."
- "My husband will probably leave me with nothing."
  Do you want this to be true?

Say instead, "If I get divorced, I will take every measure to get what's fair."

♦ "I'll never get out from under."
Do you want this to be true?
Say instead, "Slowly but surely, I am putting my finances in order."

♦ "I'm an impulse spender. I can't help it."
Do you want this to be true?
Say instead, "I spend only what I can afford to spend."

♦ "I just can't save money."
Do you want this to be true?
Say instead, "I am beginning to save a little from every pay-check."

By asking yourself this one question every time you are about to make a statement about your financial situation, you will learn to speak only in language that's respectful to yourself, your money, your future.

Sometimes—with all of us—words just pop out, or we say something before we've thought it through, but when it comes to money, listen to the words you use. If you slip, simply take it back. Say, "I didn't mean that." Rephrase what you've said to reflect what you want to be true. Align your words with your goal, remembering the power in each and every word.

THE WORDS CREATE THE VISION

I cannot stress enough the profound impact the words you use today will have on you tomorrow, which is why I want you to speak the language of wealth right now, using the present tense—"I have the courage to be rich"—to create the future you want. Beginning today.

The notion of stating your goals in the present tense rather than as

an expression of future intent is neither my own invention nor is it
new. It actually dates back to a tenth-century Hindu text called *The
Outlook of Shiva,* written by a scholar called Somananda. In it, he
instructs us to act as if we already embody our goal, no matter the dis-
parity between what we are and what we wish to become. It is important not to allow doubt to cause us to abandon our intention but to
maintain "an unwavering awareness" by affirming our goal with confidence and conviction. In this way, Somananda explains, our being
aligns itself with our intention, and the goal becomes manifest.

The wisdom of this teaching is what I draw upon when I urge you
to create a new truth by speaking it in the present tense and unifying
the sequence of thoughts, words, and actions. Become it by being it.
Be it by saying it.

PRELUDE TO ACTION

What happens next? After you start to think you can, your thoughts
become more powerful; after you start to use only words that say you
can, you start to feel more powerful. When you feel more powerful
you have the energy to propel you toward the actions that create a life
of real wealth. There's the cycle: from your thoughts and your words
to your actions. Every time you go through the cycle without waver-
ing from the goal of oneness, your assurance and determination build,
paving the way toward more.

If you learn to compose the thoughts and words of more, you're
partway there. What once seemed impossible now seems inevitable.
Richness, remember, begins with your thoughts, because your
thoughts create your destiny.

CHAPTER 3

THE COURAGE TO MAKE ROOM FOR MORE MONEY

There are so many things we imagine when we dream about having more money, when we think about what it would be like to be rich. The things we could buy, the places we could go, the problems money would solve. We think about how much better we would feel, less anxious and afraid, how much happier. We could be more generous, perhaps, donate money to charity, surprise our parents with some great present, and certainly not worry about sending the kids to college, or our own retirement. If only we had more money, we think, everything would just fall into place. If only . . .

It's true that money can buy things and solve problems, but in the fantasy, we're also imagining other things that money might provide—extra time and the capacity to use it well, a once-and-for-all cure for fear and anxiety, peace of mind, generosity, even happiness. That's a lot to ask from some paper and shiny pieces of metal. In the dream we give such powers to money because the dream is of more than money itself. Dreams like these suggest that we believe that with more money, we'd not only have more, we'd also *be* more. Richer not only in dollars and cents, but richer in soul and spirit, too. Is it possible that dreams like these can become a reality in which we are richer on all planes? I not only think it, I know it; with faith, integrity, and courage, anything is possible.

We have seen how emotional obstacles—shame, fear, anger—stand between us and more. We have seen how our thoughts and words must be in alignment in order for us to achieve more. We have seen how important it is to clear away the internal clutter that keeps us from having more, being more. But we still have to overcome one last obstacle before we can start taking truly strong financial actions that will permanently create what we want and so deserve when it comes to our financial lives. The last obstacle that must be cleared away is material clutter: the sheer volume of items in your life that you no longer value and no longer need; the confusion in your finances that allows you to obscure what you actually have and what you don't have; the chaos of all the financial tasks you intend to get to but until now have left undone.

If you are not making the money in your life that you think you should be making, if you have debt, if you cannot save a penny, I am willing to bet that clutter is standing smack in the middle of what you have today and what you could have tomorrow.

CLUTTER'S COMPOUND INTEREST

Clutter in our lives leads to more clutter—the clutter of stuff in closets, cupboards, basements, and attics. Think of your bedroom, your bathroom, your kitchen and kitchen drawers, the garage, your shelves; just think of the clutter. A huge industry has arisen to help us manage and contain our clutter. Think of the irony. We spend good money to buy stuff, to hold stuff; we pile it up in corners, under beds, in closets, where we surely forget about it, where it almost never gets used. Overflow clutter ends up in rented storage bins, at a cost, say, of seventy dollars a month or more, which can mean a loss of thousands of dollars over time. What are the items filling these storage bins and our basements and attics? Items we think we might need someday, items we are not yet ready to part with. Items that, in all likelihood, we'll never use again—yet we still won't let them go.

Why won't we let these items go, the useless items we keep around us? It is the profound fear of loss, which prevents us from gain. We keep so much stuff around us because we fear that if all our material possessions were taken away, we'd be left with nothing—and who would we be if we had nothing? It's this same fear of loss, however, that cuts off the possibility for more. You've heard the phrase *Less is more*? In this context it means that clutter blocks the way for more. Surrounded by clutter, you can't find what you need, see what you have, notice what you value, or pinpoint what's missing. In a rich and radiantly abundant life, on the other hand, one in which there is clarity, there is always room for more to come.

In the purely financial realm, when our papers are cluttered and our affairs unattended to, we create a swirl of financial chaos around us. We bounce checks, we pay late charges on our mortgage, we forget to renew our driver's license or pay our property taxes. Why? We do this to obscure where we really stand, because we can't face our true financial selves, so we choose instead to ignore it, forget it, lose it, not face it—all actions that lead us away from money, not toward it, and keep us from creating.

Money can't see its way through clutter and chaos and confusion. It hates being spent on items stuffed into a cupboard or closet and never used. It dislikes being shoved into a drawer, in the form of unopened or unpaid bills, or crammed into a wallet any which way. If you hold on to what you have for longer than you should, you're using yesterday's space to hold tomorrow's offerings. If you allow the clutter in your mind to push out the true facts of your finances, you're not leaving room for thoughts of more. But if instead you clear its path of obstacles like these, you will be able to find your money, and money will be able to find you.

UNLEASHING THE POWER
OF MONEY

As the bearer of your money, you are the one who determines—with your thoughts, your words, and the financial actions you take— whether your money will be fat, skinny, full of vigor, or listless: how well, in other words, it will treat you in return. Give it the full power of its life force, and it can provide you with every material thing you wish for, increase its value many times over, help charities, buy education, and keep you and your family safe forever. Does money have a life force, an energy force, of its own? I truly believe it does, for I have seen its force at work, in small amounts of money that, invested wisely over time, thrive and prosper into fortunes—that's the life force of money given its full rein. I've also seen it allowed to languish. A twenty-dollar bill stuffed into the back pocket of your jeans and sent through the washer and dryer is money languishing. I believe that the life force of money is vital, given all that it has the power to achieve. The condi- tions under which you and your money live will in the end determine whether your life will be a rich one or not.

Conditions have to be optimal for any force to be unleashed; a hur- ricane, for example, will lose its strength before it gets very far inland. In the same way, certain conditions must prevail in order for you to attract money, make it feel welcome, and make it want to stay with you forever and grow. Only you can create these conditions. In order for money to find you, it has to work its way through your emotions, your thoughts, words, and actions. In order for you to become a beacon that illuminates the way for money, you have to clear the way for money, clear its path of the emotions, thoughts, words, actions, and external objects—the clutter, the chaos—that are blocking the way for more money to come in. This in turn will bring you closer to your true self and light the way for more.

JOHN PAUL'S STORY

I wanted to be an accountant mostly because I love numbers, always have. I live in a small town, and I know my clients really trust me, but I've always known, too, that other accountants in town have made a lot more than I have, which has frustrated me because I know I'm a better account- ant than many of them.

Not long ago I started going out with Sherri, a woman I fell for the very first time we met. I began to think about marriage, children, a life beyond numbers, and how we could have a great future together. But Sherri came to my office one night after work, and suddenly that future began to fade. She sounded almost sad when she said she would never hire an accountant with an office like mine. I looked around and saw what she meant—dust and chaos every- where, files falling down. The place was a mess, but I hadn't noticed; all I do is look at numbers. That night I felt that I had lost her respect, and we didn't have a great evening together. At the end of the night—it was a Thursday, I remember—I told her that I would have a surprise for her on Sunday.

Friday I couldn't concentrate on work at all, but was full of energy. I had a plan. I put the work aside and began cleaning my office, top to bottom. I did the files, and dusted, vacuumed, cleaned the windows and the blinds, everything. As I was cleaning, I found many things—papers I'd mis- placed, several old checks I had forgotten to cash, bills I wasn't sure I'd paid, correspondence I hadn't answered. It really dawned on me then that it wasn't enough just to be good with numbers. Here I was, supposed to be on top of things, and my own affairs were one big mess. By midnight on Saturday I was finished, and I felt so much better. But then I looked around at the walls, all scuffed and dingy, and I thought, More mess. This is actually what clients saw when they came to my office! Sherri was right. I wouldn't hire me, either. I went to the hardware store the next morning and bought some paint and brushes. When Sherri came at noon, I had two walls painted, and the place already looked a thousand times better. She was really pleased, I could tell, but I was even more pleased. She later said that was the moment when she fell in love. That was about ten months ago, and the funny thing is that since I've cleaned up my act, my business is really picking up, too. I still have to make a conscious effort not to be disorganized, but I'm also doing so well that I'm thinking it might be time to hire a secretary. It was looking beyond my numbers that made the difference.

Being good with numbers is not necessarily the same thing as being good with money. John Paul was burying his money and potential under piles of clutter and chaos, leaving money with no ready way to find him, which in fact was turning money away. When he cleared the way for more, more came in: more business, more money, a richer life in more ways than one.

PENNY'S STORY

I'm your basic stay-at-home mom, I guess you'd call it, and I always left the finances to Charlie, my husband. With two kids, we've never had that much extra, but we always tried to put a little away into the savings account with every pay-check. We used to talk about what we would live on when we retired, but those conversations never went very far; there was too much to pay for every day.

When my father died, my mother was hit all at once with trying to figure out what she had. There was enough money there, which was a relief to everyone, but what surprised us was that Mom really got interested in her money. She said she couldn't believe how conservative Dad had been all those years, and she was seeing for the first time how much more there could have been. She joined an investment club and put some money into it which she said she wanted to go toward college tuition for my kids, who are now seven and nine. This got me excited, and I began to watch my mother's stock port-folio on television periodically throughout the day. The mar-ket would go up, then down, all day long, and I got really hooked on what was happening.

Then I started bugging Charlie about our money. I was thinking that we could do better. He has this drawer where he keeps our papers, and I kept saying, Let's go through it together. For the longest time he wouldn't, but finally we did. It was a hodgepodge of little bits of money. Six hundred dol-lars in savings bonds from when I was working, before I had the kids. Three IRAs at the bank. Two savings accounts we'd started when the children were born but had forgotten to add money to. Papers from Charlie's 401(k) at his old job. Plus our savings account. But it added up to fourteen thou-sand dollars. We were amazed. We actually had fourteen thousand dollars that we didn't know about stuffed into this drawer.

We cleared everything out and then looked into what would be best to do with it. We kept two thousand dollars in the savings account for emergencies and invested the rest in

*these great mutual funds we read about. I figured out how to
do the paperwork, which wasn't that complicated once I
actually sat down and did it. It was a great feeling, thinking
that we could actually begin to make some money.*

*Then one day, I was watching a financial show on
TV, and I thought, What am I doing sitting here, watching
money? The kids are at school, and I should be making
money instead. Charlie and I had already agreed that I
wouldn't go back to work full-time for a few more years,
but I figured I could do* something. *So I've been substitute-
teaching a couple of days a week ever since the beginning
of the school year. And all that money goes into our investments. I really feel like a grown-up for the first time, and it
feels good.*

By clearing the way through their financial clutter, Penny and Charlie
found they had more than they imagined: enough to begin to see a
clear path to a promising future. Stuffed in a drawer, their money was
neglected and suffocating. When they let it out and treated it with
respect, they were empowering it to grow on their behalf in the years
ahead. Penny then took that power to heart and, with her actions,
turned toward more.

JEFF'S STORY

*You can imagine what it's like having five kids—sheer may-
hem. It's fun for the most part, this high-energy household.
But it's also hard to keep track of everything. Meg, my wife, is
basically a saint. She runs the house, gets the kids off to
school and camp and lessons, buys them what they need, and
keeps track of the money. I'm a lawyer. I make good money,
and we live in a nice neighborhood, but with five kids, it
never seems like enough. Meg doesn't complain, but she's*

always sort of hinted that the money isn't exactly under control and let it go at that.

Then one day it all started to fall apart. It was a weekend, and I went to send a fax to a client, and the machine didn't work. No dial tone, either. So I called the phone company to complain, and they said that the line had been turned off for nonpayment. We get a separate bill for the fax line, because it was installed at a different time from the phone line. How long had it been off, I asked, and they said two weeks. Two weeks! Think of the work I might have missed, plus who wants their clients to hear that their lawyer's line has been disconnected when they try to fax you? Meg wasn't home, so I went to her desk to look for the bill and found a lot more than I bargained for.

Bills everywhere, especially for credit cards I didn't even know we had. Some bills weren't opened yet, but were already overdue. I looked in her checkbook and saw that she was paying a little here, a little there, trying to keep us afloat. Then I came across a sweet note she had written to her sister but never sent, promising to send the money she'd borrowed next month. It broke my heart, but clearly something was really wrong with the way we were living. Here I was making a perfectly good salary by any standard, and my whole family was sinking.

The timing was unusual because the house was absolutely empty—soccer games, play dates, who knows where they all were. Shopping, maybe. Anyway, I started looking around, going from room to room, and there was so much stuff. Rollerblades still in the box, toys and cosmetics still in bags, clothes everywhere, and, believe me, I wasn't exactly innocent, there was plenty of my stuff, too. I looked in some drawers and what did I find? Five rolls of Scotch tape, partly used. Five rolls! Who needs five rolls of tape? There was this pasta-

making machine in the kitchen that we'd used maybe once. Books all over the place, three children's tape players, sweaters for the dog, and about a dozen lunch boxes. I just can't begin to name all the stuff.

When everybody came home, they ran laughing and screaming into the house, and then they got quiet when they saw me. I called a family meeting right then and said, "This has got to stop." When I get serious, they really pay attention, even the little ones, and there was silence in the room. I walked them through every bedroom, even mine and Meg's, because this wasn't the children's fault. Then I said we were having a yard sale next weekend, and everyone should round up stuff to contribute to it.

We made over a thousand dollars on our yard sale, which left us with twenty-three thousand dollars in debt, five kids, and a big mess. It was Meg's idea that we go to a consumer credit counseling service, which was a big help. It got us organized and focused, and the counselor showed us how to deal with the debt first, and how we could begin to save later, once the credit cards were paid off. We sent all the yard-sale money to the credit card companies, which felt pretty great, I have to say.

I look around at my neighbors, and they have the same stuff that we had and still have. And I wonder, Do they have the same kind of debt? Or could they really have so much more money? I had a hint at the yard sale, when more than one of my neighbors said they should do the same thing. Maybe we all have too much, or maybe we all just owe too much.

The weird thing is that since we started paying attention, which is basically what we're doing now, paying attention, everything seems more possible. Last week, we got an offer for a credit card with a really low interest rate for six

*months, and Meg said, Let's do it, roll over some debt, and
that will make a difference. Then for the first time, our town
announced a summer program for kids, with swimming and
tennis—free. So the kids can go to that. Strangest of all,
though, is that just the other day I got a letter from my father,
with a check for five thousand dollars. He'd done well in the
market, he said, and wanted us to put the money toward a
college fund, a thousand dollars for each of the kids. He's
never in my life done anything like that before. Weighed
against our debt, it's hope. The debt feels lighter. We can deal
with it.*

With the best intentions in the world, Jeff and Meg filled up their
house with children—and filled up their lives with clutter. When they
finally faced their clutter, they also came face-to-face with their
finances. And made some changes. They got rid of some of yesterday's
spending, yesterday's clutter, and what's happened? Already, more is
coming in. Reduce the clutter, they learned, and you can make way for
more.

Drawing upon the courage to be rich does not mean denying yourself
the important things in life, but changing your thoughts about money,
your words about money, and the actions you take with the money
you have and the items your money has bought. In essence, I am asking you to change your current money reflexes, so that you start
thinking, talking, and behaving with money, your money, in a new
way—with clarity. If you have very little right now, I know that it takes
immense faith to believe you could have more. But you can. How can
you start a fortune with, say, twenty dollars? With faith, with that
twenty dollars, the next twenty dollars, and the clarity to see all the
way to tomorrow, when the first twenty dollars has disappeared into a
sea of plenty.

But you must start to clear away the clutter now, as John Paul,

Penny, and Jeff did. Money needs time and space to grow, and the "seed money" you plant today must be treated the way you would a garden: planted and nurtured and given time to grow. Tiny seeds can grow into huge plants, and tiny sums of money can grow into great wealth. Perhaps at this point in your life it sounds hopeless, but with faith—and, yes, courage—you can turn your life around and find the clarity in today, along with the clarity to look forward to tomorrow. Clear a path through the clutter and chaos in all aspects of your life, and you can see the way ahead and find the capacity for abundance in the clarity.

YOUR EXERCISE: FOUR STEPS TOWARD CLARITY

You make room for more by knowing what you have, by not owning anything you don't want or need or love, and by valuing every item you own. You make room for more, literally and metaphorically, by creating a place for more to enter.

Your possessions are the earthly, material objects that represent who you are, what you care about, how you define yourself: your taste and your value system. You spend hours of your life working to pay for these possessions. Over time, your possessions change, from the makeshift objects that furnished your first apartment, when you were starting out, to the items you bought later with such care, perhaps with the idea of permanence. The following actions toward clarity will take you on a tour of your house and its contents, four times. I want you to think about the value of each object—what it cost you when you bought it, what it is worth in dollars today, and what it is worth as an earthly, material representation of who you are now.

1. The first time, wander through your house, your garage, look through your drawers, closets, and cupboards with

the goal of finding at least twenty-five items that you are willing to throw away—yes, throw away. Anything from worn-out shoes, grimy duplicate can openers, broken toys, and lipsticks that were definitely a mistake to spent toothbrushes, unused cleaning products, and earrings with one half of the pair missing. Broken umbrellas, dried-up cans of paint, candle stubs. Bits of things where there's not even enough left to use. Twenty-five items. Keep looking until you find them. These items are gone, and I want you to throw them away.

2. Now go through your house again, this time in search of loose change and the occasional bill squirreled away. Look in your handbags and your briefcase. Look in the pockets of your sweaters, pants, jackets, skirts, shirts, dresses, and coats; look under the cushions of your chairs and couches, and in between the seats of your car. Do you have a penny jar somewhere? Go get it. Look through your jewelry box or where you keep your cuff links. Rummage through the kitchen drawers, any other secret places where you might have left or put some money. If you are like most of us, you will find, all together, thirty dollars or more. Then put the money you've found into a jar—call it a jar of abundance—or a bowl—a bowl of bounty—to remind you of what you didn't even know you had, and put it near where you keep your bills.

3. Go through your house a third time. This time, find at least twenty-five items that are still in good shape but are truthfully of no further use to you. Clothes you or your family no longer wear, winter coats, scarves, hats, old belts, handbags, dishes, a working appliance you have replaced, videos, a stack of books you no longer need, still-good toys. Twenty-five items that someone else could use and would be grate-

ful to have. After you have gathered everything, reflect for a minute on the money you spent, how much of it was wasted, and how little you have to show for it now.

Now clear away the clutter. Take these items to a donor bin, a charity thrift shop, a nursing home or day-care center, the Salvation Army or Goodwill. Take them, in other words, to a place where people who need them will have the readiest access to them.

Could you have a yard sale instead? You could. But I want you to begin thinking expansively. By having a yard sale, you see, you'd get only a fraction of what these items are really worth, which diminishes both your purchase and your purchase price. They are better given to someone who will appreciate them and use them gratefully, rather than sold to someone who will gloat over having gotten a bargain. This can actually raise their worth to full value. Rather than trying to make up for your mistakes, you will have made a generous offering to the world. Make your donations within one week.

Charitable giving is not only a donation but also a deduction. If you have taken the items to an anonymous place (a clothing drop, for instance), jot down honestly what you have donated—a man's suit, for example, will yield you a tax deduction of seventy-two dollars, and a nice woman's dress will let you deduct sixty-five dollars. If you have taken them to a place where you will be given a receipt for the items donated, save the receipt for tax time.

4. Now go through your house a fourth time, pausing to touch and look at the items that mean everything in the world to you, the items you would never part with, ever—photographs of your children, a ring your mother gave you, the

desk that was your grandmother's, scrapbooks, perhaps the painting in your living room that was the first big thing you and your partner ever bought together. Now think of these items so precious to you, and how little in fact they cost you. Define for yourself the true meaning of worth.

Just a rough estimate—what do you suppose your clutter cost you at the time you bought it, and how much money does that mean you no longer have today? Ten fifteen-dollar T-shirts, an ill-fitting forty-dollar skirt or seventy-dollar shirt, the toaster oven that never worked properly, the bread maker that made oddly shaped and funny-tasting bread. What did these things that you had to buy because you thought you couldn't live without them—and then didn't use them—really cost you in the end? Note, too, the items that served you well; these are items from which you "got your money's worth"—a fair and equal trade.

What I want for you to do is to begin to think about money, what it can buy and when it can serve you better kept, simply, as money. Remember that most items, the minute they're removed from the store in which you bought them, lose their financial value or are certainly worth far less than what you paid for them—you can bring value to them only by using them.

By removing the first of your clutter, you have already begun to create more—more space, more awareness, more honesty, more possibility, more hope for tomorrow, and, ultimately, more money. What you don't want is gone, and therefore meaningless clutter is out of the way. The chances are good that you've also filled a jar of "found money," to remind you that you had even more than you realized. By treasuring anew the items you could never part with, you've been reminded of the things that money cannot buy. These are lessons in more, lessons in clarity. Facing up to your money, probably for the first time in your life, will leave you with a sense of power, with the feeling that yes, you can figure this out. When clutter is in control, you leave that clutter with the last word, and clutter has only the power to destroy. When you take control of the clutter, you are left instead with the power to act and the power to create.

FINANCIAL CLUTTER

Unpaid bills create financial clutter, as does debt, and they both work against clarity. Unopened monthly checking account statements clutter up your clear thoughts about money, for when you don't know how much or how little you really have, you do not know what you can (or cannot) afford to spend.

More clutter arises from the things you know you must do—set up your will or trust, arrange guardianship for your children in case something happens to you, get your debt under control, begin investing for your future—but haven't yet done. Bank or credit card statements you don't read or understand are costing you, blocking you, and getting in your way financially. Changes you mean to make but haven't made to your 401(k) plan preoccupy your mind and keep your finances in a frozen state of chaos. Financial papers kept for years, unsorted, in a filing cabinet; a messy wallet, with the bills stuffed in or folded or out of order—these things mean you aren't paying attention to your money, which is tantamount to pushing it away. Items as seemingly insignificant as overdue library books or videos cost money by the day, clutter your thoughts, and give you the feeling that your life is in disarray. Even in the neatest and tidiest house, financial clutter can stand in the way of more.

Remember your jar of money, the money you didn't even know you had? I asked you to put it near where you keep your bills. Just leave it there for now. By stating your desire to be rich, in drawing on your courage, in taking the actions that will lead you toward more, you will also leave your financial clutter behind you. In the chapters that follow, we'll get to what you must do to create a new future. We'll get to what you must do with your found money. And it will be so much easier to move forward once you have left this clutter behind. Having come this far, you have cleared the way toward wealth, toward richness of all kinds. Now it is time to make your dreams come true.

PART II

THE VALUE OF MONEY

CHAPTER 4

THE COURAGE
TO VALUE MONEY

Not long ago, I was talking to my next-door neighbor Elysia, who was outside selling lemonade with her sister, Naomi. We were having a conversation about raising her prices from ten cents to twenty-five cents per cup. I asked her, "Elysia, what are the five most important things to you in life?"

She contemplated the history of her seven years, then looked at me and said, "First my family, then my house, television, candy, and then money." Impressed that she had come up with exactly five items, I probed a little deeper.

"Elysia, what do you need to get the candy that you love?"

"Money," she said.

"And how about the TV, what do you need to get that?"

"Money."

"And how about your house?"

"Money," she replied once again.

And then I asked, "How about your family, what do you need to get them?"

Just as quickly, she replied, "Love."

"That's right," I said, "but don't you think that maybe you have to reorder your list? You see, if you need money to buy the candy, the house, and the TV, then don't you think money should be more important than what it can buy?"

She thought about this, and then she looked at me and said, "I think you are right."

Elysia, in that short period of time, was introduced to the first law of money, a law that serves as the foundation for wise spending:

THE FIRST LAW OF MONEY

People first. Then money. Then things.

You see, most of us are just like Elysia, in that we value things more than we value money. We care more about having what money can buy than we care about having money itself. If we valued money more than we valued things, we would not part with it so freely, nor would we think of parting with money we didn't have in order to buy something on credit. This is a vital law, a law that is respectful of money, a law that, if you follow it, will keep what you have and what you spend (or don't spend) in full harmony. It is a law that, if you follow it, will make you truly rich.

People first. Those things that are created by and kept with love must always come before anything else. Family, friends, your partner, your children, yourself. The adage that money can't buy love is true, and a life without love—regardless of how much money one has—is a poor life indeed.

Then money. Can you imagine going to someone's house and having them proudly show you a room filled with thousands of dollar bills and telling you the history of how all that money came to be? You would be appalled at the vulgarity. At the same time, you would think nothing of it if you were to go to someone's house and be given a tour of a room they had just redecorated. What did it take to redecorate that room? Money. Money exchanged for furniture, paintings, carpeting, lamps, and so on. In either case, you're being shown a room full of money. The difference in your perception was the value system that you applied—a room full of things is okay, whereas a room full of money is not. That is because you value things more than you value money.

Then things. When your financial priorities are in order, things come last.

GETTING AND SPENDING

We work hard for our money, forty hours or more a week, and once we're set loose from the workplace, we go shopping. We buy food and clothes and stuff, and then we say we just don't know where the money went. But if we valued money over things, over the items it can buy, then we would know exactly where our money went. We would change our money/thing ratio so that we'd have more money than things. We would take great pleasure in seeing our money and watching it grow. Barring unexpected illness, we would have no debt—and, for that matter, no doubt. We would always know when we could afford something we wanted to buy, and we would also be more likely to be able to buy the things we truly wanted.

YOUR EXERCISE: FIND THE COURAGE, FIND THE MONEY

Our consumer culture makes us want things, and easy credit enables us to have them, long before we've paid for them. Bigger and better, or smaller and better. New. Improved. Entire new arenas of consumer goods keep opening up, enticing and seducing us. No one can say no all the time, so I'm not going to ask you to do that. I learned long ago that restricting my clients to a budget works no better than forcing someone overweight to diet—sooner or later there'll be a financial tantrum. Instead, I am asking you to start making some choices about today and tomorrow.

Not long ago I was in a gourmet and gift shop where there were giveaway samples on all the display tables, making the shopping experience feel like a party. On one table they were offering slivers of very pretty fragrant soap. You bought this brightly colored soap not in standard bars but by weight; they'd cut what you wanted from a bar the size of a loaf of bread: $10 a pound. I did a quick calculation, and figured that if I were to switch from my ordinary soap to this fancy soap, I would be spending $100 more a year on *soap*.

At another table, they were offering teeny cups and spoons with various kinds of gourmet vinegars for customers to taste—blueberry tarragon, cabernet sauvignon, cognac, and fig. They were exotic-tasting, it's true, but each bottle of vinegar cost $14—$10 more than I usually pay for my perfectly fine vinegar. Another quick calculation, and I realized that if I switched to these fancy vinegars, I would be spending maybe $50 more a year on vinegar than I do now.

At the next table I tasted some raspberry-mint jam: delicious. But worth $6 more per jar than I usually spend for jam? I don't think so.

But it is in just this way—premium this and designer that—that our spending inches up, our scale of living inches up, we upgrade a little here and a little there, to the point where those things we once thought of as luxuries have become necessities. With three relatively small indulgences at that store, assuming I never went back to my usual brands, I would have raised my cost of living by almost $200 a year.

Now, it could just so happen that soap, vinegar, and jams are items that really matter to me and that the thought of having these exquisite varieties makes me feel so great and pampered that the extra $200 a year would be worth it to me. If that were the case, well, then, I might have decided that I was going to buy them anyway, extravagant or not. But if I valued money over things, I would find that $200 from somewhere else in my life, not simply tack on to my spending an extra $200 a year in order to feel good. Because it's not just $200 today that's at stake. It's also $200 next year and every year thereafter. Beyond that, it's $200 that's being used for today's small pleasures at a far greater cost tomorrow.

If you're not on a course of getting rich but want to be, you have to change course; it's that simple. To choose rich is to make every penny count, every dollar count, every financial choice count. To erase the bad habits that make money vaporize into nothingness. To distinguish between necessity and luxury, and to choose your luxuries very, very carefully. Case in point: the fancy "designer" lemonade I also sampled that day at the gourmet shop.

Let's say I drink six quarts of lemonade a week, all three months of summer, and let's say I switch to premium lemonade. One summer's cost? $180. Let's say I don't switch but stick to the 65-cent version. One summer's cost? $23.40, which I've been paying all along anyway. I put the $156.60 I didn't spend into a good no-load mutual fund for 20 years at 10 percent interest, and it grows to $8992.

Now I want you to examine the necessities in your own life, and also the luxuries. Next, choose a few luxuries that you wouldn't mind "downgrading" to the necessity category—$500, $1000, $2000 worth each year; you pick the number that feels right. Regardless of how much or how little you think you have, you can find money by examining your expenses, trimming your spending here and there, and learning to choose and value money over things.

What I want you to do is to think about everything you own, everything you owe on, everything you want, everything you actually need. Examine your spending carefully and honestly, taking note of items you don't use, items where maybe, just maybe, you don't need the top-of-the-line version next time, areas where you're apt to waste money flagrantly. In chapter 3, we removed some of the clutter from our past, and with this exercise, we will turn future clutter into money instead. This exercise will help you find $500, $1000, $2000, or more, every year—money that you will think about and treat differently after you read the chapters that follow.

What will the money be used for? First, to speed up the process to eradicate any debt you have, for once and for all. After that, the money will be used to invest in your future.

Here are some thoughts to get you started:

♦ Your morning coffee. Do you make it at home (cheaper) or grab a cup on the way into the office (more costly)? Do you drink Starbucks or other superior coffee? One medium-size Starbucks coffee a day costs $2.75, which means you're spending $1004 a year on morning coffee. Invested at 10 percent, that's $57,504 over 20 years, $98,740 over 25 years, and $165,152 over 30 years.

♦ Somewhere along the line, did you switch from an old-fashioned blanket and bedspread to a luxurious puffy down coverlet? That's a step up from necessity to luxury. What about extra-fluffy towels, lovely scented soaps, rich shampoos, and accessories for the bath? Have you turned your daily bath into a luxury at-home spa? At what cost? If you can cut back just $10 a month on these luxuries, you will have $120 more a year to invest.

♦ Have you added to your phone line extra features like call waiting, call forwarding, or caller ID? At what cost per year? Eliminating caller ID, which costs $7.99 a month, will save you $95.88 a year today and give you $95.88 more a year for tomorrow.

♦ Cell phone. Do you really need it? What is it costing you per year?

- Designer sunglasses. How much did you spend on your most recent pair of sunglasses? Have you looked into cheaper brands? How often do you lose a pair? Are expensive sunglasses a downgradable luxury for you?

- Have you made the switch from half gallons of ordinary ice cream to pints of premium? What about cookies—do you buy "designer" brands rather than big bags of Oreos?

- Do you and your partner go to the movies once a week? Luxury or necessity? If you skipped one week a month, you'd save $200 or more a year (not to mention considerable additional savings from not eating out afterward).

- How many things are there in your kitchen that you rarely or never use? Appliances—pasta maker, bread maker, ice cream maker, popcorn popper, waffle iron? Rarely used pots and pans? How about serving bowls and platters? Do you need all the ones you have? Is all your equipment top-of-the-line? Do you use it enough to justify having the best? Might you think twice before buying something else for the kitchen?

- Do you buy books that you know you're going to read just once, rather than take them out from the library? Four fewer hardcover mysteries a year, at $25 each, puts you $100 closer to your goal.

- How extravagantly does your garden grow? Gardening is suddenly a big new "necessity" and can be a costly one. Could your garden budget take some pruning?

- Daily bread—have you decided that the best thing since sliced bread is French baguettes, bread that goes stale after one day? Have you switched from ordinary loaves of bread to gourmet bread? Luxury or necessity?

- Designer underwear—luxury or necessity?

- How many power tools are in your garage, and how often do you use them?

- How much unused exercise equipment do you have around the house? Have you discarded your old sweats in favor of slick new exercise wear?

- Must you have an expensive camera? A videocam?

- How often do you feel you need a new car? Could it be less often?

- Remember the days when every family had one TV? How many color televisions do you have now? How many VCRs? How many videotapes? Do you tape over things you've taped before or use fresh tapes every time? How many videotapes do your children actually own? Would you consider replacing an old TV with a newer model (bigger screen, sleeker console) before the old one actually stops working? If so, could you reconsider?

- Have you signed up for cable TV with all the extra channels or just the basic plan? The difference can be $25 a month, or $300 a year.

- As a kid, did you drive to vacation spots or visit your grandparents on holidays? These days, do all your vacation destinations require planes and hotels? At what cost?

- Does someone else do your cleaning? Luxury or necessity?

- Do you routinely take your clothing to the dry cleaner when all it needs is a pressing you could do yourself? If your dry-cleaning bill were just $10 less each week, you would have $520 a year to invest.

- Do you use disposable razors? Buy expensive juice boxes for the kids? Small cost, maybe, but the cost of disposables adds up.

- Have you switched from old-fashioned vegetable oil to the much more expensive extra-virgin olive oil?

- Do you drink premium beer instead of regular beer? How much, over the course of a year, is this costing you?

- Do you have a really great "designer" bike? How often do you use it?

- Do you buy a lot of costume jewelry, wear it a few times, then forget about it and go on to other, newer costume jewelry?

- Do you need a separate phone line for your fax? For your computer? Is this a genuine need?

- Luxury or necessity—that bouquet of fresh flowers you routinely pick up on the way home from work every single Friday, even if you're not going to be home much that weekend? At, say, $8 a week, you're spending $416 per year of the money that could be making your future more beautiful.

- Do you buy lottery tickets twice a week? Even one ticket twice a week can cost $104 a year, and the odds of creating your own fortune with $104 a year are far greater than the odds of your winning your fortune in the lottery.

- Do you pump your own gas to save money each week?

- Do you use more expensive whitening toothpaste rather than standard varieties? How much extra does it cost per tube and per year?

- Do you love the luxury of manicures, pedicures, and waxing so much that you wouldn't think of going without them? A $15 manicure—$18 with tip—every two weeks, costs $468 over the course of one year.

- Are your cosmetics department-store varieties or drugstore brands? Does every single cosmetic item you "need" have to be premium? How many cosmetics currently in your bathroom have turned out to be mistakes? At what cost? Could you trim $200 a year from the cost of cosmetics?

- How much do you truly spend on convenience foods, gourmet takeout, restaurants, and entertaining? Might there be a way to trim a few hundred dollars a year here and there?

- Do you have a satellite dish? Need—or luxury?
- Do you have an electronic personal organizer? Has it gotten you organized? Do you even use it?
- Did you raise your children with disposable diapers and pre-moistened baby wipes? Are there a lot of seldom-used toys around the house? Could you pare down by $200 or more the mountain of stuff you buy your kids each year?
- How new is your computer? Are you constantly trading up for faster, more powerful models? Could you wait a little longer next time?
- Do you really need all the clothes you have? Do you buy clothes simply because they're on sale? Can you trim $300 a year from your annual clothing budget?
- How often are you assessed a late charge on videos, library books, and bills?
- Do your kids have a separate phone line? Luxury or necessity?
- Have you switched to extended-wear—and more expensive—disposable contact lenses?
- Do you wear sneakers other than plain old Keds when you don't need to?
- Do you pay for "designer" bottled water and fancy fruit juices?
- Do you belong to a gym? Do you use it?
- Did you leave the barber behind years ago for an expensive hairstylist? Do you pay for coloring as well? Some stylists charge $100 for a haircut; investing this money once a month for 25 years, at 10 percent, you'd have $132,683 (not including the tip!).
- Do you have a gas grill instead of the charcoal kind you used to have? Is that another luxury you've turned into a need?
- Have you ever "needed" cosmetic surgery? Cosmetic dentistry? A massage? A personal trainer?

◆ How many compact discs do you have that you never listen to? Or tapes?

◆ How often do you go into stores or look through mail-order catalogues without any particular "need" in mind? How often do you buy?

◆ Might you be able to say no to the next high tech/high fashion/ high concept item that appeals to you, at least until you see how much other people "need" it after they've had it for six months?

Did you find $500, $1000, $2000? Here's how it will make you feel to become rich, over time. You made the money materialize, and maybe you can come up with even more. After you rid yourself of the burden of debt, you will begin to invest it. Soon, the interest begins to add up. Then the interest compounds, month after month, year after year. Then there comes a point where the money you have put away begins to matter. It begins to make you feel good. And then it begins to matter more. You begin to make decisions differently—an extra $50 toward tomorrow begins to seem much more valuable than another sweater or another dinner out or another CD to play once or twice in the car on your way to work. There will come a time when the money you have created matters more than the choices you will make in order to create it. At that point, you will choose—without regrets, in a kind of excited state—to keep pouring money into your tomorrow ($50 extra a month, $100 extra a month, or more). You will choose to value money over things. After a while, you begin to grow with your money. You stop cringing every time the bills come, the unexpected happens, the fear begins anew. When getting rich becomes your true goal, you're on your way.

That's how we get rich, financially speaking. Little by little. Every fortune in this world began with a balance of zero. Oddly enough, that's also how we get rich, emotionally speaking—by the way we make our choices and the choices we make.

CHAPTER 5

DEFINING VALUE
AND WORTH

YOUR MONEY REFLEXES

In a financial planner's version of a party game, I often ask people this question: If I were to offer you (a) $1000 a day for 30 days, or (b) a penny on day 1, two pennies on day 2, four pennies on day 3, and so on, doubling the amount every day for 30 days, which would you take? Invariably, people will start mentally adding up numbers, maybe getting as far as day 10, when the amount I'd give them would be a whopping $5.12. At that point, most people go for the sure thing and reflexively take the first offer, the automatic $30,000. A few people, even without doing all the math, will always opt for the unknown, figuring there's a trick in here somewhere; even without knowing the outcome they will just as reflexively choose b. Only very occasionally will someone actually sit down and start doubling pennies on paper and realize that by day 22 the amount I'd give them is up to $20,971.52, and know which option to pick. Pick b and you'd have amassed $5,737,418.23 by day 30.

Aside from the fact that there's no actual money at stake, why don't people want to play this game through to see where it might go? I am convinced that no one wants to play for the same reasons that most of us don't want to deal with our real money in our real lives. We prefer instant gratification (you can add up the $30,000 in a second) to what money can do over time (five or ten minutes to double up the pennies). Because we don't respect small amounts of money enough to believe that they can grow to a fortune, many people won't pick up a penny off the street. Unbelievable as it sounds, for many of us our gut reflex is to turn away from money, which essentially is turning away from what we can truly become.

Do you compete with your money? Try to prove love with your money? Try to please others with your money? Does charging something give you a kind of high from which you later crash? Do you tend always to say yes when asked to spend money or, conversely, tend always to say no? Do you hate to part with your money? Like the automatic a or b response most people offer to my game, before even playing out the possibilities, all these are reflexive responses to money, not responses of reason, and when you let your gut reflexes govern your behavior with money, or when you want money to say something to others about you that isn't true, you're in effect answering before permitting your courage its voice. You're silencing your courage, and with that action, you're not acting in your best interests.

EMILY: *"It makes me so mad. Every other weekend, the twins come home with some expensive present from their father, even though I have asked him not to buy them so much stuff. So the next weekend, my weekend, I always go out and buy them some nice present, too— nicer, I might add, than I can afford."*

Emily's reflex is to compete, not with love but with spending, with the result that she's angry at her ex-husband for overspending, angry at herself for competitive spending—and also angry at herself for conveying to her children values of which she does not approve. The courageous reflex is to look within, not without, when deciding what to spend. No child is born to expect or demand a big treat every weekend, but every child will thrive with a full weekend's worth of love and attention.

BRIAN: *"We have a 401(k) plan at work, but my employer doesn't match what the employees put in. I'm going to sign up for it anyway, as soon as I have the money."*

Each of the five years that Brian has worked for this firm, he has gotten a raise, even though he was managing just fine before the raise. The greatest pity here is that Brian, who is early into his career (and his spending/saving habits), is at a point in which time could benefit him so much more with every contribution he makes today. But his reflex is to put today's desires before tomorrow's needs. The courageous reflex is always to keep tomorrow in mind today.

LIZ: *"I am so excited about my new condo. Usually I'm not quite this bad with credit cards, but this time I kind of went overboard. I wanted it to be perfect."*

Liz's reflex is to spend money before she has it, to get to the goal without taking pleasure and gratification in the process. Do you really think that after this surge in spending and debt, Liz is going to want to listen to her voice of reason, pay off her debt, and stop making her home her dream home? With courage, you choose to put money in before you take it out.

As their words suggest, these people know that they are acting reflexively, without letting reason—and courage—have their say in the decisions they're making and the money they're spending or not spending.

When you live with the courage to be rich as a financial and emotional constant, your life will open up in a number of new ways. You will be able to temper your reflexive spending or your refusal to spend, without feeling anxious or deprived either way, because you will be making your choices from a rich place, not a place of poverty or uncertainty. When you value money over things, you will shop with a sense of calm that you don't have now, because your debt will be gone, your spending will be in harmony with your investing, and you will choose to buy only things that you value more than the money it costs to buy them. When you choose to live a rich life, you feel rich in every way, you act expansively and generously with your money, and your money responds to you in the same way.

RICH THOUGHTS ABOUT SPENDING AND VALUE

When it comes to most things that matter to us—a relationship, our job, office politics, how well our children are doing in school—we tend to obsess about them. We talk about them constantly with our friends, and we look at them from every possible angle, trying to understand every nuance, trying to make things work out in the best possible way. We'd all agree that money is important, right up there with our relationships, our jobs, the things that define us. But when we obsess about money, what do we obsess about? Maybe we're buying something important, and we obsess about getting a good deal. Often we obsess about whether or not we can afford a certain item, which almost always means that we're trying to talk ourselves into buying something we cannot afford. We may obsess about the things that other people have and how much they cost. Certainly we obsess about those things we don't have. For all this, however, we seldom pull close to the heart of money, or its true value, when we talk about money. We rarely talk about what it can do rather than what it can buy, which means that we value things, not money.

Here are some questions I want you to think about now:

- ♦ What is it in life that you truly value?
- ♦ Do you value the possessions you have around you?

- Do you value your money?
- What do you value most?

S U Z E ' S S T O R Y

For years, I played a little game with my clients to try to make them think about what was really important. I would ask them to pretend that there was a huge fire coming their way, and to pretend that they had just thirty minutes to get everything out of their house. What would they take?

It never failed. Without hesitation, the answers always came flowing back in a stream of sentiment—my wedding pictures, my mom's wedding dress, family scrapbooks, a bracelet my grandmother gave me, an oil portrait of my child.

After years of pretend fires, such a fire became a tragic reality for me and many of my clients. A number of years ago, the Oakland Hills experienced one of the worst fires in history. I was visiting a friend and will never forget looking out the window and thinking, What is all that smoke? The skies were quickly turning from a gorgeous blue to the most ominous black I have ever seen. The hills were on fire. Just then we heard from a neighbor that the fire was spreading, and if you wanted to get anything out of your house, you had very little time. I jumped into my car and headed up to my house, which was in the direct path of the fire. When I got home, some of my neighbors were already loading their cars to evacuate the area. As I began doing the same thing, in a state of sheer panic, I remember thinking, Oh my God, I am doing in real life what I have been asking my clients to pretend to do all these years. I then took a good look at everything I had packed, and sure enough, I was bringing with me the things that money could never replace. Items of the highest personal value to me, but worthless to any other soul on earth.

I drove down the hills and joined the other evacuees watching the smoke from a safe distance. I began asking others what they had chosen to bring with them, and, like me, most had chosen those items that had deep meaning only to themselves, items that money could never replace.

By the time the fire died down, at four-fifteen that afternoon, stopping about a mile from my house, some three thousand homes were lost. As I drove through what used to be some of the most beautiful areas in Oakland, there were charred ruins wherever you looked. The only things left standing were some chimneys. I thought then of the solace their priceless mementos would give to those who had otherwise lost everything.

When we are faced with a situation like this, we know beyond a doubt what has value for us and what does not. We know what to take and what to leave behind. We act in an instinctive, reflexive way—and yet perhaps this is when we behave most purely with our money. But it's rare that we're asked to make these kinds of choices. Day to day, we lose touch with these, our purest values; we obscure them in the way we spend, neglect to save, fail to take the financial actions we know we should.

The courage to be rich comes alive when you have the courage to know what you really do value in this life, when you live—and spend—with the clarity with which my neighbors and I expressed our values that desperate day of the fire. In order to be truly rich, you have to not only value what you have, but also have only things in your life that you value. You have to value doing what is right over doing what is easy. You have to value tomorrow along with today. Finally, once you internalize these qualities, you have to think them, say them, and express them in your actions. At that point, you will want for nothing, and you will have what you want. Your financial reflexes will be pure and true to your goal of becoming rich.

ASKING FOR MORE

In order to become rich, your self-worth has to rise along with your net worth—you must feel you deserve to be rich, you must never cast yourself as the victim, you must stop settling or feeling as if you're just getting by, and you must make the most of what you have. This is a hard concept for many of us to grasp, for most of us feel as if we're already doing the best we can—but are we, really?

TRACY'S STORY

My marriage was basically a disaster. We had been married for only a year when I found out that Mark was sleeping around, but by then I was pregnant, so I stayed with him for two more years before I took the baby and moved out. I'm a personal trainer, and one of my clients had a garage that had been converted into a little cottage that he rented to me for eight hundred dollars a month. I figured it was probably the best I could do, so we moved in, Maisie and I. I teach at a gym, and I also have private clients, so I figured I could get by.

The heat in the cottage didn't work too well, so I first had to buy a space heater to keep us warm, then some blankets— all the things I needed to set up house—and everything went on my credit cards. There's day care at the gym, so when I'm there I'm fine, but whenever I was training clients at their houses, I couldn't exactly bring Maisie along, so my day-care costs kept going up. Then half the time my clients had excuses for why they couldn't pay on time, and sometimes they'd call and cancel, and never pay what they owed me. So I was getting pretty desperate. It didn't help that my car needed a new transmission, which was another thirteen hundred dollars on my credit card. I was up to my credit limit, so what did I do? I got another card.

I was talking to Ron, one of the other instructors at the gym, one day, a really nice guy, and he mentioned that he had just upped his rates for private clients to sixty-five dollars an hour. What! Then he said that he had all the clients he could handle; did I want a couple of referrals? I couldn't believe it: How was it that he was charging twenty-five dollars an hour more and he had more clients than he could handle? I asked him if he ever had trouble getting paid, and he kind of looked at me as if I were crazy and said no, he always got paid up front, plus he had a policy that if a client canceled less than twenty-four hours in advance, the client had to pay a thirty-dollar cancellation fee. I felt like such a jerk. This guy does exactly what I do, and he's probably making three times the money. Not to mention having more work than he can handle.

Embarrassed, I told him what I charged and how half the time I never got paid anyway. He thought I was nuts. He told me that he wouldn't give me a single referral unless I charged sixty-five dollars an hour, and he said it hurt every one of us if we didn't all charge the going rate. Then he made me promise only to take money up front. He really got me thinking: Why not be a grown-up about this?

With my favorite clients, I couldn't suddenly raise my rates by twenty-five dollars an hour, so I told them that I was raising them by ten dollars, up to fifty dollars an hour. I was pretty scared to do it—I hate talking about money—but I did. I told my undependable clients the same thing and also told them that I had to be paid up front. Well, that was pretty much it for some of them, and I got a little panicky that I wouldn't have enough clients. But then I got three extra clients from Ron and charged them all sixty-five dollars an hour. It felt great. One of my new clients has a friend who wants a trainer, too, so that will be one more client at the top rate. I've lost a few clients, the ones who were kind of dead-

beats anyway, but I am actually making more money than I was before. And I can't tell you how much better I feel about myself.

Inspired, even encouraged, by her competition, Tracy began asking for more, stopped settling and getting by, and ceased to allow herself to be a victim of clients who had no intention of paying her. Hard as it was for her to ask for more, she did it—which was asking more of herself, as well as asking more of her clients. The result? Her self-worth rose, as did her net worth.

Tracy, in other words, began living up to an important law of money:

LAW OF MONEY

When you undervalue what you do, the world will undervalue who you are.

Do you see the connection? You cannot feel poor and undeserving and expect to become rich. Instead, you must be certain of your claim on the world, and stand up for your rights in this world even as you stand up to your responsibilities. If you don't have as much as you truly feel you should have, you must ask for more—more of yourself and more of others—as Tracy did. The act of asking is itself a rich act, a powerful act, an expansive act. By asking, you are opening yourself up to receive more, and you will—perhaps not today, but you will. People who expect more get more, it's that simple.

Money and Guilt

What if you were to have all the money you needed and your financial ducks were in a row? What then? Would you be happy? Or would you feel guilty about what you had?

If you don't have as much as you'd like to have or you spend more than you should, do you feel guilty?

Do you have enough money right now? Do you take great pleasure in it, or does it make you feel guilty?

If the relationship between you and your money is harmonious, regardless of how much you have, your financial transactions will be harmonious as well. By this I mean that you will take such pleasure in what your money brings to your life, what your money—whether large amounts of it or small—can do to help the lives of others, and what spending it on life's simple or sophisticated pleasures can do to enhance your quality of life and well-being. Let's face it, money is great. Then why does it—or the lack of it—make so many of us feel racked with guilt and miserable?

I have never met a person who feels guilty about how much they love their children, how much they love their parents, their family, their partner. I have never seen anyone hide the fact that they have a loving family. If there is lots of love in your life, if your family is close or your marriage is happy, you will tell me with pride and respect and gratitude how rich you feel, rich with love. No guilt there, not a bit. We never feel guilty when we have more than we could ever want of the things that money can't buy; it's only when money comes into the equation that guilt makes its way in, too.

L I N D A ' S   S T O R Y

I think I knew what my life was going to be like from the time I was fifteen. Jake and I were high school sweethearts, and that was that. Every summer, he worked in his father's boat-

yard, and I worked the soda fountain in my parents' drug-
store, and we just knew that he'd take over the boatyard one
day, and we'd also run the drugstore. Which was what hap-
pened. We got married after high school and now have two
children, who aren't really children anymore. Our son's fin-
ishing junior college, and our daughter is already out on her
own. But all the time they were growing up, it was a small-
town story, and we were pretty happy. The boatyard did fine,
and the drugstore pretty much stayed as it always was. Then,
about five years ago, our little town began to wake up; sud-
denly it wasn't just the fishing boats in the boatyard, pleasure
boats began coming, too. More and more people were build-
ing weekend and summer houses here, and now the house we
inherited from my parents is suddenly worth a lot. About a
month ago, we got this amazing offer to sell the drugstore. It's
on the corner of Main Street, and it's a pretty big space. The
taxes have been going up, and we were wondering anyway if
we should keep it going. But now that the town is getting
spiffed up, we're just this poky old drugstore, and people keep
coming in and asking for cosmetics I have never even heard
of. So in comes this offer, out of nowhere. Jake's ecstatic and
keeps talking about how we should take it and all the things
we could buy. The kids, too. And my friends, I don't know, I
think they're a little bit jealous. They're saying things like
maybe we'd start hanging out with the summer people
instead of them. Me, I feel really torn about it. We didn't do
anything to deserve this. What would we do with so much
money? I almost wish this had never come up.

When it comes to money, if you have it, you may feel that you don't
deserve it—guilt. If you don't have it, you may feel that you should
have it—guilt. If you are working toward having it, you may feel that
all you're doing is working for money and you are not enjoying the
process. And if it just happens to come your way, as with the offer that

Linda and Jake are considering, then guilt can keep you from taking what could be yours. Money guilt can take the joy out of what you have created as well as entice you to do things that are not necessarily in your best interest—Linda's temptation to turn down the offer on the store, for example.

If you do not have the courage to face this guilt straight-on and bankrupt its power over your money, then you really will never be able to experience true richness. The mere fact that we judge ourselves by how much we have shows what an important touchstone money is in telling us who we are. Inwardly we say we go for it, aim as high as we can, but outwardly we question why we deserve what we can attain.

At this very moment in time, each one of us holds before us an offer much like Linda's, the offer of a bigger cup to fill with riches. If you are not achieving all that you can in this world, you can change course and claim your potential. If you are in debt, you can turn away from your guilt and self-pity, methodically get out of debt starting today, and put that money you have used month after month into your future. If you have everything that you could need yet remain plagued by guilt, you owe it to yourself and your money to make yourself worthy of what you have, embrace it, and send it flowing back out into the world—through investments, through contributions to charity, through careful spending on yourself and on your loved ones' pleasure. If you have not saved a penny for retirement and feel guilty about it, you can begin saving today. I am a financial planner, not a psychiatrist, but I do know that your net worth will rise to meet your self-worth only if your self-worth rises to accept what can be yours. Feeling guilty about money does no good whatsoever, is disrespectful to you and your money, and will keep more from coming to you. If you have accepted love into your life, then you must accept money as well, for if you don't, you are implying that you are not yet worthy of money and are placing a higher value on money than you are on love—a violation of the first law of money: *People first, then money.* Make yourself worthy of money, and money will make itself worthy of you.

CHAPTER 6

THE COURAGE TO FACE
THE UNKNOWN

LOOKING AT YOUR MONEY

Your overall financial picture encompasses all that you have available to you now, all that you have put away for later, all that you owe, perhaps the equity in your home, and all that you will be able to create from now on, starting now. There's a sequence to getting rich that first involves making settlement with the past, which is to say clearing out your finances so that you know exactly where you stand and, if you are bearing the burden of debt, getting rid of it, to clear the way for what you can create tomorrow. First step: knowing where you stand right now.

YOUR EXERCISE: FACING
THE UNKNOWN

Please go to where you keep your bills, and where, if you did the "found money" exercise in chapter 3, you've placed your jar of "found" money. What's there? I want you to find out.

First, look at your checkbook. Have you recorded all the checks you've written? Have you balanced the checkbook on a regular basis? Have you made certain that the bank has credited you with every deposit you made? (Banks are not infallible, you know.) Now open all your bills, bank statements, brokerage statements, and quarterly insurance and tax payments—anything that has to do with your money, what you have and what you owe. Look at every statement and any bill that you do not pay in full monthly. Write down the balance of what you owe on every bill. Maybe you still owe your gardener three hundred dollars for clearing out a hedge, even if you've already paid him the one hundred dollars you owe him this month for mowing the lawn. Possibly you owe the skating rink two hundred dollars for this year's membership. Or you owe the dance studio for your child's ballet lessons, after you've paid only the deposit. Record every credit card bill, every balance that remains on your statements and invoices.

After you have written these amounts down, take a deep breath and total them. What do you owe? Is it more or less than you thought? Regardless of how you feel about it, at least you now know where you stand, and some financial clutter—the clutter of guessing, the clutter of estimating, the clutter of worrying—is gone, replaced by the truth, for better or for worse. You have faced your finances.

Now I want you to open up a brand-new checking account and start over, start facing your money honestly every month and with each check you write. If you don't care about your bank one way or another, go to a different bank. If you're happy with your bank, then open up a new checking account there—with a different account number, a new promise to yourself, a new approach to your money. Take with you your jar of money. Deposit a sum of money, including the money from your jar, and start fresh with this new checking account.

While you are at the bank, I also want you to ask the banker for a P.O.D. form to sign. If you have a checking account in your name, this P.O.D.—payment on death—form will enable the person you choose to have access to the money in your account immediately in the event of your death. This is the simplest possible estate-planning issue, and one of the most neglected. Without this form, depending on how your estate is set up, it might take even your next of kin months to access the money in your account; with this form, whoever you designate will be able to use the funds as soon as they're needed—value people first, remember, then money, then things. If you are on a course to richness, you want to think about today, tomorrow, and forever, and signing this form is thinking in the most expansive way possible. Don't forget to tell the designated person what you've done, and cross this peace-of-mind issue off your list forever.

As your old account is laid to rest, your outstanding checks will eventually clear, and soon you will be able to close that account and work only with your new account, fully balanced every month. It will feel great, starting over. I can't ask that you go back and balance the past, but I do know that with a new resolve, you can face your finances in a fresh new way—and a new checking account will enable you to do this. You will know what you own, you will know what you owe, and much clutter and chaos will be removed, which is the way to make room for more money. In this moment of reckoning, I want you to face the truth. Do not be afraid.

From this day on, as soon as a bill comes in, I want you to open it, look at it, write a check for it immediately, and record it in your checkbook. Put the check in an envelope, put a stamp on the envelope, and get it ready to mail. Write on the inside flap of the envelope the amount of the check and the due date. If you are customarily late in making your payments or if you dread having to sit down and pay a daunting stack of bills all at once, this technique will help you begin to deal with your money and keep your affairs in order. If you can send off the checks with the bills as soon as they come in, great. Then the bills will not clutter your physical or mental space even for a day. If you do not have the money to send off the checks right away, no problem. As soon as you do have the money and deposit it into your checking account, you are to mail off as many checks as your deposit will cover, according to their due dates. If with that deposit there is enough money to cover them all, then send them all off at once. Remember, they have already been written and recorded, so the only thing you have to do now is mail them.

And the money from your money jar or bowl? That extra twenty or thirty dollars or more? That money is to be applied to the credit card that carries the highest interest rate.

The hardest part of paying the bills is actually sitting down and facing them all at one time. It really can be overwhelming, we don't like to do it, and so we don't. We also don't like to let go of money that we have just gotten. We like to hold on to it, because we do not like to see money flowing away from us. The fact that this is money that isn't really ours but money we owe to others—to the mortgage company, for insurance, for cable TV, to the department store—doesn't make it any easier to relinquish. Simply having it makes us feel richer for the time being, and we like that feeling. Yet this is where financial clutter starts to build—and it's also the point at which we begin to create more clutter: As soon as we feel a little richer, our natural tendency is to spend a little more, and then when the bills come due, we don't have enough money left to pay them. Don't hoard the money you owe—free yourself up instead by writing and paying your bills as soon as you possibly can. If you want to turn financial chaos into financial calm, I am telling you that paying your bills in this way will make you feel clearer about where you stand and ultimately will make you feel more powerful. And it's when you feel powerful that more will come your way. What you know about your money can never hurt you as much as what you do not know about your money.

Credit Card Debt:
The Weight and the Burden

Having been in credit card debt myself and having seen many of my clients struggle to fight their way out of it, I know what credit card debt can do, to both your net worth and your self-worth. When you're in credit card debt, you and your self-worth are in a kind of free fall, because you're literally worth less than you have, which makes you feel less than you are—a negative balance on both accounts. Deep in credit card debt, you can't see your way out—the minimum payments get you nowhere, you're constantly juggling payment due dates, and simply by looking at the monthly finance charges (if you can bear to look at them at all), you know, even if you can't run the numbers, that the situation is hopeless. In terms of self-worth, you feel that you're living a lie. Surrounded by things you don't own, you have the odd sense that nothing is yours but the debt—to the extent that you become the debt itself. And what is a debt? It is less than zero. And that's what you feel you are. That's the inward manifestation, and it's with you all the time, like a Greek chorus, reminding you that, financially and emotionally, you're trapped.

There's often an external manifestation of debt, too, which one of my clients and I discovered together.

A M A N D A ' S   S T O R Y

Amanda, a longtime client of mine whom I had not seen for quite a while, came to see me one day a few years ago, and when she arrived, I noticed that she had put on a lot of weight. Obviously, I said nothing about it—she had come to see me about her money, not her weight. We were going over her current finances, and because I had consulted my notes from our last meeting just before she came in, I noticed that this time Amanda had twenty thousand dollars more in credit card debt than she had had a few years previous. When I asked her what had happened, she said that her business had gotten into trouble and that she was taking cash advances from her credit cards to keep it going.

As I went through her papers, I noticed, too, that Amanda had more than $20,000 in a savings account, so I asked her why she was incurring debt on her credit cards and not drawing on her available cash. She replied that if she did that, then her husband would know that her business wasn't doing so well. "You mean your husband doesn't know you have twenty thousand dollars in credit card debt?" I asked.

"That's right," Amanda said. "I pay the bills, so he has no idea." I then asked her how she felt about that, and she said, "I feel as if I am carrying the weight of the world on my shoulders."

I asked Amanda how long she had been hiding the debt from her husband, and she said for a year. Summoning up my courage, I also asked her when she'd started gaining the weight. She began gaining weight, she answered, about a year ago as well. With that, flashbulbs went off for both of us, and our conversation very quickly turned into a financial Weight Watchers meeting. We couldn't be sure, of course, whether her weight gain was the result of anxiety over her business, over deceiving her husband, over the debt itself, or whether it was the result of something else entirely. But we could both see that she had to do something to relieve her stress.

After talking it over, we agreed that she must tell her husband the truth about their finances. Amanda promised that when she went home that night, she would tell him everything. She called the next morning and said that even though the discussion was a little rough at first, they decided in the end that they should take the money out of their available cash and pay off the credit cards, which, as far as I knew, they did.

About six months later, Amanda called to say that her

business was doing even worse than it had been, and wanted my reassurance on their decision to close it down and stop throwing good money after bad. After reviewing the numbers, I said with confidence that I thought that was a good idea. Before she hung up, she said, "By the way, I've lost fifteen pounds and am feeling much better about myself." I thought about this when I went to her folder to update her records and read my notes from our last meeting: Has gained weight, does not know why. Business failing, hiding $20,000 debt from husband, is to tell him tonight. Called to say she told him, they will pay off the debt with their available cash. *As I was about to write this update*—Is closing business, lost fifteen pounds, sounds great—*I began to think again about Amanda's weight gain and loss. It clearly hadn't been caused by her business. Her business continued to fail after she came to see me. Still, she had lost weight. What was different was that: (a) she had gotten rid of the debt, even if it left her and her husband with no savings; and (b) she was no longer holding on to the secret of hidden debt. And with that I began to follow my hunch that perhaps the weight of debt is not simply an emotional burden but a physical burden as well.*

From then on, when clients came into my office burdened with debt and *weight, I would try to find out, as politely as I could, whether their weight had risen commensurate with their debt. I am not claiming to be a sociologist here, but surprisingly often the answer was yes. I would then try to find out whether they were hiding the fact of their debt from someone they loved; again, more often than not they would say yes. My clients, I found, were carrying the weight of their debt in more ways than one.*

One of the most disrespectful and powerless ways to live a life is to live a lie, and when you are mired in credit card debt, I am sorry to say that you're living a lie. You're presenting to the world as your own possessions things that do not belong to you, things that you cannot afford. If your debt is carefully hidden, particularly from those closest to you, you are not only living a lie but also putting your loved ones' financial lives at risk. You are being dishonest about yourself and your future, because juggling credit card debt today jeopardizes all of tomorrow's dollars. You are also being disrespectful of money itself, because the way to treat money is to value it and enable it to grow, not to send it off to credit card companies in interest payments higher than the cost of an item in the first place. True richness is attained when our net worth and self-worth have met the challenges of life and risen above them.

Good Debt, Bad Debt

There is a place at times for debt in all our lives, but the debt, if it is to be worthy debt, must be in alignment with the other goals in your life.

Student loan debt, for example, is in alignment with your goals for the future, for this kind of debt enables you to pursue your dreams in a way you couldn't without incurring the debt. Student loan debt is debt to feel proud of.

A mortgage, assuming you can truly afford the house, is worthy debt, for it enables you to pursue the dream of home ownership and to create a safe haven from the world for yourself and your family. You can be proud when you get to the point where you can qualify for, and afford, a mortgage payment.

If you have stretched beyond what you can afford today in order to help your parents, then you have achieved worthy debt. *People first, then money.*

If you have gone into debt to cover medical expenses for yourself or a loved one, then your debt is honorable for the same reason as above.

If you have taken out a car loan, assuming you need a car and can afford the payments, then your debt is worthwhile, because a car is a necessity for most of us, and to pay for it all at once is beyond the means of most of us.

A loan from a friend or family member to cover a cash-flow crunch, when you know for certain that the money will be coming by a specific date, is a loan of convenience and needn't be a burden.

Extending your limits for extenuating circumstances, such as getting through a pregnancy or an adoption, is a finite loan, and, assuming you have figured out when and how you will dispense with it, will not cost you your future but will help you create it.

Overspending on credit cards merely to accumulate things to wear or display or to satisfy the desire for traveling, eating out, or entertainment is paying tomorrow for today's pleasures. This is the most dishonorable kind of debt there is.

CREDIT CARD DEBT

Whenever I ask people whether they have credit card debt, those who don't have debt invariably answer with a triple negative: "No, uh-uh, not me. I pay my bills in full every month." In their vehemence is discipline and pride. If they do have credit card debt, on the other hand, without fail their reply is always in the form of a question: "Do I have credit card debt?" or, more often, "Who, me?" even if we are the only two people in the room. I puzzled over this for years, until one day I had my answer. I was watching a group of kids play that round-robin children's game "Who stole the cookies from the cookie jar?" Each child, when accused of stealing the cookies ("Suze stole the cookies from the cookie jar"), replies with a question: "Who me?" ("Yes, you"; "Couldn't be"; "Then who?"). Each child is accused of stealing the cookies, denies it, and then accuses another child as the game comes full circle.

The people who answer my question about credit card debt with another question are those who have stolen the cookies from the cookie jar. They are trying to buy some time to think about how to answer the question. In fact, they don't want to have to answer it at all. Not only do they not want to face the truth by answering the question aloud, they also don't want me to know.

If you have credit card debt, do you think, do you really think, you're the only one who has messed up in this way? Do you really think you're alone with this dark secret? And is it really such a source of shame that you can't even admit it aloud to someone else?

Do you see the damage your debt is causing, not only to your finances today and tomorrow but also to your sense of self-worth? I have said this before, but it bears repeating: *You are not a bad person because you have credit card debt, you are simply a person who has managed your money badly.* There is a huge difference between those two. What others think of you is far less important than what you think of yourself. If you think less of yourself because you have debt, most likely your thoughts, words, and actions will render you unable to get out of debt.

If you proceed with your financial life the way it is now, you are settling. You are doing absolutely nothing to change your situation. In order to live a life of richness, a life free of the bondage, weight, and burden of debt, you have to summon from the deepest recesses of your soul every ounce of courage you have and put the process of getting out of debt in motion. You must turn your fear into action, your self-pity into resolve. You can no longer grant yourself permission barely to get by, to float the debt from month to month and year to year, or to ignore your situation. Getting out of debt is without a doubt the single most important action you can take on behalf of your future financial and emotional security.

DENIED CREDIT?

Over the years, I've received many letters from people who've been denied lower-interest-rate credit cards and want to know what they can do about it. Credit card companies, banks, mortgage lenders, and credit unions buy information about you through credit bureaus. They use a procedure called "scoring" applicants when deciding whether to approve or deny credit. Leaving the issues of the scoring process aside, here is what you need to know about what your credit report contains and how to fix incorrect information.

You are entitled to a free copy of your credit file within 30 days if you have been denied credit by the bureau that reported the information. I recommend that you check your credit status from time to time anyway, in order to make sure that it is accurate. If you've been denied credit, you must apply for your file within 60 days of the denial.

The information that is contained in a credit file is your full name (and any previous names), Social Security number, telephone number, current address, employment history, marriages, divorces, liens, bankruptcy information, and, most important, your credit history. It will list the names of your creditors—including retailers, card issuers, and other lenders—and your payment history on these accounts for the previous 24–60 months, including your credit limits and current balances. It will also state who is paying the accounts—whether it is you, a collection agency, or another type of service such as the Consumer Credit Counseling Service. If you are currently disputing a charge, this too will appear in your file. Also it will list the names of people or companies that have requested your file within the last six months (two years if the information was given to an employer or potential employer).

Upon receiving your file, review all the information to see if everything is accurate. Make a list of everything that is incorrect, out-of-date, or misleading. In particular, look for mistakes in your name, address, phone number, or Social Security number, and for missing or outdated employment information. You'll also want to look for: bankruptcies that are more than ten years old, any negative information about you that is more than seven years old, credit inquiries older than two years, credit accounts that are not yours, incorrect account histories (especially late payments when you've paid on time), a missing notation when you've disputed a charge on a credit card bill, closed accounts incorrectly listed as open, and any account that is not listed as "closed by consumer," because if it doesn't note this it will appear to have been closed by the creditor.

Once you've made the list you can use the "Request for Reinvestigation" form that accompanies your credit report. If you did not receive this form, write a letter requesting one. List on the form each incorrect item and explain exactly what is wrong. Be sure to make a copy of the form before sending it back. The reinvestigation is free.

Once the credit bureau receives your reinvestigation request, it must get back to you within a reasonable time. That usually means 30 days, although many bureaus will get back to you within 10 days. This is an easy process for them, since they are all linked by computers. If you have found errors—and don't be surprised if you do—you might be concerned that other credit bureaus might also have this misinformation on your credit rating. It's a good idea to obtain copies of their reports as well and to go through the same process.

Here's how to contact the credit bureaus:

Equifax
P.O. Box 740241
Atlanta, GA 30374-0241
(800) 685-1111
(800) 997-2493 residents of Colorado, Georgia,
Maryland, Massachusetts, New Jersey, or Vermont
Order online at http://www.equifax.com/consumer/consumer.html

Experian (formerly TRW)
P.O. Box 2104
Allen, TX 75013-2104
(888) EXPERIAN
http://www.experian.com

Trans Union Corporation
Consumer Disclosure Center
P.O. Box 403
Springfield, PA 19064-0390
(800) 888-4213 to get your credit report
(800) 916-8800 to ask questions about your report
http://www.tuc.com

If you don't hear from the credit bureau by the deadline, send a follow-up letter. Sending a copy of your second letter to the Federal Trade Commission (6th & Pennsylvania Avenue NW, Washington, DC 20580, Main Office) will really grab their attention.

If something in your credit report is incorrect, or if the creditor who provided the information can no longer verify it, the credit bureau must remove the information from your file. Many times bureaus will remove an item without reinvestigating it if the item is more bother than it's worth.

If you feel something is wrongfully in your file and you want to explain a particular entry, you are entitled to add a 100-word statement to your file. Because the bureau is required to set down only a summary of what you wrote, be extremely concise and clear. You can also add positive things to your file—for example, accounts that you've paid on time. Just ask in writing that they be added to your report.

Finally, if you feel the bureau is not abiding by the law or has treated you unfairly, you can send your complaint to the Federal Trade Commission (at the above address). Be sure to send a copy of your correspondence with the bureau about which you are complaining. If a credit bureau insists on reporting out-of-date or inaccurate information, writing to the FTC can put an end to it.

For further information about repairing credit, I recommend the books *Credit Repair, Nolo's Law Form Kit,* and *Money Troubles* by attorney Robin Leonard, published by Nolo Press (www.nolo.com), or you can contact National Foundation of Credit Counseling at (800) 388-2777 or www.nfcc.org. (Formerly known as Consumer Credit Counseling Service.)

YOUR DEBT SET POINT

How much debt are you carrying right now? Does it make you nervous and uneasy? If it does but you haven't taken any action to eradicate it, then you haven't yet reached the "set point" of your debt. I believe that each of us has within us a point at which anxiety over our debt turns to panic, and it is at this point that we are finally moved to take action. One person's set point may be $2000; another's may be $20,000; still another's may be in the six figures. You know your set point instinctively—without a doubt you'll know it when you reach it.

What I have noticed is that often there is a correlation—an inverse relationship—between this set point and a person's self-esteem. The lower the self-esteem, the higher the set point. If you are spending money you don't have, and continue to do so even as the possibility of paying it off becomes more and more remote, then you are probably spending money not to *have* more but to *be* more. The less self-esteem you have, the more debt you create.

The first step, then, is to work on your self-esteem. Easy to say, but how do you do it? Start by knowing that you are more than the negative balance on your credit card statement. Begin to tell those close to you about the debt you are carrying, relieving yourself of the burden of secrecy. Know that you are not a bad person because you have credit card debt, simply a person who has managed your money badly. Once you free your notion of self-worth from the bonds of material things, you will "need" less and you will spend less. As your self-esteem rises, your debt will diminish. Call it a law of financial physics.

PAYING OFF CREDIT CARD DEBT

With credit card debt—among the rich and the poor—at epidemic proportions in this country, there have been many television programs and dozens of articles about how to get out of debt. The subject is well covered in books, too; in my book *The 9 Steps to Financial Freedom*, I offer a step-by-step plan. In short, there is plenty of help available to show you how to get out of debt. You already know why you should do it; now I want you to take the actions that will enable you to reach that goal. Millions of people have done it, and so can you—but only if you raise it to a top priority and keep your vow to become debt-free.

Having covered the topic at length elsewhere, I am not going to summarize it here, because if you have debt, you should learn everything you can about paying it off. However, here are some important points to keep in mind:

1. Face your debt by telling others about it.
2. If you are in credit card trouble, you must cut up all of your credit cards now, with the possible exception of one card for emergencies; do not carry this card in your wallet, however.
3. Call the credit card company of the one card you've kept and ask them to lower your credit limit to a level that will provide you with security in the event of an emergency.
4. You must pay more than the minimum payment every month, as much more as you possibly can. Here's an example to illustrate why: If you owe a credit card company $1000 at an 18.5 percent interest rate and you just pay the minimum of $17 every month, it will take you about 12.5 years to pay it off and cost you $1550 in interest. Pay just $10 extra a month and you will cut down the payback time to 4.6 years and pay $512 in interest. That's a savings of over $1000. Higher balances take exponentially longer to pay off; a balance of $3000 can take up to 30 years to pay off if you just pay the minimum due every month. You can

calculate the amount of time it will take you to pay off your debt on the FinanCenter, Inc., Web site (http:// www.calcbuilder.com).

5. You must pay off the credit card with the highest interest rate first, and the rest in descending order.

6. You must negotiate for yourself the best interest rates, even if it means switching credit cards every 6 months.

7. You must understand everything about how your credit card works—all fees, how the company charges you, all about the so-called grace period—everything.

8. You must honor all your debts equally—whether it's the money you owe Visa or the money you owe your brother.

9. After you pay off one credit card, you must apply the money you have been paying that particular company to paying off another credit card.

10. If you doubt that you can do this by yourself, you must get in touch with a wonderful nonprofit agency the National Foundation of Credit Counseling; they can be reached by calling (800) 388-2227 or visit their website www.nfcc.org. They will help you organize and consolidate your debt.

11. You must never let this happen again.

12. After all your debts have been paid off, you are to apply the money you were paying all those months toward creating your future.

BANKRUPTCY

I can't tell you how many letters I have received from people who have gotten into financial trouble and are now wondering if bankruptcy is a viable way out for them. After all, more and more people are claiming bankruptcy—the number in 2000 was up to 1.22 million people.

So far as I know, there has always been a provision for declaring bankruptcy and a way to start over. Sometimes, for no apparent reason, anyone among us can be struck by illness, death, a natural disaster, a financial blow that sends us farther back than zero, to a place where there is no reasonable way out, hard as we may work. Yes, yes, then, of course, we should be permitted to start over.

If your financial troubles arise instead from credit card debt, if you're overextended because of irresponsible actions, should you then be permitted the legal means to start over? That's another question entirely, and one you have to answer yourself. Why? Because even though your financial record may be cleared after seven years by declaring bankruptcy, there is also the record of your soul to consider, and that record has no stated time frame. If you declare bankruptcy, someone will have to pay for what you are not paying for. It might be the merchant you cheated, or your debt might be passed along to the rest of us to absorb. Declaring bankruptcy is not simply a way to cop out on overspending. And should you choose to do it, you must understand that fact for your own sake, not just for the sake of the rest of us, who will surely, one way or another, be required to pick up the pieces.

If you are in a position where bankruptcy seems the surest way out, then there are excellent books published by Nolo Press for you to consult—just go to the library. If you decide to take this course of action, you must understand the magnitude of what you are doing, you must understand what you are asking of others, you must understand the sacrifice you are making as well as what you will gain. There is a time and a place for declaring bankruptcy; otherwise we wouldn't have a provision for it in our system. And if you do decide that it is the right solution for you, I hope that you will take your actions to heart, know that it is your only way out, then start over from a place of pride, not shame—pride that will never allow you to find yourself in this situation again. If bankruptcy is truly your only way out, then face it with courage.

CHAPTER 7

RICH THOUGHTS

RICH THOUGHTS ABOUT CHILDREN

Every parent dreams of the world for his or her child; trouble is, the dream gets a little fuzzy when it's not reinforced by action. Presenting the world to a child—teaching a child what to expect, how to conduct daily life, what responsibility means, and how to handle money—is perhaps the most awesome prospect any parent faces in a lifetime. Yet, for all the care and concern with which we teach our children, we rarely stop to reflect carefully about what we want to teach them about money or what kinds of lessons our own actions convey.

If you want your child to have good table manners, you will constantly remind her to hold a fork properly, to keep her elbows off the table, and never to slurp the soup. It becomes a reflex, a refrain, and you keep repeating the lessons until her table manners are excellent—and automatic. At the same time, you know that if you want her table manners to be good, your own table manners must be impeccable, because she'll watch you, study you, learn from you—and catch you when you slip up. Your child will learn about money from you in the same way: by intuiting what you think, hearing what you say, and mimicking what you do.

With the twentieth century behind us, what will your child need to know in order to prosper in the twenty-first? No one can say for certain, but he or she will need financial skills much more sophisticated than those that many of us learned. Your child likely will not work all her life for some benevolent corporation that looks after her and sees that she gets a pension to keep her safe in the long years of her retirement. With many kids mastering computer skills even as toddlers, your child will have to be adept with the tools of the future. With technology continuing to advance at such a staggering pace, your child will need to know how to think and adapt.

So often I'm at an ATM and observe a parent letting a young child pull the money from the machine. Kids know what money is and does, they love it, and they adore this transaction, pulling out a hefty stack of bills and holding the cash. "Let's get some money from the cash machine," the parent will say—and in that there is a big lesson, for I have yet to hear a parent explain to a child that in order to get the money out of the machine, you first have to put it into the machine. Yesterday's children learned that money doesn't grow on trees. Today's child learns that it comes from machines.

Do you see? Allowing your child to hand over the plastic credit card to a clerk in a store or pull the money from the cash machine is not teaching your child about money. Only you can decide the money values you wish to impart to your child, but I am asking you to stop and give some real thought to the lessons your child learns about money and values. In the swirl of everyday life—school lunches, daily bathtime, play dates, missing mittens—it is easy to turn the lessons of wealth (the lessons of more, of less, of possibility) into afterthoughts. For the sake of your child's future, I ask you to turn often to the subject of money, to teach your children confidence and competence.

Nowhere is this truer than when it comes to planning for your child's college education. Providing a top-notch college education is a part of every parent's dream, yet only 48 percent of today's parents are actually saving for the college education they dream about providing.

Too often, then, the scenario works something like this: As the time to pay for college grows closer and closer, your anxiety grows greater and greater. In this case, less money really does translate into more—more anxiety and more guilt, that is. But here's the catch: Your children are inevitably going to intuit the anxiety, which passes a troubling message down to them. How do you think it makes them feel to know that their mere existence and desire to better themselves through a college education is causing a financial hardship to those they love most? Always, when this happens, the size of the child's internal bank account diminishes.

Then what happens? Let's say that, one way or another, the child gets to college. If you do manage to send him to college, he goes knowing that he is taking from you more than you can afford. Feeling poor and "less than," he responds to the solicitors that our colleges actually invite to campuses to entice credit card debt. Having received unclear or ambiguous money messages from you, he somehow thinks that using this credit card, which he doesn't quite understand, will help ease the burden. Before even starting out in the world, he gets himself in debt, a position of powerlessness. When that child enters the job market, he or she will enter it from a place of fear, guilt, or abject gratitude—not, in any case, from a powerful place. In essence, at this point your child's self-worth will come to be determined by your net worth and your feelings about your net worth. And this is the stance with which he enters the adult world.

It does not have to be this way. Attend to matters now. If you do not think you will have money to send your children to school, tell them as soon as you can. It is not a statement about how worthy a person or parent you are if you cannot pay for a college education, nor does it make your child a victim. There are many ways to finance an education if you can't pay for it outright; I have discussed these in *The 9 Steps to Financial Freedom.* But don't spring it on a child at the last minute. The time to start communicating the truth about your financial situation to your children is when they are young. Do not be ashamed to talk about money, about what you think you will be able to contribute, for being honest and forthright about this important subject is one of the most valuable lessons you can ever impart.

If, on the other hand, you have the means—or plan to have or create the means—to save for an education, the sooner you take action the sooner you will assuage your (and your child's) anxiety, thus beginning to pass on a positive money message. With a savings or investment vehicle in place, you are far likelier to save or invest. Taking action also makes any far-off prospect seem suddenly real. Think about it, take action toward it, and talk about it—with your children.

RICH THOUGHTS ABOUT CARS

If it's not a component of the American dream, it's certainly a component of our collective consumer machismo: You are what you drive, for as long as you drive it. Cars are our ultimate symbol of success, and they display the level of success we've achieved—or the level of success we want others to think we've achieved: This is who I am, because this is the make and model I drive.

Now it's true that most of us need a car, but even a modest car is a big-ticket item, one of the biggest purchases we will make, not just in terms of today's dollars but also—especially—in terms of tomorrow's. I am asking you here not to let what you drive today drive your destiny tomorrow. I am asking you to value money over things. I am asking you to value your money over your car.

In the first place, think of the language we use when we talk about cars. "I bought a Toyota Camry." Done deal, even if the bank played a part in the purchase, and the car is somehow a past-tense item, over and done with. What if instead you were to say, "I invested in a Toyota Camry"? An investment is something you nurture, care for, and expect to grow in value on your behalf in the years to come. Shouldn't something as important and expensive as a car, any car, be accorded that respect? Instead, we tend to treat our cars like junk, forget to change the oil, neglect to keep them clean so they don't rust, skip the engine tune-ups. We say things like, "Well, they don't make cars like they used to; this car simply won't last that long." Not true. What kind of a way is this to treat such a big investment? Is this showing respect for your money? You are not what you drive.

In the second place, think what you might well be spending over your lifetime in order to drive. What if you were to buy a car, take out a five-year car loan, pay off your car in five years, and then drive it for another five years. What if you continued to "make" your car payments once the car was paid off—investing that money rather than letting it drift back into your pool of available cash? You could make yourself a lot of money.

Let's say you were to buy 5 cars over the course of 50 years' driving, and drive each car for 10 years. You spend 25 years making car payments and the other 25 years investing the money you'd been using to make your car payments. And let's say, for argument's sake, that those car payments remained a steady $350 a month. Investing $350 a month at 9 percent for 25 years will yield you $392,392.67. If you've invested the money for long-term growth and earn 11 percent on it, you will have, at the end, $551,646.65.

Or let's look at it another way. Let's say the car you decide to buy in round one costs $25,000. You make a down payment, take out a loan, and pay it off, at $350 a month, in 5 years. You will end up having spent $26,172 for your car. Now for the next 5 years that you keep the car, you invest the $350 each month at, say, 8 percent. At the end of 10 years, when you decide it's time to buy a new car, you will have nearly enough invested with which to buy a new car outright—over $25,000. From then on, taking this approach throughout your lifetime, you can have a new car every 10 years in effect for "free."

What about leasing—no money down, basically. Isn't that the wisest way to own a car? No—because to begin with, leasing means you will never own your car.

Low down payment, low monthly payments, then start all over with a new car in three years—sounds great, doesn't it? That's probably why 30 percent of the people driving new cars last year leased instead of buying. But I want you to keep the big picture in mind—tomorrow's dollars and not just today's. Would you rather lease your life or own it?

When it comes to a car, buying a reliable model, paying it off in four or five years, and planning to own it for at least eight or ten years may not sound like the sexiest decision you could make, but it will ultimately free up more money for you, now and in the future. There's a reason most dealers are encouraging you to lease, and it's because it's in their best interest—which means, too, that it's probably not in your best interest.

Let's say in this case that the car you want costs $15,000. A typical ad will offer a lease with no money down, a significant sum—let's say $1200—due at the signing of the lease, then a great monthly lease fee, let's call it $250. (The small type at the bottom may mention a few additional fees—let's say $300—due when you sign.) You're leasing for 3 years, and are given 12,000 miles per year on your lease. The car will cost you $10,500 over the term of the lease. (Unless, that is, you drive more than 36,000 miles, which will cost you a penalty for every mile over, you turn the car in with a dent or something broken, or your circumstances change and you decide to turn the car in early, all of which will result in additional fees or penalties.) At the end of the lease, you have nothing and have to start all over with leasing fees and monthly payments. If, however, you bought the car and kept it for a number of years after it was paid off, you would have a car still worth something in a trade-in, as well as the money you'd invested after you paid off the loan.

Bottom line: Are you the make and model of the car you drive? Yes, you are.

RICH THOUGHTS ABOUT TAXES

Whenever I ask people what's the one thing, when it comes to their money, that they have the hardest time with, a surprising number say to me: taxes. As inevitable as death, as inevitable as springtime, taxes are inevitable for all of us; we postpone facing them, we brood about doing them, we worry about what they will cost each year (even if we already know, give or take), and we let them take up a great deal of our psychic financial energy for at least the first several months of the year—every year.

Why do we do this? Over the years, all the tax write-offs we used to hear about or take advantage of have been disappearing, one by one. Rich or poor, there is very little you can do this year to manipulate your tax bill into being less than it is destined to be, and very little you can do to ensure that your tax bill will not be more than it's destined to be. It's true that you can invest your money with the tax ramifications in mind, but that's rarely the main concern among sophisticated investors; making money is. In fact, people who have power over their money, people who are in control of their money, people who are certain of their goals for their money are the least likely to worry about taxes. Rich or poor, you will worry about your taxes if you feel powerless over money, and you won't worry about your taxes if you feel in control of your finances.

For all the talk of a kinder, gentler IRS, our taxing authority, faceless and mysterious, is a powerful organization indeed. They have the power to collect vast amounts of your money. They have the right to audit you, whether you made a mistake, didn't mean to make a mistake, or didn't make a mistake—just because they think you might have made a mistake. Now, that's power. They have the power to make you organize all the paperwork they ask for, and they have the power to make you feel faint every time they send you a letter. Most people can't find one good thing to say about the IRS.

Despite all this, fear and loathing of tax season is a waste of your time, a waste of your energy, and most likely will not make one bit of difference when it comes to your finances, for you will owe what you will owe, and there is nothing you can do about it. Spending many anxious weeks over taxes causes emotional clutter and it won't save you any money or paperwork, or even undo anything you did in the past year.

And you know what else? If you pay more in taxes than the next person, it means—bottom line—that you made more, and that you'll get to keep more. In fact, the most rich and expansive way to think about taxes is this: I hope I pay a lot more in taxes every year, because it will mean that I am making a lot more money. I'm not going to ask you to go as far as to do that (it's a hard one for me, too, believe me), but at least think about it.

Is there an upside to taxes?

If you can think of tax time as your annual clearing out and cleaning up of your finances, then it still may not be your favorite time of year, but it can certainly be a productive one in which you get your financial life in order. Some things to think about:

- If you are not a whiz with computer tax programs like Quicken or not totally up to date on tax law, or if your returns are in any way complicated (for example, by possible deductions, investments to figure into the overall picture, or earnings from self-employment), then do seek a good tax preparer to help you file your returns.

- One of my financial planning refrains is that getting a tax refund is a waste of money. If you are due a refund, this means that you have been paying too much to the IRS throughout the year. The money is returned to you, but without any interest. So in essence you are giving a tax-free loan to the government. However, if you are a real spender, this might be a great opportunity to save. Losing interest is better than losing the money altogether. Rather than blowing your tax refund in one lump sum, it would be such an expansive act—to yourself and your tomorrow—if you were to take that tax refund and fund your Roth IRA (see chapter 20) or other retirement accounts that you are eligible for with it in that one lump sum.

- Use this time of year to eliminate financial clutter.

Doing Away with
Financial Clutter

Almost always, whenever new clients would come into my office, I would encounter a whole new variety of clutter. Some would arrive with their papers jammed any which way into large manila envelopes; some would arrive bearing shopping bags of statements. Others would bring orderly clutter, papers rubber-banded into neat stacks but in no particular order. Others still would choose folders to enclose the clutter. Occasionally, clients would dispense with the clutter altogether, arriving with just a few sheets from a notepad with some random numbers on them. As my clients presented their papers, I knew that they were presenting their lives to me; the event always took on the air of a ceremony. I saw my job ultimately as sending my clients home with the power and courage to create abundance. But first, my job was working to help to organize the chaos.

Many times clients arrived literally with years of stuff—bank statements going back a decade, stacks of paycheck stubs, so much of their financial past that it made it hard to see their financial present, let alone tomorrow. In order to see where you stand, I want you to use tax time to bring your finances totally up to date.

- ♦ First, get rid of taxes from the past. If your taxes are relatively simple, keep the documentation for three years, which is how long the IRS has to audit you after you've filed. Keep your return, W-2 forms, 1099 forms, records of investment income and any other income (rental income, for example), and tax deductions.

    If your returns are more complicated (by capital gains or losses, if you have your own business or are self-employed, if you have inherited considerable sums of money, or bought and sold a lot of property), the IRS can audit you as far back as six years, if they think you have not reported all your income. Keep seven years' worth of returns and documentation, just to be on the safe side.

If the IRS suspects you of big-time cheating or fraud, they can audit you for whatever year they want. If, God forbid, you have committed fraud, your papers won't do you much good, but you probably ought to hang on to them anyway.

- ♦ For retirement accounts, stocks, and investments outside retirement funds, in most cases you will receive statements either quarterly, every six months, or each time you deposit more money into the vehicle. Hang on to these interim statements until the end of every year, then keep only the year-end record.

- ♦ If you suspect you may be headed for divorce or if you are thinking of selling your home, hang on to all household bills for at least the past six months. In the case of divorce, you will need to demonstrate what it costs you to live month to month. If you decide to sell your house, a potential buyer might ask to see what you spend on utilities, oil, and so on, and the more cooperative you can be, the better.

- ♦ If you are self-employed, keep all bills until you do your taxes, then discard anything that is not remotely an itemized deduction.

- ♦ It is not necessary to keep every ATM printout. When you balance your (new) checkbook every month, throw out all ATM receipts.

- ♦ If you are disputing any bill, keep the bill until the dispute is resolved.

- ♦ If you are withdrawing money from retirement accounts, if you have sold real estate, or have cashed in investments, keep records of those transactions for at least three years.

- ♦ Keep all your medical records for the entire year, and hold them until you file your taxes and can see whether they add up to enough for a deduction.

- Try to be organized in keeping permanent records, such as the deed to your house and records of capital improvements, your marriage certificate, birth or adoption certificates, insurance policies, the title to your car, pertinent death certificates, veteran's records, contracts or warranties involved with big-ticket items—both for the sake of insurance and in case you need to use the warranty.

- One last thing. While you're taking inventory, let's see what else you have. If you haven't yet received one in the mail, call the Social Security Administration office at (800) 722-1213 and ask them for a copy of a form called "Request for Earnings and Benefit Estimate Statement." This form will enable you to estimate, based on what you have put in to date, the amount of Social Security money you can expect to receive upon retirement. Once you complete the form, you will receive your statement in about a month. Review it carefully for mistakes. Please check it against the tax returns you are about to throw out, then keep it in a permanent file.

RICH THOUGHTS ABOUT TOMORROW, TODAY

As an old adage has it, the rich get richer; and rich and poor people alike believe it, as if it were some fundamental principle about money, like compound interest, say, or investing for growth. But is it true?

Well, it's true in the sense that the more money you have in place to earn money, the more money you'll earn over time. That's indeed a fundamental principle of wealth. Nevertheless, remember that most rich people didn't start out that way. How did they get there? By taking rich actions. And you can begin to think rich, too, no matter how little money you have right now.

As we've seen, scaling back your luxuries here and there can create a lot of money to invest today for tomorrow. You can find much more money in addition to that, but you have to look for it. Another old adage states the importance of making every penny count—and, I might add, counting every penny. How many of us do that? The rich do, I can promise you that.

How can you create more money? By looking at every penny you spend. With the baffling array of long-distance telephone choices, for example, have you ever really figured out which one would actually save you money, even a little bit of money, every month? Why not? Ten, twenty dollars a month—it's a lot of money to create, and it could be worth so very much more, over time. Do you buy in bulk when it makes real financial sense to? Why not? Do you skip over coupons for items you buy regularly and neglect to pay attention to weekly supermarket specials? Why? Have you tried, where available, a generic version of every item you use? Why not? One more adage: A penny saved is a penny earned.

Another way of creating money by redirecting your money. You see, most of us think of our money as existing in a pool: Here is the pool of what I have to spend this month. And, no matter what, the pool gets drained every month, replenished, then drained again. But think about this. So many of our expenses are finite—we pay for a one-time item or some expense goes away. Then what happens? The money we have been paying for an expense that is now behind us simply goes back into the pool and gets drained away, one way or another, with the rest of our money today, when it could instead be redirected into money for tomorrow. For example:

♦ Let's say your child has been in day care or a preschool program, or has had a baby-sitter or nanny in her preschool years, then "graduates" and moves on to public school. You now have $200 a week or more that you no longer have to pay for your child's care. What do you do? If you put that money back into the pool, you will spend it and never see it again. If instead, with discipline and respect, you redirect that money toward tomorrow, you will be investing at least $10,400 a year toward your future.

♦ You bought a dining room set for $2400 and paid $100 a month over two years to acquire it. If you put the money that went toward making those payments back into the pool, it's gone. Redirect it toward tomorrow, and you will have an extra $1200 a year to invest.

♦ You needed a water-treatment system when you moved into your house, and bought it through the bank at $65 a month for five years. Finally it's paid off, but it was never that big a deal—just $65 a month. Put that money into the pool, and where will it go? Redirect it instead, and that's $780 a year toward tomorrow.

♦ You are a family of four with a food bill of $300 a month, give or take. Your older child goes off to college, and your food bill is cut by roughly one-quarter. That's $75 a month, or $900 a year. Unless you isolate that money, you will never see it again. If you redirect it toward tomorrow, you will.

♦ You finally decide you are going to get out of credit card debt, and though it takes you five years at $400 a month, you do. Drop that $400 a month into the pool, and it will cause ripples but eventually be absorbed. Keep it out of the pool, redirect it, and you will have an extra $4800 a year toward your future.

♦ You are managing perfectly well, and you get a raise. What do you do with the money? Redirect it.

Redirecting money is taking money that you have been paying every month anyway, or have had added to your income, and reclaiming it to work for your future.

PART III

FOR
LOVE
AND
MONEY

CHAPTER 8

THE COURAGE TO OPEN YOUR HEART,

THE COURAGE TO OPEN YOUR HANDS

Think of all the money that will flow through and around you every single day of your life. Your parents' money and possibly money that filters down from their parents. Money to be apportioned among you and your siblings. Money that arises as an issue between friends and colleagues. If as an adult you marry your future to another's, then you are also combining your fortunes. Your money will flow to your children, if you have them, and perhaps on to theirs. And yet, despite its constant presence in our lives, money is a subject we draw away from, even in our most intimate relationships. It's hard to face money directly, to ask for what you want, to claim what's yours, to learn what you have every right to know. If it is your intention to be rich, then you have to introduce the vocabulary of richness into your relationships. It takes courage to open yourself up to money, to ask others to do the same, to make true wealth one of the goals of true love.

LOVE AND MONEY

It never fails. When everything is working out between two people, they think love is so simple. Yet when the disagreements start, love becomes a complicated venture indeed. Often, the central complication is—surprise, surprise—money. Couples are always saying things like "Oh, money is killing our relationship" or "We were doing fine until money came between us." When I hear this, all I can think is that money has never done a thing to anyone, never hurt a fly. Money is just money. But it is the power you give your money, or your attitudes toward and your fears about your money, that can wreak havoc on the most important relationships in your life.

Not surprisingly, by now you may realize that you are in a relationship with money, whether you think of it in these terms or not. And like the other relationships in your life, this one needs work to make it successful. You must take actions that will create possibilities rather than destroy them, actions that will help you feel secure rather than afraid, and above all else, actions that will establish, in your private world, the sense that you are unconditionally loved for who you are and not for what you have. The first law of money states: *People first, then money.* It is also an essential law of relationships: *People first, then money.*

Which doesn't mean that money doesn't matter when it comes to love, because it matters a great deal. Of all the kinds of intimacy there are—physical, emotional, domestic—financial intimacy is perhaps the hardest to achieve, and, it could easily be argued, the most important in the long run. You can turn over your body, heart, and soul to someone, but the union will never be complete unless you link your fortunes (and misfortunes) together, too, for better or worse, and forever.

THE FINANCIAL COURTSHIP

You have met the person of your dreams. You have never loved any-one so much in your entire life. Finally you decide to get married or join lives and live happily ever after, till death do you part. The vows truly are holy, and you mean them with every ounce of your being. Could money get in the way of this love of yours? Not possible, you say. Until it does.

If you haven't walked carefully and honestly through all the money issues ahead of time, I can promise you that money will one day become an obstacle in your relationship. Even if you think you have the subject well covered, you'll probably find that money becomes a problem later on: you change, your partner changes, the money grows or fails to—all potential reasons for disagreement. Arguments over money trigger divorce in more cases than you can imagine—argu-ments that are not necessarily based on deceit or lies but on how we deal with money. Because most of us deal with it very, very differently.

This is so hard to understand ahead of time and so painful to dis-cover after the fact. On your own, you handle your money your own way. You worry, sure, and sometimes perhaps you spend money you shouldn't—you go overboard on gifts for yourself and others, occa-sionally you're late in paying your bills. Yet when someone else has a stake in your money and you have a stake in theirs, sloppy habits or reckless spending or even wildly divergent views on how to manage money can strike at the core of how safe and secure you feel and can make you feel violated in a very intimate way. When the first argument over money erupts, most of us are taken by surprise. And the only— the only—way to protect yourself and ensure that your relationship will thrive is to look at money issues in the most naked and honest way you can. Before you utter a single vow, and many times thereafter.

You must open the dialogue. Not just "Oh gosh, who's going to pay for what?"—which we'll get to. But you must attempt to talk together in a rational, candid way about the serious side of money, matters that over time go from being background issues in a relationship to those of the highest priority—how you spend, how you save, how well you share.

- How do both of you feel about saving money for the future? How committed are you both to investing for tomorrow? Do you both agree that money you've saved shouldn't be touched, or would one of you be willing to tap into your savings for such luxuries as vacations or a hot tub or a new sound system?
- Are your investment styles—be they aggressive or conservative—in sync?
- Can you talk together, no matter how young you are, about retirement?
- Are you in agreement over who does the bookkeeping and pays the bills?
- Do your notions of generosity match?
- Do you agree about your responsibilities toward your respective families?
- Do you have a prenuptial agreement? Do you want one? How does that make each of you feel?
- In the case of a job transfer, whose job takes precedence?
- If your incomes vary greatly, who is expected to pay for what, and how do you come to that decision?
- If you have children, what will happen if one of you wants to stay at home with them? How will the money work then?
- Do you feel the same about the financial aspects of child rearing—public vs. private schools, etc.?
- Are relations with any ex-spouses clearly defined?
- Do you know how much your partner earns? How much he or she spends every month? How much his or her bills are every month?
- Do you both pay your bills on time, or is one of you consistently late?

♦ Is any past credit card debt, school loans, or bankruptcy being brought into the relationship?

♦ Do both of you have a good credit report, or does one of you have the credit rating from hell?

♦ Are you both prepared to share your assets or your income, or does one of you feel the need to keep some aspects of your financial life separate? If so, why? Can you both live with that?

Do you still think love holds all the answers?

A M Y ' S   S T O R Y

After three years of dating, you'd think I would know enough about my husband when it came to money. Boy, was I wrong.

I thought I was falling into heaven. I met Bob and thought right away that maybe things could be different. We had always been so poor, my mom, my sister, and I. My father had split when I was nine, and Mom always had to work two jobs to make ends meet. Not that she didn't do a good job. She did, and we always felt very loved, but my sister and I grew up with the knowledge that life is very difficult. That's what I believed. My mom even managed to find the money to put each of us through junior college, and so what did I do? I had a baby in my second year, my wonderful daughter, Caitlin. And then my life cycle became like my mom's—working around the clock to make everything work out. Caitlin's seven now, and I have held down two jobs ever since she was born. But I found a decent apartment for us, and we were managing just fine when I met Bob. I was knocked out by him, he was so self-assured and seemed to have everything under control. And he was amazed by me. He loved Caitlin, plus he always seemed so impressed by the way I handled everything that I felt impressed by myself, too, maybe for the first time.

I felt like I was managing the world. Then it got more amazing. It turned out that Bob was from a wealthy family, and they took us in, Caitlin and me, as if we were their own. We'd go to their house for barbecues, and it wasn't hot dogs and hamburgers, it was grilled salmon—really elegant. For the first two years everything was wonderful. And it kept getting more wonderful. When we decided to get married, Bob's parents made the down payment on our house as a wedding present. I was so excited—our own house! We closed before the wedding, and I couldn't believe how lucky I felt. I painted Caitlin's room myself and was so proud I could give her her own room; I never had my own room growing up. The deed to the house was put in Bob's name alone, which his parents felt was fair, since they gave the money for the down payment, and I thought, Fine. Everything was perfect. I gave up my apartment when we got married, and we moved into our house, like in a storybook.

We hadn't really talked about money much, other than to agree that we would split everything, and I thought, Fine, it's all our money now anyway. I made $36,000 between my two jobs, and Bob made $60,000, working in the marketing department of a big corporation. At first, it seemed like so much money, but then I began to feel poorer than I had before, when I had my own little apartment. My half of the mortgage was more expensive than my rent had been, and on top of that there were insurance and taxes. Since the house was bigger than my apartment, my half of the utilities was as much as or sometimes more than what I had been paying before. Then there was the cost of the extra food. I spent most of my savings on new furniture for the house. The expenses kept adding up, but it all seemed okay, because we were building this great new life.

I guess the scales began to fall from my eyes when Bob bought his new Jeep, which he paid for in cash, with money I assumed he'd gotten from his parents. And here I was, driving around in a fifteen-year-old Buick. All my money went into our life and the house, all of it, but then Bob had enough to go buy this new Jeep. What really hurt is that he didn't seem to care that I was still working two jobs, which sometimes meant eighteen-hour days, and I got so tired while he worked an easy nine-to-five and had lots of extra money. When I tried to talk to him about it, he said, "Hey, I'm not asking you to do anything you weren't doing before we were married." He got really angry. Then I thought about how I was paying half of the mortgage, so I asked him when my name would be added to the deed. Never, he said; that was the deal, his parents were protecting their investment. I didn't think it was fair because, after all, I was paying half, but he said if I were paying rent on an apartment I wouldn't have an owner's stake in it, so why should I care?

Caitlin loved Bob, and she was happy, so I stayed in the marriage, even with all the anger—and I couldn't believe the anger. But finally, I had to go, and after only three years of marriage we separated. Was the divorce fair? No way. I had lost my affordable apartment and had spent too much on the house—and I got nothing. No child support, because Caitlin isn't his child. No alimony, because I had been pulling my weight all along. Nothing except the furniture to show for all that I'd put into the house and the marriage. Caitlin and I are poorer than ever, living in a studio apartment. My savings are gone. I married this rich man, hoping for a better life, and lost everything.

Amy started out with such high hopes and had quite realistic dreams of the life she and her husband would lead. So where did it go astray? Remember, in order to follow a course toward wealth, what you think, say, and do must be one. Let's track Amy's thoughts, words, and actions.

What Amy thought was that when she and Bob got married, her life would get easier, not harder—fair enough. She thought that she would no longer have to carry the financial burden all by herself, and that she and Bob would join forces to make a better life for all of them. She was no gold digger—in fact, proportionately she contributed more to the marriage than her husband did—but had thought that, with the two of them working, she might be able to give up one of her jobs so that she wouldn't have to work so hard. She thought that she could have an easier life than her mom had had, that she could give a better life to her daughter. She thought that Bob would want this for her as well. What did she say about it to Bob—before the marriage? She said nothing and kept on doing all the things she'd done before, working two jobs and so on. Then what happened? When her marriage didn't fulfill her desires, she got angry. Angry at Bob, angry at herself. From that point on, everything she did—whether it confused him, hurt herself, or destroyed any chance at compromise—resulted from her anger.

How could it have been different? Amy could have communicated with Bob, at least enough to make him aware of her fierce need to provide for her child. She could have shared her hope—ahead of time—that life might become easier for her after their marriage. If he had balked at that, everything might have been different. If Amy had known how Bob felt about splitting bills, whose name the deed to "their" house would be in, as well as all their other financial differences, Amy might have decided right then and there, even though it would have broken her heart, that Bob was not what she wanted—not what she could afford. It wasn't as if Amy was waiting for a knight in shining armor to save her. Amy had tremendous courage and was doing fine on her own. When she fell in love with Bob, however, she thought that life could be even better. Had she and Bob each understood the other's position, it could have been. In the end, though, Bob felt used, felt as if Amy was trying to change the ground rules of their relationship. She, too, felt used, because she thought the ground rules would, and should, change with their marriage. Whatever love they had was lost to money. And, in this case, Amy and her daughter ended up poorer, financially and emotionally.

FINANCIAL PREVIEW

Even if Amy wasn't comfortable initiating intimate financial conversations, when she thought about it, she saw—with the inevitable clarity of hindsight—that Bob had many financial habits that should have clued her in to what he was really like and what she was getting herself into by marrying him. Whenever they went out to eat, for instance, they always split the bill fifty-fifty. Same with the movies and any vacations they took. On shopping trips, Bob would routinely go to Banana Republic, while Amy shopped for herself and her daughter at Kmart. If he borrowed her car, he never filled it back up with gas. Once he even put a little dent in the car and showed it to Amy, but never offered to pay for the repair. She was definitely not marrying a man with an "our" sensibility, and much as she hoped for more, he never gave her a glimmer of a reason for that hope.

Every day you see how the person you love acts with, and reacts to, money. The big things, like whether debt is a part of the picture. And the little things—the man who has to have every high-tech gadget there is, the woman who loves to buy shoes—which, if they irk you now, will irk you much more over time. At first you ignore what you don't like, in a much more forgiving way than you would other bad habits—personal hygiene, for example, or bad manners, or constant broken promises. Money is at once too small a subject for confrontation ("I don't want it to seem like I don't trust him!") and too great a subject, for you have given it the ultimate power, the power of silence. But listen closely. Money is one of the most important parts of life—my life, your life, the life of the person you love. If you sense your partner will put his or her money above the needs of your relationship, then I ask you to have the courage to admit to yourself what you already know in your heart.

What you see now is what you'll get later, although you may feel different about today's financial qualities as they play out farther down the road, when there's perhaps more at stake. The little things get bigger over time, whereas qualities of prudence, which may seem a little

stuffy now, become far more important in the long term. There is no
way to see clearly into the future, but you can certainly face what you
see today. This quiz offers a sampling of financial habits, good and bad,
all of which suggest character traits. Please circle the letter of the
habits which apply to your partner. Somewhere in this quiz, too, you
might find yourself.

A.   Fails to tip waiters and other service people adequately as a
     matter of course
B.   Seems unusually taken with luxury items, like wildly expen-
     sive cars, clothes, or gadgets
C.   Has a weekly date with friends at the racetrack
D.   Never balances the checkbook, or regularly bounces checks
E.   Keeps the checkbook balanced at all times

A.   Invites you to dinner, chooses the restaurant, then com-
     plains about the prices on the menu
B.   Expresses material longings for things—vacations, jew-
     elry—way beyond his or her budget
C.   Buys and sells stocks constantly for the thrill of it rather
     than as wise economic moves
D.   Seems to regard his or her parents or others as a source of
     income
E.   Is saving the maximum allowed by law in retirement
     accounts and monitors these investments to make sure they
     are performing to the best of their ability

A.   Complains about child-support obligations
B.   Tries to impress your friends by bragging about money
C.   Prefers to take vacations in places with gambling casinos
D.   Has a messy wallet, or a wallet full of maxed-out credit cards
     but absolutely no cash
E.   Never buys an item to impress others or brags about money

A. Talks about using his or her work expense account for personal items
B. Cannot pay off credit card bills at the end of every month
C. Cannot get up and walk away from a gambling table, even if losing badly
D. Spends money on a new pair of shoes even though other bills are overdue
E. Loves to talk about finances and is open to teaching you

A. Seems uncomfortable using the pronoun "we"
B. Can never go into a store without buying an item, whether he or she needs it or not
C. Is constantly baffled as to where the paycheck went
D. Receives calls from bill collectors
E. Is charitable and generous and does not define him- or herself by how much is in the bank account

A. Would never put loose change into a donation box after making a purchase
B. Gives you unusually expensive gifts that you know he or she can't afford
C. Is constantly placing bets, be it on a backgammon game or an office pool
D. Avoids talking about money and acts like everything is just fine when you suspect it isn't
E. Pays all the bills on time and rarely carries a balance on credit cards

Scoring: Count how many of each letter you have circled and record the number below.

A____   B____   C____   D____   E____

The letter with the largest number reveals your partner's primary money traits.

KEY

A =   PENNY-PINCHER

B =   SPENDTHRIFT

C =   GAMBLER

D =   FINANCIAL WRECK

E =   FINANCIAL CATCH

While it's true that we all have our financial quirks, any of these un-desirable financial qualities taken to their worst extreme could signal trouble ahead—and you don't want to end up with a penny-pincher, spendthrift, gambler, or financial wreck, or someone with qualities of each. Hard as it is to do so, you must open a dialogue about money with your partner now, because it is impossible to join hearts without your purse strings interlocking as well.

If you're close to commitment or in a long-term arrangement but still not comfortable with the way you communicate about money, begin the dialogue now. Can people change their money habits just by talking about the subject? Yes, they can. Once you open the dialogue honestly, you will be better able to see each other's perspective and to act out of compassion for your partner's fears and concerns. Maybe the changes won't come all at once, but I've seen many people open up about money, change their habits, and work together toward a har-monious financial relationship. If you can state clearly what you find problematic or troubling, then at least there's a new perspective out in the open. Expect changes to come not at once but over time, as you initiate a chain of compromises. The most important catalyst for improvement is opening the dialogue in the first place. And being open to change yourself.

When talking in an intimate way about money, it is essential that you do it from an understanding and compassionate place, not spurred by anger or defensiveness. It is not necessarily true, for example, that penny-pinchers are stingy—most are simply afraid of losing what they have; they think that there isn't enough money to go around. In the same way, a spendthrift often uses money to try to make up for low self-esteem or self-worth. A financial wreck also needs to be addressed with great care. It has taken him or her a long time to get in such terrible financial trouble—and there's a reason someone actively goes about making his or her own affairs chaotic. In the case of a gambler, the damage may call for professional help. Regardless of the tendency that signals trouble to you, silence on your part will only prolong and worsen the damage.

YOUR EXERCISE

I want you to sit down together and figure out a sum of money that feels like a generous discretionary amount, an amount that would enable each of you to buy something to show for it, something you cared about. Use as your starting point the amount of money you each spend each month on things you want, things for yourself. Maybe the sum will be the same for you both.

More likely, one of you has more money and should therefore choose a discretionary amount that's proportionately higher. Maybe the figure is two hundred dollars, three hundred dollars, less than that, or much more. You decide, but it has to be a sum of money that matters.

Now go to the bank and withdraw, each of you, your amount of money, in cash. Put it into an envelope and give it to your partner. The rules are that you must neither talk about what you plan to buy nor report on your purchases until the end of the month. Keep the money in the envelope, apart from your own money, and keep all receipts. What should you buy? Anything you want, things that you'd probably buy anyway, somewhere down the road. Anything that you'd buy with your own money—because if you're thinking of merging money, this will, one day, be your money.

At the end of the month, open the dialogue, with honesty and compassion. Here are some questions for discussion: How did it feel to be spending the other person's money? How did you feel, knowing that the other person was spending your money? How do you feel about what your partner bought with your money—pleased, angry, resentful, surprised? Did one of you buy things with both of you in mind, while the other bought things with just him- or herself in mind? Did one of you have money left over at the end of the month? Did you both do a good job of keeping track of where the money went?

Keep your discussion limited to this money as you answer these questions. You have been playing house, but it will give you some idea about what it will feel like to be keeping house.

FINANCIAL INTIMACY

What if your particular lovebug spent the three hundred dollars you apportioned on car parts, while you spent it (in your view) judiciously, buying the ingredients for a romantic dinner, a few cosmetics you had run out of, a birthday present for a mutual friend whose party you were both attending, and two tickets to a play? Add years' worth of car parts that only your partner enjoys against spending with both of you in mind, and the result is not going to total an equal partnership or a happy one. True, the money was to be spent as discretionary income, but if your ideas about spending in general are worlds apart, you must bring them closer, through dialogue.

Perhaps the formula is pretty simple now. Let's say you're playing house in a scrappy starter apartment, each earning about the same amount, splitting things pretty much fifty-fifty, with enough left over to buy what you want. So what's the problem?

Any little twinge about money you feel now is going to be amplified later. Our ideas and compulsions about money change as we age—none of us is the same financial being at twenty-five or thirty-five as we are at fifty, when we begin to internalize the fact of retirement and the eventuality of mortality. We may change our money habits, too, as we make more money. Buy a house together, a house that needs a new roof, and then see how you feel if that money goes to car parts. The addition of children to our lives changes, sometimes drastically, our ideas about the money we have and the money we need. It's a process, learning about someone else and money, and it can last a lifetime.

A relationship deepens as the stakes get higher. At the beginning, it's easy to say what's yours and what's mine, when very little is "ours." As time goes on, though, those easy boundaries blur, and what's "ours" begins to take precedence. The house, the furnishings, the car, the children, the family and friends you share, and the rituals you establish can make the marriage a rich place to inhabit. A relationship counselor will tell you to keep close track of the emotional pulse of your relationship. As a financial counselor, I can tell you that the financial pulse is equally important, because the financial stakes in a marriage start out high and only get higher.

LEGAL INTIMACY

It is essential to disclose to each other your personal financial histories, money habits, and financial likes and dislikes, and it is also essential that, whether you decide to live together or get married, you know your legal obligations to each other. In particular, marriage, where the financial issues are considerable, must not be entered into lightly. Nor should you agree to purchase a large asset together without thinking things through completely, considering every possible eventuality. A marriage that goes sour and ends up in divorce can leave scars that even the best financial plastic surgeon in the world cannot cover up. Scars that could have been avoided. Few things are as difficult for me as a financial planner as meeting someone forced to start over by a marriage gone bad, especially at an age when he or she should be about to enjoy retirement. Such people are riddled with anger and fear, but they also feel hurt and humiliated.

It's beyond the scope of this book to set forth all the contractual obligations of marriage or those that can arise from a long-term non-marital relationship, which in any case vary widely from state to state. I do know, however, from the many financial questions that have arisen in my office, how few of us, whether we're entering into a life-time partnership or a marriage, think through—or talk through—ahead of time all the responsibilities we may one day have to face up to. Here are some of the questions I have had to answer for my clients:

Am I liable for the debts my spouse incurred before our marriage?

No. You don't marry debt. But as soon as you commingle assets, any joint account you set up is fair game for prior creditors. You can get around this in some states by keeping or opening a bank account in your own name, which creditors theoretically can't touch. Even so, the IRS has the power to put a lien on a refund due when you file a joint tax return. So his or her prior tax liens are the scariest debts to marry.

Am I liable for debts incurred after our marriage that are only in my spouse's name?

Yes. It depends on the state, but in most states, for all intents and purposes, you're responsible for each other. Creditors will always try to get you to pay, and you'll be the one who has to go to great lengths (and expense) to prove you're not liable.

Is there any advantage to trying to keep our monies separate by filing separate tax returns?

The answer, in most cases, is no. Filing separately can deny you tax advantages. Even couples involved in bitter divorce disputes tend to file together as long as they can if it results in a tax benefit. (However, in California, for example, an ex-spouse's tax return can be subpoenaed by the other party to determine adjustments in the amount of child or spousal support. A new spouse might want to keep his or her information out of the picture, and filing separately would achieve that—even though it usually costs more in taxes to do it that way.)

If my spouse has a former spouse and/or children he or she is required to support, will my income be considered by the court when deciding how much the payments will be?

Technically no, but the court will look at your household income and expenses, and if your spouse has more *disposable income* because of your combined incomes, it's hard to keep non-parental income out of the picture. Your income may be exempt from consideration if you keep your monies separate, although in some states the court can subpoena your income tax returns to find out your combined household income before setting (or changing) the amount.

What happens if my spouse files for bankruptcy?

The creditors may be able to come after you for the entire amount of the debts—even if your spouse is actually an ex-spouse now—if you were legally married when the debts were piling up. If you're liable for the debt, one spouse's discharge of the debt in bankruptcy court will not relieve the other spouse of the debt, which may show up as a ding on the "good" spouse's credit report. What this means is that if your ex-spouse claims bankruptcy, it may show up on your credit rating reports because you are also responsible for the debt that was accumulated in both, or either, of your names when you were legally married. Just because your ex got out of it does not mean you have, even if the debt was in his or her name alone while you were married.

What are the presumptions with respect to custody of children?

Many states assume joint custody is best for the children and will not award sole custody unless there's a strong showing of proof of unfitness. Others won't award joint custody unless both parties agree to it. This is one issue that can't be predisposed in a prenup.

If my ex-spouse doesn't pay child support, can the court still enforce visitation rights?

Yes. Financial and custodial arrangements are viewed by courts as distinct and separate issues.

Who is responsible for an incapacitated child?

The father and mother share equal responsibility for an incapacitated or disabled child. When the child turns 19, he or she is considered a *conserved adult;* the parents become the conservators and manage any state or federal money for which the child is eligible. In return, the state can access money that you or your spouse have put aside to be held for the benefit of the child. If you have a child (or, for that matter, a parent) who will need long-term assistance, please see a good trust lawyer who deals with asset protection.

Are there common-law marriage rights that accrue to a person who lives with you as a spouse for a long period of time?

It comes as a big surprise to a lot of people, but in many states you can hold yourself out as husband and wife, file joint returns, and so on, but if you're not married you get nothing if the other person dies or leaves. It's even possible that if a common-law loved one were in an intensive care unit, the other partner wouldn't be allowed in—because he or she is not next of kin. Establishing a durable power of attorney for health care (see *The 9 Steps to Financial Freedom* and *The Road to Wealth*) is the way to protect yourself against this possibility and is a crucial consideration for unmarried partners.

Can I throw my spouse out of my house, especially if I owned the house before our marriage?

That "neither spouse may be excluded from the other's dwelling" is a staple of state law. If a domestic situation becomes violent, barring the violent partner requires a court-issued restraining order.

Can your spouse leave you, move to another state, and sue for divorce there to get a better deal for himself or herself?

Yes, although divorce laws vary widely from state to state, particularly those regarding residency requirements before filing for and granting divorce.

If I move from one state to another, can it change my marital property rights?

Yes, sometimes drastically. For example, if you move to California and own property in another state, acquired during the marriage, it may be considered *quasi-community property* and you may have to split it in the event of a divorce. Quasi-community property is an asset that would be considered community property if it was acquired or located in the state you are in when you divorce, but may not be considered as such in the state where it is located.

In a divorce, can a spouse take back a gift given specifically to you—or at least claim his or her "half" of such a gift?

Maybe. It's very hard to prove intention, especially if you don't have any written instrument to show it was a gift to you alone. In the case of an inheritance, that's generally considered separate property—unless you commingle it.

Can I disinherit my spouse?

Not always, but it depends on which state you live in. Most states allow a spouse to take what is known as a *forced share,* the

amount any spouse is entitled to by law, regardless of the other spouse's wishes. The amount varies from state to state, but it can be up to one-third of the estate.

Do I have a legal duty to support my spouse during marriage?
Yes. Husband and wife contract toward each other "obligations of mutual respect, fidelity, and support." This applies if a spouse becomes ill or loses—or quits—a job.

If you are in a same-sex relationship or you have chosen to live together but remain unmarried, you still have some serious questions to consider, such as the following:

If we're unmarried but own property together, what happens if we break up?
The property will be divided according to who holds title or whose name is on the account, unless the unnamed party can claim that he or she had an agreement with the partner to share the asset. The dispute will be resolved in the business division of the local court, rather than the family law division, and contract law rather than family law will apply.

If we're unmarried and haven't bought any property together, can either of us still face financial obligations toward the other?
In just about every state of the union, contracts between unmarried couples are legally binding. It's better for the contracts to be in writing, since proving a contract is pretty hard to do if it isn't written down, and oral contracts are rarely enforced. But if you strongly believe that you and your partner had a firm contract and you can afford to fight for your rights in court, you may be able to prove your case.

Do unmarried partners ever owe each other alimony after a breakup?

Not unless there is proof of a contract to provide such postseparation support, which is rare unless the contract is a written and legally binding one.

Are unmarried couples liable for each other's debts?

Not unless they co-sign on a loan or have a clear contract with each other to accept such liability.

These questions are not meant to scare you or dissuade you from making a commitment. Rather, they point up just how solemn lifetime commitments, especially the legal institution of marriage, really are. You must be emotionally ready to marry, it's true, but you also must understand the financial and legal ramifications of the institution, because there's more at stake here than your heart. If you are in a troubled relationship and any of these questions struck too close to home, please think carefully before you put at risk all you have today and all you might have tomorrow.

CHAPTER 9

THE BUSINESS OF LOVE

When two or more people enter into a business relationship, legal documents are usually drawn up to explain how the business is going to run, who is paid what, and who owns what. These documents may also contain a clause stating that if something was to go wrong—let's say the business partners wanted to break up—how the partnership would be dissolved. Details might include a predetermined formula as to how the business would be valued, as well as a calculation of what each partner would have to pay to buy out the others and how that process would be carried out. It is also not uncommon for the principals of the business to purchase an insurance policy known as *key man insurance,* which protects the surviving partners in the event of an untimely death of one of them. None of this suggests that any of the partners expects the business to fail—quite the opposite; otherwise they wouldn't be going into business together in the first place. Rather, it means that the partners are wise enough to lay all their cards on the table ahead of time, that they want to protect one another and themselves, and that they want to get on with the business.

When it comes to the business of marriage or a long-term commitment, however, most of us would never think of enacting such a plan or muster up the courage to talk about it—but make no mistake about it, marriage is a business, and one with a 50 percent failure rate at that.

The time to talk about the what-ifs in marriage or a committed unmarried relationship is the same time we'd talk about it in starting a business, when we are most optimistic—at the outset. When we love and trust each other with all our hearts, before we know what the future might bring.

S U S A N ' S   S T O R Y

I can't believe the way it turned out and what I might have lost. Mark was not that eager to get married, especially since he felt he had lost too much in the divorce after his first marriage. We'd been together for about five years, though, and then I got pregnant. He said he would marry me, but he wanted a prenup. I hated that; I would never take more than my share from anyone. I said yes, but I felt hurt about it for a long time. He went to a lawyer to have the prenup drawn up, and then I showed it to a girlfriend of mine who's a lawyer. The prenup was all about Mark's future earnings, that he should get to keep his retirement plans and everything if we got divorced. My friend said fine, that was okay, but she added to it that I could keep all my future money, too. What did I know? I was thirty years old, working as an administrative assistant in a start-up computer company. Mark had much more money, and he was already a financial officer at a big utilities company. Fine, I said, and we both signed the papers.

For a long time everything was great. When Max was born, Mark fell in love with him; he was a great father. I kept working and began to really enjoy it, because the company was growing by leaps and bounds. The more I got into programming, the more I loved it. There was a program at work where the company would pay tuition for relevant classes. I decided I didn't want to be an assistant forever, so I signed up for some courses and did really well. It was as if all of a sudden everything clicked, and there I was, getting promoted, installing software for lots of companies. I'd never thought about having a real career; I always thought I would just have a job, but this was great. I bought a BMW, plus some stock options in the company, and began to feel really good about what I was doing. I had a retirement plan at work, too, and little by little, that money was really adding up. And I could work from home a lot, which meant I was there for Max.

Mark was doing great, too. He got a promotion about the same time as I did, so we were both happy. It didn't seem competitive or anything. We bought this great house and put Max into private school. And for twelve years everything was so good—until three years ago.

Mark was basically downsized because of office politics. Everyone at the top was moved around, and two of his good friends were also fired at the same time. It was awful. Here he was, forty-six years old and out of a job. The severance package seemed good at the time, and he got to take his retirement money, but he was shell-shocked. His company sent him to a headhunter, but nothing came of it. I knew it would take him some time to get back on his feet, but months went by and he didn't even try to find work; he just sat at home watching television. I thought maybe he was depressed and tried to get him to go to a doctor, but he wouldn't. Now we're in the gym phase—he goes to the gym every day for a couple of hours. It's been three years. Both his friends have jobs—not great jobs, but they're working. Mark is resentful toward me all the time, and God forbid I should buy new clothes for work or do anything nice for myself. His severance money is long gone. He says he's trying to find a job, but I'm home enough to know that's not true. After this year, Max will have to go to public school, and I don't know what's going to happen to the house. I'm doing everything, and I am miserable. Mark won't even write the checks to pay the bills. Not long ago, I blew up and asked for a separation. We haven't mentioned it again, but I'm walking on eggshells in this marriage. I really am thinking of getting out. I was so supportive for so long, but one person can't do the whole thing. Three years is enough.

I don't see another way out. And you know what? I'm so happy he made me sign that prenup. If we get a divorce, I won't have to pay for him to sit around feeling sorry for himself. I have my job, my stock, and my retirement money. I can take care of me and Max. And maybe then, finally, Mark will take care of himself.

PREMARITAL AND COHABITATION AGREEMENTS

What I would ask you to do is unconventional: I am asking you to plan for the what-ifs while you are still totally in love. In the name of love, plan for anything and everything that could happen. Decide now how things will be split up should your feelings for each other change, and put it in writing. Have a legal contract known as a *premarital agreement* (or *prenuptial agreement,* or *prenup*) drawn up before you are married, or, if you intend to stay unmarried, draw up what's known as a *cohabitation* or *property agreement* before you solidify your relationship. If you have the courage to take this bold step out of love, not greed, out of wanting the best for each other, not only now but forever, regardless of what happens, then you have nothing to lose. If you stay together happily, so much the better; the agreement will never come up again. If, however, the marriage ends, and you do end up getting divorced, you will have planned for this eventuality ahead of time. If I ran the world, I would definitely pass a new law: Before anyone could get married, there would have to be a prenup.

Time and time again, when I raise the subject, people say to me, "But Suze, why do I need a prenup? I don't have any assets to my name." Those are words of poverty. Prenups are for tomorrow, not today, and no matter how deep your love is today, nobody—not you, not your partner—can see what tomorrow might look like, to see ahead to what you might have in the years to come, and what you might stand to lose.

The myth is that the very subject of prenups will cause contention. In reality, it's a way of bringing to the surface your deepest concerns about money and security and the unknowns of the future. It's not a sign of greed, weakness, or fear to want the reassurance that you both will be safe, whatever happens, and, in my experience, opening up these issues can bring partners closer together in ways they rarely comprehend until they do it.

WHO NEEDS A PRENUP?

Years ago, prenups were for those who had considerable wealth they wanted to protect. Today, with living arrangements so much more diverse, that is no longer the case. Even people who have, as yet, no assets enter into prenups to protect what they might have tomorrow, to protect themselves against debtors if a would-be spouse is not responsible with money, and, ultimately, to protect themselves, no matter what happens, forever. Two-career couples might want to keep future earnings or stock options separate. Also, given that second marriages are so very common today, prenups are becoming popular among couples who want to make sure to put into writing the assets they want to keep safe for their children from earlier marriages.

Today, too, many couples—younger couples just starting out, older couples who, for various reasons, prefer not to marry, and same-sex couples—are living together and buying property together, and need the same kinds of protection that married couples do. Here are some scenarios in which prenups come into play:

- You have been through a nasty divorce and you know very well what can happen and how costly it can be to decide who is going to get what, and you want to make sure that you never have to go through that again.

- You built up or inherited an extensive portfolio, or maybe a successful business or considerable real estate holdings before you were married. These holdings may take considerable time to maintain, possibly by both you and your spouse, and you will both reap the rewards during your marriage. Even so, you want to make sure that this property and its growth remain in your name alone should the marriage dissolve.

- You are in a fast-track career, stand a good chance of becoming extremely wealthy one day, and want to protect what you hope to earn.

- One day you'll inherit your parents' vacation home—they've already laid the legal groundwork for this. As your parents no longer use the house very much, you and your fiancé have begun using it every weekend and are full of plans to fix it up. Even so, this house has been in your family forever—and you want to make sure it remains in your family.

- You are not rich, but you are about to marry a rich man. By the end of the marriage, he could claim (possibly correctly) that everything he has derives from his separate property and that everything earned during the marriage was spent—thus claiming that there is nothing to split. Even if he's wrong, he has the money to fight you in court. You need a prenup so that you will know where you'll come out in the event of a divorce.

- You are a widow (or widower) with children, and you want to protect their father's (or mother's) money for them before you remarry.

- You are remarrying and don't want your grown children to be suspicious or resentful of a new stepparent. A prenup will demonstrate to them that assets due to go to them one day will in fact do so.

♦ Your future spouse came to work in your business and was so devoted to the business before you fell in love that you want to put some of the business into his or her name.

♦ You have managed to save about sixty thousand dollars, which you are willing to use as a down payment for the house you and your fiancé, who has no savings to speak of, plan to buy. Should something happen, you want to make sure that your life savings is protected.

♦ You've been working for twelve years at a great corporation and to your surprise have accumulated a substantial amount of money in your 401(k). The man you are marrying is younger and just starting out at another corporation. While you agree that you will share retirement plans from this point on, you'd like to keep your present benefits protected in the event of a divorce.

♦ You know that your future spouse has debt or is prone to spending unwisely, and that you do not want to be responsible for debts he or she incurs in his or her own name while you are married.

♦ You are in a committed long-term unmarried relationship. You want to live together and share some assets, perhaps even buy property together, but you aren't ready to commingle all your assets.

HOW PRENUPS WORK

Below are questions and answers detailing the main points that you need to consider with respect to prenups. Pay particular attention to the questions pertaining to debt, for that is one area that usually goes unexplored until it is too late. Please note that every state has different nuances when it comes to these contracts, so you must check with an attorney in your particular state to make sure you are creating a prenup or cohabitation agreement that will protect both of you and also stand up in a court of law.

What exactly is a prenuptial agreement?

A *premarital* or *prenuptial agreement* is a legal contract you enter into before marriage which states how a couple's assets as well as debts are to be divided in a way that is fair and reasonable to both spouses in case of a divorce. A *cohabitation agreement* works in the same way. You can also enter into such an agreement while you are married (a *marital agreement*) or, in the case of a cohabitation agreement, while you are living together.

Do judges really pay attention to prenups? If not, is it worth making my fiancé sign one?

Until recently, judges weren't favorably inclined toward prenups. Years ago, many states did everything they could to discourage divorce; they did not want to honor prenups, because the belief was that they encouraged divorce. They have since decided that this is not true and in fact recognize that sometimes people are better off if they do get divorced. So now, generally, the courts enforce these agreements. However, they will not honor the contract if the court feels that it gave one spouse a powerful incentive to end the marriage, for they see this kind of a contract as one that promotes divorce—which they still don't look favorably upon. The contract won't be enforced if it's viewed as a contract to evade creditors illegally, or if the court believes that one party was intimidated during the process. In some states, it's required that each partner consult with his or her own attorney before signing the agreement.

What is the best way to go about getting a prenup?

Prenups must be put in writing and signed by both parties. My best advice is for each of you to retain an individual attorney to represent your interests or at least to review the contract and advise you about its implications before you sign it. These contracts can be complicated, and you want to make sure that each of you knows exactly what you are signing. Not only should both partners sign the agreement, so should both attorneys.

Do prenups have to be witnessed and/or notarized to be valid?

This too varies from state to state. For example, in New York a prenup must be notarized to be valid, but in some states, neither witnesses nor notaries are necessary.

Do I need to disclose everything I have?

If anything, err on the side of more rather than less. Disclose it all—your assets, debts, income, expenses, and anything else that will affect the value of your estate, now or in the future. If you are not completely honest and open with each other, a court could reexamine your agreement and refuse to honor it.

Does a prenup only have to do with property ownership?

No. Other items such as debt, say, or future stock options or retirement benefits can be designated in the agreement. There have been prenups that covered everything from who will get the season baseball tickets to who has to feed the dog. Almost anything can be covered as long as it does not violate public policy—such areas, for example, as insufficient child support, because you cannot contract away a child's right to support.

What, exactly, is the definition of property?

In most courts of law, property includes everything from your sewing kit to your retirement funds. It also includes debts, patents, intellectual property (such as novels and screenplays), artwork—you name it. When it comes to the definition of property, expand your thoughts to go way beyond things like your car, boat, furniture, jewelry, or house. Property essentially includes everything.

What's the connection between prenups and debt, present and future?

In most cases, when you enter into a marriage, you are not responsible for the debts that your spouse incurred before the marriage. You will, however, be responsible for any debts incurred while you are married, whether both names appear on the credit card or not. Clearly, if it's a joint credit card issued in both names, you are both responsible. Less clear is what happens with cards issued in a single name. What about the credit cards that your husband or wife was issued in his or her name alone, for his or her own purposes? Let's say your spouse runs up significant debt, then you get divorced, and after the divorce he or she claims bankruptcy. Even though your name was not on the credit card, the company has the right to come after you for that money. Why? Because there was a question in relation to marital status on the application, and if he or she checked "married," then in very tiny writing the application stated that the spouse is also responsible for the debt unless otherwise noted. In some states, you can protect yourself against this by having a prenup that specifies which debt you will not be responsible for. You could have stated that any credit cards in your spouse's name alone are not your responsibility. However, this option may not be available to you in your state. Check the laws in your state, to see if you can protect yourself by sending a copy of your prenuptial agreement to all pertinent credit card companies, including those with which you set up new accounts.

How is property that I acquired before the marriage regarded by the courts?

Property acquired before the marriage is known as *separate property.* It remains separate property as long as you keep it in your name alone and your spouse has no access to it whatsoever. Even so, it doesn't hurt to have it detailed in the prenup. A problem can arise, however, if your partner contributes time or money to the maintenance of a premarital property, thus increasing its value. In some states, whether or not your partner contributes time or money to the asset, the *appreciation* may be considered a joint asset in any case.

What if I'm left an inheritance or will be given a gift by my parents after I am married? Is that property considered joint property?

No. If those funds were given specifically to you, and you keep those funds in an account in your name only, or you buy something with those funds in your name only, they'll remain your separate property. However, the longer a marriage goes on, the more boundaries between separate monies can blur. Let's say you buy some mutual funds, for example, and it's most convenient for the moment to name your spouse as joint owner. You may have just converted your separate property to *joint,* or *community, property.* Where you want such assets to end up should be spelled out in the prenup.

What if I owned rental property before I was married and continue to earn from it during the marriage—is the rent still my separate property?

This can be tricky. In some states, if you both invest your labor in the management of the property, the current income is considered a joint asset, since it's the product of both partners' labor, rather than a passive investment. If you use a management company, on the other hand, the rent is more often considered a separate asset. The laws on this vary widely from state to state, so check the law in your state. Again, however, it doesn't hurt to clarify ownership in the prenup.

I live in a community-property state. What exactly does community property mean?

Community property states include Arizona, California, Idaho, Louisiana, Nevada, New Mexico, Texas, Washington, and Wisconsin. *Community property* is everything acquired during the marriage except gifts, inheritances, or anything else agreed upon by both parties, regardless of whose funds are used. (An exception is income generated by separate property.) When you acquire something that falls under the classification of community property, then it is considered to be owned equally by each of you. This is true of debt that you accumulate as well as property and other assets. If you wish to handle your property or acquisitions in another way, you can so specify in a prenup. The biggest impact of community property is that upon dissolution of a marriage, it is divided fifty-fifty. In non–community-property states, the court can divide the joint assets however the judge thinks is most fair, depending on the financial needs and abilities of the parties upon dissolution.

If I live in a community-property state, am I responsible for the debts of my spouse?

The answer again is that your separate funds cannot be attached for any debts incurred by your spouse before the marriage. Nevertheless, creditors can come after your half of the community-property funds to pay for a debt that your spouse incurred before marriage. They can even attach your wages if they want—unless you specify otherwise in a prenup or deposit your wages in a separate account to which your spouse has no access whatsoever. Do not commingle these funds, or you cannot keep them safe. If you live in a community-property state and your spouse comes into the relationship with significant debt, you must discuss setting up a separate account for your wages. Again, make sure that your prenuptial agreement states your intention to keep your earnings separate.

If I draw up a prenup in one state and then we move to another, what happens?

It is important that you have the original contract checked by an attorney in the new state. If anything needs to be changed, your attorneys in the new state can make those changes.

What if, after the contract is drawn up, we want to make some changes?

No problem. You basically follow the procedure that you followed when you had the contract drawn up in the first place. Have the agreement witnessed and notarized, if necessary, and state expressly whether you're replacing the earlier document with this one or simply amending certain terms listed in the previous agreement.

If we have a prenup and the way in which we decide to divide our property is different from that dictated by the laws of the state where we live, will our prenup stand?

Yes. If the contract is drawn up correctly (even if you live in a community-property state), your agreement will allow you to modify or even contract out of the state property system and implement instead an agreement that better suits your needs.

When should the agreement be signed?

Do not sign it on the way to the chapel. The court will throw out your prenup if it feels that in any way either party was under duress when signing, or that the parties did not have ample time to think about it and to seek professional help. Make sure that you draw up your agreement under normal circumstances. Normal circumstances means that the person signed of his or her own free will and without any kind of gun-to-the-head coercion.

Yours, Mine, and Ours

All your adult life you've been managing your own money your own way, and now you're supposed to share everything? Not just the rent or the mortgage, but everything? This has been the traditional idea behind marriage: total financial togetherness. From football tickets to facials, everything that the two of you need and want is supposed to come out of your suddenly "joint" funds. This presumes that you will both want the same things at the same time, that your money habits (balancing the checkbook, for instance) will blend harmoniously, and that you both come from families where money is handled and treated in approximately the same way. It presumes, too, that if one or both of you become more successful, you'll be able to grow together financially as well as emotionally, and that you'll be able to survive the financial down times together. And it presumes that if children enter the picture or aging parents get sick and need your help, you'll be able to accommodate these new responsibilities peaceably. All this, in other words, presumes a lot, and presumes a transition that most of us, when we get married or start living together, can't make all at once.

Merging finances means compromise, it means sometimes putting someone else's interests and needs ahead of your own, and it requires negotiation and careful thought. No two couples are alike, and no two couples manage their finances in quite the same way—whether they manage them well or poorly.

K A T H E R I N E ' S   S T O R Y

We got married almost nine years ago, and I guess we didn't really talk too much ahead of time about money. It was pretty clear-cut at the time. I moved into Richard's condo before the wedding, actually, and we didn't make many adjustments. He owned it, and he kept paying the mortgage and mainte-nance, plus the electricity and so on, and I began paying for food and everything else I could. I bought some houseplants and window shades and a nice halogen lamp and fresh flow-ers every week. Still, it continued to feel like his place—I think he wasn't quite used to my being there all the time—and I never made an issue of how to divide up the expenses. I just tried to pay for every single thing I could. Plus the condo felt temporary. We were already talking about buying a house together, so I figured we'd just let the money stuff evolve.

Eventually we did find a house to buy. We also sold the condo really fast, and the profits were enough for a down pay-ment. Even then it was okay. We decided that he'd pay the mortgage, taxes, and insurance, plus a few other bills, and I would pay pretty much all the rest—food, cable, the gardener, dry cleaning, the oil bill, phone, garbage removal, electricity, whatever. At the time, Richard was making more money, and splitting things, about two-thirds to one-third, seemed fair to us both, I think. Or at least I don't remember very many fights about money this early on.

But then the bills started to escalate. The "everything else" part, the part that I was paying, just kept going up. There was suddenly a chimney cleaner, then firewood for the fireplace, and the windows were filthy, so we called a window washer. The house ended up needing a lot of work. Richard paid for some things, and I paid for some. There was work to fix the leaky basement, which he paid for, then I paid for the new hot-water heater, and it just kept going on. I was trying to think of it as "our" money—who cared who paid, anyway, so long as we had the money?—but there was no way to do that. Richard had his checking account, and I had mine, no joint account, and he'd always talk about "my" money and "your" money. Soon there was no way to keep track of the one-third, two-thirds split anymore. I'd go to the drugstore and he'd ask me to get him some things. When I got home, he'd say, "I'll pay for my things, how much are they?" But then he'd usually forget to pay. As I began to earn more money, I knew I was paying more, which would have been fine if he hadn't been guarding so carefully what was supposedly his. It was also getting to the point of absurdity—we couldn't get through a day without talking about his money or mine, and how he was going to chip in for this or that. It was really hurtful. Here I had gone into this marriage with my whole heart and all the money I made, and he was still trying to go Dutch treat. We were doing fine and making good money, but the pleasure was gone. There was nothing to show that we were in this together.

Then two things happened that really drove me crazy. The first was with this mutual fund that we were investing in. We had the account together. We were both putting some money in every month, but he was usually putting in more than I was, although I kept adding more when I could. The market started doing very well, and one day I opened the statement and said something like, "Gosh, Richard, we're really making money here." He got funny, and said that most of the money, give or take, was his. He didn't see it as ours at all, even though we were both paying as much as we could and even though we were married. He just wanted to be able to take out his money and earnings and run. When I told him that according to the law, if we got divorced, half of it would be mine anyway, he didn't speak to me for three days.

The second thing was that we wanted to have a baby. Aside from the money fights, everything else was good, and we both wanted a child. Well, we had to go through fertility treatments, which I put on my charge card. By the time I got pregnant, the bill was up to about eight thousand dollars— but who cared? We had a wonderful son! What made me so angry was that Richard thought of it as my debt—his baby, my debt. Not his problem. It was my credit card; why should he help pay it off? It made me want to run, just take the baby and run. After a fight, we paid most of it off with our tax refund. I finally paid off the rest.

By this time, the arbitrary split had been thrown out the window. It is really expensive having a child, and how do you split those costs? Child care, clothes, diapers, toys, formula, birthday parties—it goes on and on. We're still trying to do home improvements, his share, my share. He opened up another mutual fund account, but he opened it in his name only. It's very discouraging. We are doing fine financially, but I feel totally on my own. I used to feel that the way to do it was just to plunge into the marriage and be generous, but now I think I'd have been better off guarding my own money and keeping tabs on everything. Last month his parents came to visit for a few days and I went out and bought all this stuff to make really nice meals, and the only thing he could say was something about how he wanted to pay for "most" of it. Most of it? What, his share and his parents' share, but not mine? By now the arguments are so familiar, they're like a running joke—only they're not funny.

True Marriage: A Shortcut to True Wealth

You can construct all the formulas you want for financial harmony, but they won't necessarily work for long. Life is not a simple equation, and when it comes to money, we may have a common currency, but each of us has a different emotional currency. When you think about it, financial intimacy may be the most profound closeness there is. Many couples share a bed before marriage, some even share a home. We confide fears and painful stories of our pasts, and we certainly share our hopes and visions for the future. But talk about money? Possibly the last frontier of intimacy. A frontier that Katherine and Richard, even after nine years of marriage—a marriage that should be flourishing—have not yet crossed.

For a marriage or any partnership to work in the long run, you both have to go into it wholeheartedly—and not only with your whole heart but also with your checkbook. It's true that, with your prenup, you might have kept some assets out of the picture or might be able to work out an unconventional formula for managing your money that happens to work for you just fine, but that doesn't violate the underlying assumption of marriage, which is that the two of you will be richer together, in every way, than you would be on your own. Two people, contributing small sums of money, can build up a fortune much, much faster than one person. Two people working at it together can make a mortgage vaporize or send their children through school. Two people, even if one of them doesn't work outside the home for money, can together create a life with greater depth and texture and richness than most of us can on our own. That's what marriage or living together, at its best, is about, and it implies a full commitment.

In some cases, your fortunes can grow by leaps and bounds if you both work, and learn to live on one salary. I have good friends who met and married when they were both thirty-five, knowing full well that the woman, an attorney, would always make more than her husband, who works for the city. Their decision? To live on her salary, which would provide a comfortable but not luxurious life for them together, and invest every single penny of his. That was twelve years ago, and today, they both know that within three years they will have enough money to live on comfortably forever if they no longer want to work. Their commitment was to each other and to their future, but it was their financial commitment to the marriage that built the fortune and made their dream materialize. No fine lines here of "yours," "mine," "ours." It was all "ours."

Or take the arrangements in which one party stays home and the other goes to work every day. Here's another chance to build great fortunes, if that's the direction the commitment takes. Only one set of professional clothes in this household, perhaps only one car. One salary keeps the family in a lower tax bracket, and the stay-at-home spouse, according to the couple's agreement, cares for the house and the children, makes dinner, keeps everything running smoothly so that the working partner can devote his or her full energy to making money. Old-fashioned? Maybe. But if it's a whole-life commitment you're talking about, and it makes domestic and fiscal sense, this can be the road to riches.

In my opinion, the first law of money should be part of the marriage ceremony itself: *People first, then money.*

This is a lesson Katherine and Richard have yet to learn. If you're not together financially, then your marriage will not reflect a full commitment; it's that simple. And where there is divisiveness, it is much harder to create and sustain wealth, for conflict gives way to hoarding, counting, and, eventually, even deceit—all qualities that work against wealth. It takes courage (and, perhaps, a leap of faith) to enter into financial free fall with someone else, trusting that you will be better off by relinquishing your money for the sake of the greater good of your marriage. But if you can think of your money and marriage in the most expansive, generous way, then there will be plenty of room for both money and the richness that comes from love, from valuing achievements, both financial and otherwise. There's the money coming into the relationship, but there's also the love and energy that bring a life-

long relationship its vitality—the care spent creating and caring for
the home, entertaining and planning to see friends, the actual work of
raising children, shopping, cooking, paying bills, all of it. You can't put
a price tag on every element that makes up a life. If you share joyously
and willingly, if your commitment is financial as well as emotional,
your partnership will be a rich, happy place to inhabit. Here are some
issues to consider:

- *Bookkeeping.* Who's paying the bills? There is nothing more
  frustrating, if you're sharing a joint checking account, than to
  pay the bills and then have the phone ring off the hook
  because the checks bounced, when, according to your figures, there should have been more than enough money in
  the account to pay for everything. You call the bank, only to
  find out that your distracted sweetheart forgot to deposit
  your last paycheck, or perhaps forgot to record a couple of
  checks, or made a large cash withdrawal from the ATM and
  spent every penny of it without ever saying a word. Each one
  of us has our own financial housekeeping preferences—
  some of us balance the bank statement every month, some
  never balance it. Some of us will pay the bills as soon as they
  come in, while others have no problem being late every
  month. Regardless of how you deal with your money, it is
  essential that you work out a plan that will meet the needs of
  both of you in handling the coming and the going of your
  money.
- *Full disclosure.* Even if you decide to relegate the actual
  bookkeeping to one person, it is essential that you both
  know everything there is to know about your money—that
  you both know what it costs to live and what the bills come
  to every month; have a clear idea of the cost of food, clothing, and shelter; have an understanding of what the children's expenses are, and everything about where your
  money is going. This is the only way for you both to be

respectful of the money, and respectful and protective of each other, because it is unfair that the burden of bills fall on just one of you. My own feeling is that hands-on contact with the bills and the checkbook is important to bring you closer to understanding your money, so why not pay the bills together every month? If that doesn't work for you, one of you might do it one month and the other the next, or switch every six months. But see that you both touch, know about, and deal with your money.

♦ *Spending*. You must together reach an agreement about spending values. How often will you get a new car? What do you each have in mind when you talk about vacations? How much will the holiday season cost? Do you give presents for every occasion? Bottom line: You must talk about and compromise on or agree on what you need, what you want, and what you can afford.

♦ *Saving*. You must have a vision for tomorrow, and a means of getting there beginning today.

THE FORMULA FOR FINANCIAL SUCCESS: A STARTING POINT

It's true that what works for your friends or neighbors might not work for you, and any plan you start with will inevitably need some fine-tuning—if not today, then later on, when your circumstances change. Nevertheless, you have to start somewhere. Here are some principles that work for my clients:

Since we've decided to split the bills up proportionally, is it necessary that we have a joint account?

Remember Katherine and Richard? A joint checking account or money market fund (see chapter 17) with both of your names on it is essential, for the simple reason that you are not going to split the bills but share them. You are joining lives, and therefore money, and this account is financially symbolic of that union. Unless you want to start calculating who drinks more orange juice or uses more toothpaste, you must have a place to house money to pay for those bills and items that you share.

How much should we each contribute to the joint account?

This will depend on how much money each of you is making. Let's say Melissa is making $100,000 a year, but Ted is making only $25,000. It would be very hard for Ted to contribute the same amount as Melissa. This is what I suggest: Add up all your joint expenses—the rent or mortgage, telephone, utilities, food, movies, etc. Then add 10 percent to the total, because we always under estimate what it costs to live, day to day, week to week, month to month, and because the joint account is also meant to cover the relationship through any down times as well. You want to build this account up, not use it up, and create a slush fund, let's call it, for the bad times or unexpected bills that come your way. The idea here, remember, is to tap into the courage to be rich—and the richer your marital funds are, the richer you are, too.

Let's say that your joint expenses plus the additional 10 percent add up to $4000 a month. Melissa and Ted each should contribute the exact same percentage of what they are making toward paying these bills. In this case, after taxes, retirement contributions, health insurance, etc., Melissa takes home $6000 a month and Ted's take-home paycheck is around $1800. Add the two take-home checks together. This comes to $7800 ($6000 plus $1800). Now divide the total of your joint expenses, $4000, by the total of your joint take-home checks ($4000 divided by $7800). This equals the percentage, in this case 51.28 percent. That means that Ted needs to contribute 51.28 percent of his take-home pay, or $923 a month, to the joint account, and Melissa needs to contribute 51.28 percent of her take-home pay, or $3077 a month. This way, all the joint bills are covered and each one of you is paying the exact same proportion of your disposable income, which makes the equation totally equal. Remember, the *amounts* do not have to be the same to make something equal, only the *percentages*.

But it doesn't seem fair that I have to contribute more, even though I make more.

A larger dollar amount does not mean you work harder and therefore have more power or are entitled to more. The world, in fact, isn't a fair place—if it were, women wouldn't make seventy-four cents to every dollar a man makes. The measurement in a committed relationship is only this: Is each partner bringing everything he or she can to the relationship? That is the only measure that counts.

Maintaining equal power is a very important area of your relationship that you need to discuss now if you haven't already. The amount of money that you make when you are in a committed relationship is not what makes you more important or more deserving. Many people do incredibly meaningful work, vital work, yet are totally underpaid, while others are paid exorbitant amounts for work that in the long run may not make a difference to one single soul. Do not—I repeat—*do not,* value yourself or your partner by how much either of you makes. Enter the relationship, and continue in the relationship, as equals—remember, *People first, then money.*

If we have a joint checking account, do we need individual checking accounts as well?

Individual accounts in addition to the joint account are, in my opinion, a must. Grown-ups need discretionary income, and autonomy is an essential ingredient in any relationship—how degrading it would be to have to ask for money for a new lipstick or fishing tackle. You're partners, remember, and there are three entities here—yours, mine, and the big one, ours. But yours and mine count, too.

I make very little, but my spouse or partner makes a lot—and says it's okay if I use my money for my own needs and don't contribute to the joint household bills. Will this work?

This won't work. If you do this, the chances are good that as the years go by, it will backfire. When one person pays for everything, what usually ends up happening is that person tends to feel a sense of ownership toward everything, as well as a silent resentment toward the other person. In a joint life, you both have to pay. What's more, the person who is not contributing financially ends up feeling less and less powerful, and has less and less of a right to make joint financial decisions, which is everyone's right in a committed relationship. It is our nature to value our self-worth in dollars and cents. When you are working for money but not contributing financially, your inner radar will start to devalue your own opinion of yourself. It is far better to contribute on a fair percentage level, even if it comes out to just a few dollars a month, than to contribute nothing.

What if I decide to stop working for money, but stay home to take care of the children?

Then you will be doing equally important work. First you must ask yourselves: Is this financially feasible? In such a situation, I would recommend that you and your spouse add up all your expenses—everything from the mortgage to food to clothes for the children. How much is left over each month? If there's very little or nothing left over, and you both decide that this is the right course to follow anyway, then you must share equally in the responsibility of caring for and spending your money. If there is some discretionary money, it should be split fifty-fifty, regardless of who's bringing it in.

If I am going to stay home with the children, how do we work the money?

There is no simple formula for handling the money in this case, but the most important factor here is that you both agree that you will stay home with the children, because resentment on either side should tell you now that the arrangement won't work. You must agree, too, that any assets that build up belong to both parties, not just to the partner earning money. You must work together to find your formula, whether it means seeking a higher-paying job for the partner earning money, moving to a more affordable place, or giving up certain luxuries. And you must find a way to ensure that you both know that the partner staying home is a full, equal partner, with equal rights.

How do you do this? In a perfect world, the solution would be that the partner working outside the home pays you, the stay-at-home partner, a "salary" equal to what you were earning while you were working outside the home, and you continue to apportion the bills as before. Most of us don't have that luxury, however. Another method is to attach a price tag to what you are actually doing. If you were not staying home with the kids and you had to hire a nanny or the equivalent, how much would it cost you? Let's say that amount is $1500 a month. Every month your spouse should write you a check for that amount of money. You should deposit it into your individual checking account and then figure out, proportionately speaking, how much needs to go back into the joint checking account. Remember, the discretionary amount is yours to spend as you please. It is not meant to cover expenses for the house or for the children; these costs come out of the joint account.

Why go through that exercise, when you could just have your spouse give you some discretionary money of your own? The answer is *Because people forget*. If you do it that way, eventually the person who is getting up every morning and going to work will from time to time forget the true worth of what you are doing. Money must change hands, one way or another, because neither of you should have to face the degrading experience of asking for or explaining every little bit of money you may want or need. When a check is written every month, the tendency to forget is not so easy. Also, we ourselves forget what we are doing and what we are worth. This process serves as a reminder.

What if the one who was making less money starts making more?

Time to rework the deal.

The way we divided things up, my husband contributed the money for the car payment, but now that the car is paid off, he says he shouldn't have to put that money into the joint account anymore.

Big opportunity for getting rich. When something gets paid off or a former expense (day care, for instance) disappears, the money, which was benefiting the partnership anyway, should still be paid out every month—into the investment vehicle you both choose—and put toward your future.

What if I lose my job?

If you lose your job through sickness or downsizing, through no fault of your own, through bad luck, then the relationship must stretch to sustain you. Remember the extra 10 percent you were putting into the joint fund all along? That money is to help you both in times of trouble. This is true to the law and the spirit of marriage. Your part is to get back on your feet as quickly as you can.

Once our joint accounts and individual accounts are set up, how do we save for our future together?

The percentages calculated for what each of you would contribute to the joint account were calculated from take-home pay, which presupposes that your take-home pay has already had taken from it the maximum 401(k) or retirement account contributions at work or in your IRA. (Or, if you are self-employed, that you have funded your SEP-IRA or KEOGH plan to the max.) As your circumstances improve, you'll want to invest in non-retirement-plan savings toward your future as well. Again, use a proportional approach to create money for your future, to be shared equally. If one of you makes much more money than the other and wants to invest more, it is up to you (or your prenup) to decide to whom that money will go in the event of a divorce.

THE SPIRIT OF MONEY, THE SPIRIT OF MARRIAGE

It is very important to know the enriching lesson that Richard, Katherine's husband, has not yet learned, which is that even though different percentages may be invested in your future, when the money comes out it comes out fifty-fifty unless you specify otherwise in a premarital agreement. Let's say, for instance, that over the past ten years you each have been putting 5 percent of your paycheck into joint investment accounts. For you that may mean $100 a month and for your spouse or life partner that may mean $500 a month. You now have over $109,000 (assuming an 8 percent return) in this account. In reality, the one putting in $500 a month really contributed over $91,000 to that pot and the one putting in $100 a month would have accounted for roughly $18,300 of it. Regardless of what went in, what comes out has to be equal—even in the most acrimonious divorce. These are the fruits of your marriage, of your partnership. Half of that money is yours and half of that money belongs to your mate. In a few states the laws will say that this pot must be divided in half. In most states, however, the law says that it does not necessarily have to be divided in half. But sharing equally goes beyond the legal system; in truth, it should be governed by the law and intent of marriage, the law of the heart. You were equal partners, and so you share in the partnership as equals. Know this up front and make it part of your commitment, which will be all the stronger for stating and following this course from the beginning. While you are together you reap the harvest of your marriage equally. Remember, when it comes to money it is not about doing what is easy, it is about having the courage to do what is right.

CHAPTER 11

The Courage to Transcend the Pain of Divorce

When you got married, you and your mate gave your word to honor each other for better or for worse, forever. If you are now facing a divorce, you are breaking your vow, but you must still honor the "for worse" part of that promise, if only for your own sake. Your thoughts, your words, and the actions you take at this time will direct your way into your future. Remember, your thoughts create your destiny. If your thoughts and words are full of hate, anger, and rage, then those emotions will direct your actions, and they will be actions of poverty. No matter how hateful and angry you feel right now—and, by the way, hate and anger may be perfectly appropriate emotions for you to feel, depending on your situation—I ask you to recognize the power of your anger to impair your judgment, to negate the good in your past, to set the tone of your future. If, on the other hand, you can carefully and deliberately draw on your courage, faith, and grace during this time, you will be drawing on qualities of richness and taking those qualities with you into tomorrow. Dissolving a union can be one of the most painful experiences in life, and though it may seem hard to believe when you are in the throes of it, you will be much better off in the end if you do everything you can not to make the situation any worse than it already is. Whether you are the one who is being left or the one who is leaving, the way in which you behave during this period will live on with you, long after the pain of the divorce has faded.

This realization surprised me, and it may sound shocking to you, but after working with many clients who've experienced divorce or the death of a spouse, I have come to believe that a death—whether forseeable or unexpected—is almost easier to cope with, over the long term. With death, there is no blame. Everybody loses with a death. A life is gone. The community surrounds you in mourning, and friends and relatives check in often to see how you are. If you have children, they draw closer to you. There is no ambiguity. The house is yours to sell or keep as you see fit, the car is yours, the retirement account, the life insurance policy, the possessions all are yours—everything that was "ours" is now yours. When you lose someone you love, the loss is great, to be sure. But you never lose the love. The love remains pure.

In a divorce, however, everything is different. If you are the bereaved party in the event of a divorce, you may be faced with a partner who is living a perfectly happy life with someone else. You may feel that for all you gave to the relationship, you got little back. Perhaps you are making do with less, while your partner is living on more. If you have children, your partner may take them away from you one night a week and every other weekend, and show them a great time. The children themselves are likely to be confused and angry. As for the community, not everyone is rallying around you unconditionally, the way they would have if your spouse had died; no one's dropping off supper for you. Rather, some of your friends aren't feeling very comfortable around you, and some of them are taking his side, thus compounding your loss. To rebuild your life from this point of disequilibrium will take great courage, and I want you to start, for your own sake, from the highest place you can.

CHARACTER LINES

I want you to think about this: Every action you take today will have an effect on your tomorrow. Actions become etched in our character, in our soul, whether they're actions based on anger, hatred, and rage, or when—despite the anger, hatred, and rage—we consciously and deliberately and purposefully "act" (and it may be the acting job of your life) from a higher place. Have you ever run into an acquaintance or friend you knew way back when, someone you haven't seen in a long time, and thought to yourself, My God, how old this person looks. I wonder what's happened in his life?

What you're seeing may be determined in part by genetics, but you're also seeing the outward manifestation of all the emotions that your friend has felt and expressed. You're seeing the external effects of his impure thoughts, his impure words, and especially his impure actions. You're seeing whether he's been mean in the past, and whether he is bitter today. You're seeing his character etched in the lines of his face. Maybe your friend has money, maybe not, but the life he's leading is anything but rich.

ACTING FROM CLARITY

There are many things you must do financially and legally to effect a divorce, but also things you must do emotionally—again, for your own good—to make sure that those financial and legal actions originate from a place of clarity, not a place of vengeance. Listen carefully to the language of breakup and divorce:

"I've never been so angry."

Acting from anger not only threatens to hamper your good judgment when it comes to making vital decisions, it can also increase your attorneys' fees. Working with clients going through divorces, I have noticed a direct correlation between the amount of the bills and the amount of anger the person has. What usually happens is that those who angrily refuse to settle end up in court, and end up paying a lot more; generally, an in-court divorce trial will cost at least three times as much as an out-of-court settlement. Ironically, those who go to court haven't a clue as to how their case will end up, because through the lens of their self-righteous anger, they can see only one side—theirs. If the court's decision is at odds with their expectations, they get angrier still. Even if they "win," there is no guarantee that their anger will subside, for what often happens is that a disgruntled ex-spouse may refuse to comply with the court order, and then the anger escalates to a whole new level. Please don't allow your anger today to cast a dark shadow upon your tomorrow.

On the other hand, if your estranged spouse is being unreasonable and there's no amicable way through the impasse, do not be afraid to go to court to have the judge determine the final accounting, pay off the debts, divide any remaining assets, and settle issues of child and spousal support, attorneys' fees, and so on.

"I don't care what happens."

So many times I hear these words from my clients: "I don't care what happens. I just want to get on with my life."

Remember that words are very powerful and that when you say you don't care what happens you are in effect creating a situation that almost surely will prevent you from getting on with your life in a rich, productive way. You may spend many more years divorced from your spouse than married to him or her; therefore the decisions you make during this crucial time will affect you for many years to come. Do not take this casually. Divorce is as serious a commitment to the future as marriage was. You must be involved in every decision, you must give a damn, for it is your life. Take control, cut through your numbness, and summon words of wealth: "I want to get on with my life, but I care deeply about what happens now, because what happens now will affect me and possibly my children forever." Say the words to your attorney, to your ex, and say them with grace until they become true. They are words that others will respect, will help make the sentiment true, will help you to care, and will help assure for you a richer tomorrow.

"I don't care about the money. I just want him [or her] back."

So many times when divorce is imminent, the person being left refuses to face up to what is happening. She ends up thinking thoughts such as, "I can get him back if I do whatever he wants." When you give up your rights to money and make it seem so totally unimportant, you are not one iota likelier to save your marriage. All you are likely to do with this kind of thinking is impoverish your future. Logic like this will rob you of what little power you have left. Remember: Respect and power attract money; disrespect and powerlessness repel it. With thoughts and words like the ones above, you are about to serve yourself a double whammy. Not only will you start to repel money, money that is rightfully yours, but the person you are trying to bring closer will be repelled, too, by your lack of self-respect and your powerlessness. No one is attracted to weakness. Maybe you can put your marriage back together, maybe not. But please don't predicate your financial actions (or, for that matter, emotional actions) on a tenuous possibility.

"I know we're going to get back together."

Unfortunately, you don't. No matter how much you may want to get back together, there is no guarantee you will, and possibly little reason for hope. If you go into denial now, or let hope overshadow all reason, you may be setting yourself up for an emotional and a financial letdown. If your partner wants out, you have little choice but to believe it and to do everything necessary to protect yourself. Preventive action on your part will have absolutely no effect on a possible reconciliation, I can promise you that. If anything, should the possibility arise, your actions now—strong, powerful, clear, graceful, and, yes, rich—will better the chances for a reconciliation.

"I'll never get through this."

Watch your words. You will get through this, just as you have gotten through other difficult times in your life. How you get through this, however, will largely be determined by whether you can reach for your courage, or whether you turn away from it toward your pain. During this transition period, you are going to have to make quite a few decisions, and it is vital that when you do so, your mind and body are as strong as possible. Act with strength, which itself will create strength. Eat well, exercise, allow yourself plenty of sleep. Even if the motions feel hollow, the actions are powerful, and powerful actions will nourish your courage.

"I hate the person who came between us."

Of course you do, if you're being left for someone else, even given the probable truth that the person who came between you didn't come uninvited. Nevertheless, if all your energies are devoted to hate, you will have little left for more constructive pursuits. If you think about this hate all the time, then you'll talk about it, and act on it, and you will be building a hateful, vengeful foundation on which to live the rest of your life. Try to pull away from the hate as much as you can, and instead expend your energies on caring for yourself.

"I'm going to take him [or her] to the cleaners."

Interesting expression, because it suggests he (or she) emerges clean, and where does that leave you? Dirty? Banish this thought, if only for the simple reason that the law won't let you impoverish your spouse. There's room to maneuver in some divorce cases, it's true, particularly when there's a lot of money involved, but the law (or at least the spirit of the law) has been created to protect you both. If your thoughts originate from a higher place—I am concerned only with getting what's fair; I want only what is rightfully mine; I do not have to settle—then you are starting with thoughts of power.

"I don't want anything. He [or she] can have it all."

Don't be a martyr. You were half of this marriage. You are entitled to half, you deserve half, and if you push away this money now, how are you going to learn to draw money toward you later on? Please let the laws and the spirit of marriage give you what is rightfully yours. Better yet, insist on it—with your attorney, with your spouse.

"I'm not worried about the money. I know he [or she] will be fair."

When it comes to dividing up assets—which means giving up money—people behave very strangely, and a person you once thought the most generous in the world might seem to have been transformed overnight into someone entirely different. The person who must protect, nurture, and look after you now is you. Maybe you're right. Maybe he (or she) will be fair and decent all the way through, and I hope so. But protecting your own interests will not get in the way of your partner's decency.

"Not today."

Powerful words indeed. During the first years, your emotions are going to go up, down, and all over the place. One day you will feel great and the next you will be wretched. On the days that the blues hit you big-time, take a break. Do not make decisions on those days. For the first six months, I always had my clients rate themselves on a scale of one to ten twice a day—when they get up and about eight hours later—a one rating being extremely happy and ten being miserable. If ever they felt they were a five or more, then they were not allowed to make any decisions regarding their money or divorce on that day. If asked to, they were simply to say, "Not today, thank you," let it go at that, and address the matter when they felt better. Check yourself twice a day, because sometimes a phone call, a song on the radio, a comment from a friend, or even two people walking down the street holding hands can set off a chain of emotions changing a one to an eight before you know what hit you. "Not today, thank you" is an expression of self-respect, coming from a position of power.

THE ONE WHO LEAVES
AND THE ONE LEFT BEHIND

This is not a contest to see who can get through this divorce with the fewest breakdowns. If you are the one who has been left, do not be surprised if your spouse seems to be doing much better than you are. Please remember that the chances are good that he or she has been thinking about this for a long time, long enough that the shock at the idea has worn off, whereas for you, the shock is brand-new and devastating. Your job now is to rebuild your life and act in your best interests. Do not get pushed into doing anything during this time. Start doing your daily ratings immediately and take action only when you are ready. You have the power to set the pace of the divorce. You have the power, too, to drag it out, but that won't help you. Use your power to proceed, but only as you are ready to.

If you're the one leaving, your responsibilities are immense. Regardless of your feelings today, you have most likely just delivered a terrible blow to the person who was once the love of your life. For your own benefit, as well as your spouse's, proceed slowly and with compassion. Your marriage failed. Now it is your responsibility to conclude it as successfully as possible. How you end something as profound and important as a marriage is a reflection of how you live your life—financially, emotionally, and spiritually.

SEEKING HELP

No one can go through a divorce alone, even with help from the guidelines offered here. Divorce laws vary substantially from state to state, and you will need help to understand the particulars of the laws in your state and what they mean in your particular case. If the divorce is relatively amicable, you may be able to settle the issues at stake with a mediator—or a mediator may provide a starting point. If you have been married just a short time, have few assets, and both know that the marriage was a mistake, your state may permit a summary dissolution, in which you go to court without an attorney, and the court simply affirms the allocation of your assets. This is basically a "short form" divorce—easy to conduct yourself when you have no children, support, or property issues. Otherwise you will need an attorney, and the more you know about your situation, the easier (and cheaper) it will be to work with your attorney. With respect to your attorney, however, remember that he or she is there to represent you legally—not emotionally. However compassionate the attorney may be, seek your emotional support elsewhere.

I urge you to seek therapy or counseling if you can possibly afford it and/or to consult with a member of the clergy. It is one thing to receive emotional support from family and friends, who will probably provide you with all the sympathy you need. But if you constantly let them see you at your very lowest point, it will be harder for you to restore the equilibrium of your relationships later, when you feel stronger. They may simply go on seeing you as a victim, and treating you like one, which would make it all too easy for you to continue acting like a victim. Plus, what if you need more than sympathy? A professional counselor's impartiality may help make you stronger, both in the short and long term. If there are children involved, a counselor may also help you in dealing with their pain and deciding whether they, too, need professional help.

DON'T FIGHT OVER THE ORANGE TOWELS: AN OVERVIEW

In the suite next to my office is an attorney who deals with family issues and divorce, and her rule-of-thumb advice is to choose your battles carefully. If there is a lot of property to be divided, concede gracefully on the smaller stuff and you'll be on higher ground when it comes to the items that really matter.

In general, the court system is in place to see to the division of property and debts and to settle issues of spousal support, child support, custody, and visitation. The following are some of the points the courts ultimately consider:

- The duration of the marriage
- The earning power of each party. How well is each of you equipped to maintain your present standard of living?
- The marketable skills of the party seeking support; how long the party who has been supported until now has stayed at home; whether children will make it harder for the party seeking support to find work; what would be involved (time and expenses) to educate or retrain the stay-at-home partner for the current job market. The court's goal is that the party seeking support will eventually be able to support him- or herself. The trend is to award support for half the duration of the marriage, without regard to fault.
- The means of the partner who is being asked for support
- Child support and custody arrangements. In determining child support, the courts often look to the percentage of time the child or children spend with each parent and the respective incomes of both parents.
- Age, health, and extenuating circumstances, such as whether you're caring for an invalid child or parent

SETTING THE DATE OF
SEPARATION / DIVORCE

Separation is defined as no longer living together and no longer having the intention to reconcile. In most states the divorce may become final within six months to one year after you've filed for divorce or the other party was served with papers. Depending on the state, the date of separation can matter a great deal in determining the financial outcome in a divorce and can affect, among other issues, how you'll divide retirement assets, how much alimony may be at stake, your right to a share of your present spouse's Social Security payments, and your responsibility for any debt incurred by your spouse. If you know or sense that you may be headed for divorce, try to plan the separation date with all factors in mind.

PENSION PLANS, RETIREMENT ACCOUNTS,
AND STOCK OPTIONS

I learned firsthand how important setting the separation date can be when the husband of a very good friend of mine came home and announced, apparently out of the clear blue sky, that he wanted a divorce. He asked her to move out as soon as possible. I couldn't figure out what happened, and why it was all so sudden and urgent. A few days later, as my friend was preparing to move, I happened to read in the paper that the company her husband was working for had just been bought out, and in two months all the employees were going to receive stock options and a generous pension plan. My friend's husband knew that if this took place after he and his wife were officially separated, there was a good chance that he wouldn't have to share that windfall with her. It was a tense two months, but she waited them out before she made her move.

Many states will value the retirement plan and/or benefits from the date of *separation,* not from the date of the divorce, because this date marks the point at which a couple's common interest ended. For instance, many employers make their contributions to their employees' pension plan at the end of the calendar year. If you separated from your spouse and moved out on December 24, and on December 25 the employer made the annual pension contribution, you may very well have missed out on your right to claim any portion of that year's contribution. (Many self-employed people, on the other hand, put last year's retirement money into their KEOGHs or SEP-IRAs at the very last minute of the tax year, in April, and this should be considered as well.)

Make sure you know how your and/or your spouse's pension plan works. When are the valuations of it made? If a pension plan is involved, consult an attorney before making any move and obtain a copy of the benefit schedule for both your and your spouse's retirement plans.

SOCIAL SECURITY

Another client of mine decided that she wanted to divorce her husband and she wanted to do it immediately. Luckily, it promised to be a very amicable divorce. They had seen an attorney and had papers drawn up, which she was about to sign when she called to ask me a question about their investments. They had both been clients of mine for a long time, and I wondered how long they had been married. When I asked her, she told me nearly ten years. I suggested she wait, because if she went ahead and signed those papers right now, she would not, when the time came, be entitled to Social Security benefits based on her spouse's earnings. Social Security benefits are based on the date of *divorce,* not the date of separation. Since my client had never worked outside the home and hadn't built up Social Security of her own, signing the divorce papers before their tenth anniversary would have turned out to be a big mistake. If she wanted to, I told her, she could move out, they could separate, and for all purposes go on with their lives as if they were divorced. Then, after their tenth anniversary, they could sign the papers to make it legal.

Please note: Claiming your share of your spouse's Social Security benefits is a right you are entitled to by the federal government and does not diminish your spouse's Social Security check in the least. So don't fail to claim your due because you think you will be taking something away from your spouse; that is absolutely not the case.

ALIMONY AND THE SEVEN-TO-TEN-YEAR MARK

This ten-year mark could have affected not only my client's Social Security but also her alimony. The seven-to-ten-year mark is an important signal, for many states use these anniversaries as benchmarks for what constitutes a long-term marriage. A long-term marriage judgment may play very favorably for purposes of spousal support for a spouse who has not worked outside the home or who was earning very little during the marriage.

THE HOUSE

The hardest decision most divorcing couples face is who gets to keep or stay in the home that the two of you built. It is hard to give up not only a person but also the space that you felt safe and probably happy in for a long time. Who keeps the house and who moves out is a fuzzy legal area, in that the law does not mandate who must move out. Of course, when there are children involved, it's another story. The primary caretaker usually stays in the house with the children. If you want to be the primary caretaker, please see an attorney before you do anything. If you've moved out, and there's a subsequent custody battle, many judges lean favorably toward keeping the situation as it is rather than disrupting the children's lives yet again. If there's any physical threat to the children, then you would have to seek a restraining order from the court that would prevent your spouse from staying in the house. Other than that, though, the decision will most likely be made between the two of you, or with the aid of legal counsel or a mediator.

With respect to the division of the value of the house, this is set on the date of *divorce,* not the separation date. In other words, let's say you decide that the marriage is over, and you separate and move out. Two years later, the divorce is final. If the value of the house has increased over those two years, you will get to participate in that increase in value.

If you are unmarried, the house issues will be resolved according to the property laws of your state. In most states this means that neither one of you has the right to buy out the other one; if you can't make a deal amicably, the court will sell the house and divide the proceeds. These are usually divided equally unless one of the partners can prove an agreement to the contrary. For these reasons, working out an amicable settlement in which one party buys out the other or they sell the place jointly is always the best solution.

INCOME TAXES

From the date of separation, all income you earn may, if you choose, be filed on a separate tax return. There may be tax ramifications, possibly negative, when you decide to do this, so make sure you consult an accountant. If you have any doubt as to what you should do, or if you and your spouse cannot decide how you should file your taxes, file separately. The law allows people who file separately to amend their taxes within a three-year period of time and file again jointly, but the law does not let people who file jointly amend their taxes later to file separately.

If you file separately, you and your spouse must decide together how you will divide deductions—the home mortgage interest, charitable deductions that both of you made, property taxes, day-care expenses, etc.

When filing jointly, you are each liable for what the other person puts on that joint tax return. Be particularly wary if you distrust your spouse when it comes to money. If your spouse overstates deductions or understates income and the IRS catches it, you as well as your spouse will be held responsible for all back taxes and penalties, plus interest. If your now ex-spouse cannot pay, the IRS will come after you. So if money has been a problem between the two of you, you might want to protect yourself and file separately for peace of mind, even if it will cost you more.

DEBT

In most scenarios, the date of separation in a final judgment or decree officially determines when you are no longer responsible for the debts that your spouse has incurred. Make sure all joint accounts are closed or divided when you separate. Make sure, too, that you divide all debts and know who is responsible for each one. Before doing so, set up an account in your name and make sure that you qualify for credit, since sometimes your individual credit rating can be affected if you close out an account. Contact all professionals and service providers (doctors, lawyers, dentists, etc.) and inform them in writing that if any work is being done for your spouse, you will not be responsible for the bills. Even if all these precautions are taken, it's still possible that creditors might come after you seeking payment for bills your spouse incurred. Thus the more accounts you can close, the better off you are. Note, too, that most likely you will be responsible for debts your spouse runs up for the necessities of life during the separation period. Necessities of life include housing, food, clothes, the children's expenses, and medical expenses.

CUTTING TIES

The hardest part of divorce, for many people, is money. People can move away from each other and start new lives, but often they seem unable to cut the financial ties quite as cleanly. Sometimes letting go of jointly managed money seems like the ultimate move, and they're not ready to do that yet. In other cases, guilt keeps the money together. Or the person who has always handled the money keeps handling it because it's familiar and easy, or because both parties are simply too lazy to separate the funds. Whatever the reason, it is wrong to remain financially intimate after you have severed domestic and emotional ties.

I have seen it time and time again: Apart from child support and alimony, when someone continues to foot the bills after a separation, resentment builds up on one side and, on the other, there is an unhealthy dependence. At issue may be the house payment, let's say, until the ex-spouse can find him- or herself a new place to live, or a car payment. Whatever the case, power and respect are going out the window on both ends.

If you decide to pay for items for your spouse after you have separated, it is very important that a start date and a stop date are delineated. Set a time limit. The particulars of any financial arrangement between the two of you should be put in writing so that there is no misunderstanding. Remember, when one person is in shock—most likely the person who is being left—he or she is not going to hear things accurately or remember things clearly. Do not set yourselves up for additional misunderstandings. With your attorneys' help, put your temporary agreement in writing, both of you sign it, and both of you keep a copy.

TENDING TO MONEY ISSUES IMMEDIATELY

Once a separation seems inevitable, you must turn your attention to money issues as quickly as possible. If you prolong these actions, you may one day find that you are responsible for credit card debt that was incurred after you moved out, or that one of your joint accounts has been wiped clean of all its assets, or that the home equity account that was there in case of emergencies now has a loan against it for twenty thousand dollars, for which you are responsible. Do not be afraid to separate your accounts immediately. If you should end up getting back together, you can always open these accounts again.

FINANCIAL CHECKLIST

What follows is an overview of everything that should be done immediately when it becomes clear that a separation is imminent:

- Consult with an attorney regarding divorce laws in your particular state.
- If you don't already have one, open up an account in your name only.
- Close all joint accounts. Don't freeze accounts, because one or both of you may need access to the funds for any number of reasons. With your attorneys' approval, split the money from joint accounts equally.
- Make copies of all the financial documents that show your true debts, assets, and expenses, including household and credit card bills, bank records, expenses for the children—every penny you spend to live month to month.
- Start keeping track of all debts incurred and money paid to each other after the date of separation. This includes money spent on joint bills, improvements to the home, moving expenses, children, insurance premiums—everything that could pertain to the two of you. If you decide to pay support to your spouse while you are working things out, make sure that all these sums are documented and that you have an agreement in writing as to what these funds are for. If you

put this in writing these payments may be tax-deductible, although they will be considered taxable income to the spouse receiving support.

♦ See a tax specialist to decide whether you are going to file your taxes jointly or separately.

♦ Sit down and really figure out what you are worth as a couple. First determine the worth of everything you own together—household furnishings, real estate, cars, everything. You can do this by hiring appraisers or by getting estimates from real estate agents. It is essential, too, that you work with a tax specialist who can inform you of the tax consequences of every move you make.

♦ Gather documentation about all your assets—any investments, retirement plans, bonds, mutual funds, savings or money market accounts, etc. In addition, a tricky and relatively new area is that of stock options, which are given to employees at great discounts but may not be exercised until years later. If your spouse has any stock options, you must see an attorney at once, as most states are still sorting out whether, in a divorce, a stock option that you hold today should be considered a joint asset when it is able to be exercised, however many years down the road.

♦ After you determine what you have in assets as well as your expenses and income, try to sit down with your spouse and see if you can work out something that is equitable. Don't do this before you have all your documentation, however, because you can't negotiate without the facts, and don't agree to anything without consulting an attorney.

LEGAL SEQUENCE

♦ Know your legal rights and responsibilities either by doing research at your local library or bookstore or by consulting an attorney. Make sure that your attorney and any books you consult are familiar with the laws of your state, because, as noted above, divorce laws vary from state to state. Many divorce lawyers will do a one-hour consultation either free or for a small flat fee, so don't hesitate to seek a second or third opinion.

♦ Now this is where courage really comes in, because this is the point at which you truly separate—which is to say, make the separation legal, the requirements for which differ from state to state. During the separation, one of you will file a *petition for divorce* or a *complaint,* and this will start the formal divorce proceedings.

♦ One of you may need to file a *request for temporary child and spousal support,* and for *custody, visitation rights, alimony,* or anything else that may apply to your situation. You will receive a *temporary order* soon after this filing, and eventually a *permanent order* once the divorce is final. Even after that, the court retains jurisdiction to alter child support provisions until the children are emancipated; thus both ex-spouses can petition the court for a change in support payments or custody arrangements until their children become legal adults. In addition, the court retains jurisdiction over spousal support until that is terminated.

♦ Now begins the process called *legal discovery,* which determines exactly what must be divided. This information is used to calculate, if applicable, the amount of child support or alimony that you will have to pay or receive.

♦ Once all this is done, it's time to negotiate the settlement. If the marriage has been very short, without children, and there are negligible assets (or debts) to divide, you may be able to divorce through a *summary disposition,* which is basically a streamlined way to file for divorce. In some states, too, the courts have set up an arm to help you represent yourself, called *in pro per.* If your case is amicable and relatively uncomplicated, look into settling it in the easiest and least expensive way possible.

♦ If the way in which the property will be divided is clear-cut to you both, you are in full agreement about custody arrangements, and you are certain to behave like adults, then a *mediator*—a negotiator who acts impartially, with no allegiance to either party—may be all you need to propose a marital settlement for the attorneys to draft.

♦ In cases where custody arrangements or property division is complicated, or when emotions are running high, you each will need an *attorney*—and possibly even a *judge.* The attorney's role is to represent your interests, suggest appropriate settlement terms, convey settlement offers, advise you as to what the court is likely to do in your situation, and help with the division of property and debts. The attorney, in other words, will fight your battles for you and insulate you from your estranged spouse.

♦ Once the terms have been settled on—who gets what and when—either by the two of you or with a court order, a *marital settlement agreement* or *stipulated judgment* is drafted, which is then used for the final judgment of divorce. If you cannot come to an agreement, you will end up settling your dispute in court.

BEWARE THE BUYOUT

In some instances, the spouse who is required to pay spousal support may instead offer you a one-time, lump-sum offer of *settlement,* which in effect is a "buyout" of any future obligations, excluding child support. Emotionally, a once-and-for-all settlement can be a clean break. Financially, however, a settlement is a gamble, because the spouse required to pay is using today's dollars to settle what might be a significantly higher amount tomorrow. If you are considering a settlement,

consider all the factors, not just by today's standards but also by tomorrow's.

COURT: THE LAST RESORT

The court system, when it comes to divorce, is set up to make sure
that the division of property is handled fairly and to ensure the welfare
of any children involved. When you go to court, the outcome is solely
in the hands of the judge. This means that you are putting the fate of
your future, your home, your children, and your pension and retirement plans in the hands of a stranger. If you can somehow try to work
it out between yourselves and reach a clear resolution, you may be better off. If, however, you cannot resolve your differences, then don't be
afraid to put the matter in the hands of the court.

Even if you are committed to taking your spouse to court, an out-of-
court settlement may be reached days or perhaps minutes before the
case is to begin—and this is the time when big mistakes are often
made. Ninety percent of divorces are settled out of court, no matter
how hellbent both parties are on having a judge hear their case. Imagine this scenario. You are about to go into the courtroom, nervous and
high-strung as can be, probably shooting daggers at your ex from a few
feet away, and vice versa. Your lawyer, who has been talking in hushed
tones to the lawyer representing your ex, approaches you and says
your ex is willing to settle the case right now if you give in on these
few points, but the decision has got to be made right away, because
once the trial begins it is too late. You agree and instantly feel a wave
of relief . . . until two months down the road, when you realize that
you may have made a mistake. Do not make decisions that will affect
the rest of your life when you feel pressured. If you have come all this
way, unless you know the precise ramifications of everything you may
be agreeing to, do not accept a last-minute settlement.

FREE AGAIN

You are single again. Now you need to make sure that all your documents—the deed to your house, the title to your car or boat, your will or trust, insurance policies, every investment or asset that was previously held jointly—reflect your new status. Please don't let this paperwork slide, for financial decisiveness will help the healing, the closure, and make you feel stronger for having put your financial past behind you. With this financial clutter behind you, you'll be freer to put your energies into starting over.

CHAPTER 12

THE COURAGE TO LIVE AFTER A DEATH

To have someone you love taken from you forever creates a pain so deep that there is little anyone can say or do to help. Hard as it is to believe in the days, weeks, and months after a death, healing is a function of faith, courage, and time. Having faced the financial aftermath of death many times with my clients, I have come to believe that we never quite know the meaning of life until we draw close to death. Often only then do we seem to learn what has true meaning and what does not. Everything is put into perspective, and in our grief, most of us put thoughts of money at the bottom of our list of priorities. Which can be a terrible mistake. The death of a partner is an event that forces us not only to deal with a new emotional reality but also to accept a new financial reality.

SUZE AND KATIE'S STORY

I was sitting at my desk in the bullpen area with the other brokers at Merrill Lynch, waiting for a new client. I was nerv-

ous, I remember, because I was still new to the business and didn't yet have many clients, and the man I was expecting, whose name was Allen, had a substantial sum of money to invest. The receptionist called when he arrived, and I went out to greet him. As I approached the reception area, I saw a burly man of about fifty-five with a kind face. I introduced myself, and he reached out to shake my hand. He asked if he could possibly have a glass of water, and I told him I would get it for him and be right back. As I was walking away he said, "By the way, what time is it?" I looked at my watch and said, "Five after one." I was gone only a few minutes, and when I returned with the water, he was resting in the chair with his eyes closed. "Here is your water," I said, but he didn't reply. In a louder voice I said, "Excuse me, Allen. I've got your water," but again he did not respond. I shook his shoulder, and with that he fell forward onto the floor. I realized that he must have had a heart attack and screamed for help. The receptionist frantically called nine-one-one, and in seconds, another broker who was trained in CPR started administering mouth-to-mouth resuscitation. The paramedics arrived, huddled over Allen, then looked up and said that they were sorry, but he was gone. I remember thinking, Gone where? I couldn't comprehend what they meant with him lying right there in front of me. His last words had been a question: "What time is it?" Did he somehow know that this was his last moment on earth and want to know the hour of his death? Deeply shaken, with the fact of this stranger's death coursing through me strong as life, I knew all I could do was go home.

About a month later, Allen's widow, Katie, came to see me to ask me what had happened. She wanted me to recount the last minutes of her husband's life. Which I did over and over again. It was as if she wanted to prolong those final moments forever. Clearly, she was having a hard time coming to terms with his death and with the fact that she was supposed to carry on alone. Alone not only emotionally but financially as well. I asked her if she knew anything about money. She said no. All she knew was that they had a savings account at the local bank that she had been using to get her money, but there was not a lot left in there. She knew, too, that Allen had had a life insurance policy, but she had not looked into that yet. She was hoping that since Allen had come to see me, I could tell her more about their finances. But now she learned that he had never even had the chance to do that. She didn't know what she was going to do, and she asked if I could help her.

This was one of the most heartbreaking days of my professional life, for there really was very little that I could do. I felt so powerless. I remember thinking that now was not the time that this woman should have to learn about money. She could barely deal with her grief as it was, let alone take on a task that to her was absolutely intimidating and terrifying. I felt a helpless anger rising up at the man she called her husband. I wondered, If he could see her, would he see not only her hurt but also her confusion? Would he realize that it didn't have to be this way? I knew that she was not totally without blame herself, that she could have asked to learn about their finances, forced the issue, but how many of us voluntarily do anything that scares and intimidates us? And there is nothing so formidable to most of us as death and money.

I am sorry to say that this was not the last time that I encountered someone in precisely this situation. Over the years I have been called upon many times to pick up the financial pieces scattered after a death. Some people were lucky; when their spouses or life partners died, they had a friend or someone they could trust to help them on their new financial course. But many bereaved souls had sought the advice of a so-called professional when they were most vulnerable and ended up losing everything, or nearly so. By the time they found their way to me, many people had already handed over their life insurance proceeds, portfolios, their futures to con artists posing as concerned professionals or to commission-hungry salespeople. It is hard enough to have the courage to go on living after you have lost your emotional equilibrium, but it is almost impossible when you have also lost your financial stability. Hard as it may seem to you now, in the early stages of your grief, I ask you please to keep your financial realities in mind as you come to terms with the death of your loved one. The actions you take at this time will have important effects later, when the death and your grief are not so new and raw.

IF I SHOULD DIE BEFORE I WAKE . . .

The death part of life's equation cannot ultimately be prevented, but we most certainly can prevent the financial confusion, and at least some of the emotional uncertainty, that so many of us seem to face when death is introduced into our life.

I strongly believe that in order to assure yourself a smooth passage through this lifetime, you must, out of respect for yourself and your loved ones, plan carefully for your death as early and as thoroughly as you can. Whether there is very little money at stake, or a lot, those who survive your death deserve to grieve without the further burdens of fear and confusion about what will happen to them after you are gone.

In my books *You've Earned It, Don't Lose It, The 9 Steps to Financial Freedom* and *The Road to Wealth,* I wrote about estate planning—everything you need to know about wills and trusts, durable power of attorney for health care, protecting your assets, and protecting your heirs. Please take the necessary measures to see that your loved ones are provided for in the most caring (and financially efficient) way you can, and please do it now.

I beg you, too, not to wait to learn about your finances. Discuss with your spouse or partner everything you need to know about your estate—including insurance, the children's best interests, the location of all documents, and a list of whom to notify. I urge you to make your preferences clear—whether you wish to be buried or cremated, where you would like your remains to rest, what kind of service or ceremony you would like to have. It is so overwhelming when someone dies that having some of the details worked out and a sense of purpose for those first painful days will provide some relief.

AFTER A DEATH

The shock of losing someone you love is devastating and paralyzing—but you must take care of the business of death, which at the time can seem as complicated as the business of life. Here is a checklist of matters that will require your immediate attention, whether you feel like attending to them or not. If you have a friend or a relative who can help you, please ask for help. Even though you may think you are aware and totally capable, you are most likely, whether you know it or not, in shock. Your numbness may prevent you from collapsing under the intensity of your pain—but it also can impair your ability to make the best and most appropriate decisions.

The first job that you will be faced with will be making proper arrangements for the burial or cremation of your loved one.

Before you do anything else, if you are not sure of his or her wishes, please check to see if there is an organ donor card on the back of his or her driver's license. If there is, please contact the nearest hospital authorities so that these wishes can be carried out. Now you must contend with the remains, surely one of the most painful tasks, but I want you to take care and pay attention, for these first moves can become emotionally and financially costly if you or someone close to you is not vigilant and well informed.

+ If the death took place in a hospital, you will be asked the name of the funeral home that you would like them to call.

They will do so and take care of transporting the remains to the home.

♦ If the death took place at your home or anywhere other than a hospital, then you will have to contact the funeral home or cremation society of your choice, which will then make arrangements to transport the remains.

♦ If you want the burial or cremation to take place in a different state from the one in which your loved one has died, again, either you or the hospital will place the call to the out-of-state funeral home or cremation society you want to use, and the funeral home will take care of the transportation arrangements for you.

♦ If you don't know which funeral home you want to use, ask your friends, your clergyman, or an administrator at your local place of worship for a recommendation. Most churches or synagogues will have a list of funeral homes for you to call. If you do not have this outlet, and none of your friends can make a recommendation, call your local hospital for assistance.

THE COSTS AND THE DANGERS

When you are trying to live through a loss of great magnitude, it is all too easy to lose touch with reality—the reality of life and the reality of money. Especially money, since money seems so irrelevant in those first few days after a death. Nevertheless, there are costs of death that are unavoidable. Beyond the funeral and during your period of mourning, how are you going to pay for the everyday expenses that will continue to come your way? So often we find that every penny we have is in a retirement account, in a life insurance policy, or locked up in equity in our home, where we can't readily get to it. We are left with very little cash to draw upon. If you haven't before, you will now have to try to estimate your monthly expenses and take that figure into consideration before you make any choices regarding funeral and burial services. For instance, let's say you have $8000 in a savings account and your monthly expenses total $3000. If you spend $8000 on the funeral, you'll be unable to pay your bills.

Even if you have a life insurance policy, the insurance company may not release the funds for many months. This is particularly the case if the cause of death is unclear or appears to be a suicide. I have a friend whose brother died in a car-racing accident. It just so happened that he had raised his life insurance policy from $50,000 to $250,000 the month before his accident. Because of the timing, the insurance company did not release the insurance proceeds until they had thoroughly investigated the possibility of a suicide. In the intervening months, his widow was left in terrible financial straits.

In other words, before you start spending what you have, it is essential that you have a clear picture of what you are going to need to get by for the next few months, and where that money is going to come from. My advice, as always, is to have an understanding of your finances long before you find yourself in a tragic situation.

THE CEMETERY PLOT

Unless you have planned for this ahead of time, the funeral home or cremation society also will discuss with you whether you need a burial plot, and can assist you in making the arrangements to purchase one.

PLANNING THE SERVICE

When it comes to planning the service, carefully consider your options. You needn't try to prove your love by choosing the most expensive options available. Dignity, remember, costs not a penny. If you know what kind of service your partner would have wanted, so much the better. One often hears of people who choose the music they'd like to have played at their funeral services, and the survivors cherish that music forever. If you don't know of any clear preference, your options are many. The service can be held at the funeral home or a place of worship. The burial can be public or private, or you can hold a private burial at once and a memorial service later on.

Again—a lot of choices. But so often, a "nothing but the best" attitude prevails, where "best" translates to most expensive. There is nothing honorable in a send-off you can't afford, so I ask you please to aim for restraint. Public and private good-byes can be dignified, holy, and simple at the same time.

KNOW YOUR RIGHTS

To make sure that you are not taken advantage of during this time, the government many years ago passed a law called the Funeral Rule, which states that a funeral home must provide you with a full disclosure of its practices, services, and fees. This includes: the cost of caskets, obituary notices placed in newspapers, and embalming; any payments made on your behalf for flowers, funeral escorts, honorarium to clergy, limousines, copies of the death certificate, memorial cards, and musicians' fees; and any additional service fee that the funeral home may charge you. If you wish, you can obtain this list from a number of funeral homes so that you can compare costs. If you are not happy with the funeral arrangements for any reason, please talk to the funeral director first, and if the problem is still not resolved to your satisfaction, contact your state licensing board.

VETERAN'S BURIAL

If your partner or loved one was a veteran, you may investigate whether he or she is eligible to be buried in any of the 115 national cemeteries free of charge. If this is the case and you so desire, it is possible that veterans' assistance will also provide transportation of the remains to the nearest veterans' cemetery, and a marker or headstone. In this service, a United States flag will be used to cover the casket and then presented to you. If you choose a veteran's burial, you will have to document the fact that the deceased was a veteran. You will need:

- Rank
- Branch of service
- Separation papers (Form 214)
- Date of entry into the service and date of departure
- Date of birth and date of death
- The deceased's Social Security number (as well as your own)
- Name and address of executor or trustee of the estate

If you decide not to have the burial in a national cemetery and choose instead to use a private cemetery, you still can apply for a burial allowance, a flag, and a government headstone or marker from the Veterans Administration. If you did not know of such an allowance, you have two years from the date of death during which you can apply for a reimbursement. To apply, just look in your phone book to find the number of the VA office nearest you.

CAUTION

Because obituary notices tell the time and date of most funerals, they make your home a target for burglars. As sad as this may seem, please have someone stay in the house during the service to make sure that you do not come home to yet another loss.

THE BILLS GO ON

I would also suggest you ask whomever you have chosen to help with the arrangements to collect your mail for the next few weeks and to keep it all in one place. It would also be helpful if he or she could see if there are any bills that need to be paid immediately and keep track of when the rest of the bills come due. If you are corresponding through the mail with respect to any financial matters related to the estate, please make sure that copies are made of any outgoing mail. It is always important to be able to document everything that you said or that someone said on your behalf during a time of sorrow. Later you may remember these early days only as a blur of pain and confusion.

CALL AN ATTORNEY

The way your spouse has set up his or her estate will determine the extent to which you will need an attorney to help you get on with your life. If everything the two of you owned was in Joint Tenancy with Right of Survivorship, and you are the sole beneficiary of the life insurance proceeds, IRA, or retirement accounts, or if everything was held in a living revocable trust for your benefit, then settling the estate will be quite easy. Once the appropriate places are presented with a certified copy of the death certificate and whatever other papers those particular institutions may want to see, everything will simply switch over to your name. If, on the other hand, your partner had many separate accounts, had only a will, had the house title in his or her name only (even if the intent was that it should pass on to you)— if, in other words, the paperwork of death is in chaos, then the process will be a longer one. Either way, you should contact an attorney within the first few days. If you do not have an attorney already, please find one who specializes in estate planning to make sure that everything is in order or to help you organize what must be done.

Whether you have an attorney or not, there are many ways to save yourself some money, because there are certain things that will need to be done that you could do by yourself or with the help of a friend. For example, a friend could call the insurance companies and the bank or brokerage firms to find out what paperwork needs to be done to report the death. The most important part of your immediate job will be helping to locate and describe all of your loved one's assets and liabilities—debts, outstanding loans, everything your loved one owed to the world.

THE "LEGALESE" OF DEATH

- *Decedent:* The person who is deceased.
- *Executor/trix:* The man or woman the decedent has designated to carry out the terms of the will.
- *Co-executors/trixes:* The people (more than one) who are designated to carry out the terms of the will.
- *Administrator/trix:* The title of the person whom the court assigns to oversee your estate or your spouse's estate if there is no will.
- *Personal Representative:* In some states, when no executor or executrix has been appointed, this is the title of the court appointee, whether a man or a woman.
- *Trustee:* If the estate is held in trust, then this is the person who is responsible for carrying out the terms of the trust.

FINANCIAL CHECKLIST: SPOUSE

The duties that a spouse or life partner must carry out vary from that of the executor/trix, etc. Below is a list of what you must do as a life partner, spouse, or next of kin, whether or not you are also the executor/trix.

- Order at least 15 certified copies of the death certificate. You will need these in order to collect insurance proceeds and to change names on bank accounts, deeds, and other assets. Please do this right away. The funeral home usually will get the number of certified death certificates you request. Otherwise, the county has an office of vital statistics at the county court-house, where death, birth, and marriage certificates are kept and can be obtained upon request for a fee. It's easiest to have the funeral home handle this, and I recommend that you request them to do so immediately—you need certified copies of the death certificate for many purposes, and it will prove time-consuming to request them from the county later.

♦ If you do not already have one, please open up a bank account in your own name.

♦ If you do not have a credit card in your own name, you may want to wait to notify the credit card companies where you have cards listed in both of your names. While it is illegal for a company to cancel your credit card because your spouse has died, it is not unheard of for them to lower your credit limit if the limit was based on the deceased's income. (It's always a good idea to have a credit card in your name alone, so that over the years, you will build up credit.)

♦ Do not pay off any credit card debts that were not yours before you check with your attorney or executor. Some attorneys or advisors might advise you not to pay off most of the deceased's debts, because it's unlikely that creditors will spend the money to come after the estate to recoup small amounts of debt. I disagree with this advice, because I believe that honoring the debt, if possible, is honoring both the dead and the living. If there isn't enough money in the estate to pay off all debts, the probate court has a "schedule" specifying which debts are given priority and the order in which the debts are to be paid—which is why I want you to check with your attorney before you begin paying the debts.

♦ Review any insurance coverage that the deceased may have had with banks or credit card companies. You may be sur-prised to find out that some things slipped through the com-munications cracks. For instance, offers for life insurance often come in the mail via a bank statement or credit card bill, at just a small cost every month. Your spouse may have impulsively signed up for such coverage. This kind of thing happens more often than you think. You may have more than you know. Call every credit card company and bank that your partner or next of kin had accounts with and ask whether there is also an insurance policy in the name of the deceased.

♦ Consider whether you will have enough money to live on in the coming months or will need money from the estate before it is settled. If so, please go through six months of your and your late spouse's records, and estimate your monthly expenses. If there is not enough money in your existing accounts to cover your projected expenses, the amount you need will be requested from a judge in *probate court,* where the estate will be settled. The judge will decide on a family allowance while the estate is being settled.

♦ Contact your local Social Security office—or the national office at (800) 772-1213 or http://www.ssa.gov—to see if there are any benefits that you qualify for. You will qualify for benefits if:

  ♦ you are 60 years of age or older.
  ♦ you are 50 years of age or older and disabled.
  ♦ you care for a child who is under age 16 or disabled.

♦ If your surviving parent is 62 years of age or older, and you are your parent's primary means of support, you will qualify through Social Security for survivor's benefits.

♦ In addition, Social Security allots a small amount of money—$255—to surviving spouses or minors, if they meet certain requirements. Do not overlook that, for sometimes every little bit can help.

♦ If you and your spouse both were collecting Social Security, you might want to stop collecting yours and switch to your late spouse's if that amount is higher. In any case, you have to choose which one you will receive.

- Your children will get Social Security if:
  - they are unmarried and under age 18.
  - they are under age 19 and still in school full-time.
  - they are disabled, no matter how old they are.

CHANGING YOUR WILL/ BENEFICIARY FORMS

Do not forget that your own will or trust should be changed now, for most likely you have left everything to the person who has just died. Make sure that you change the beneficiary designation on your IRA, life insurance polices, pension plans, 401(k) plans, and any other investment or retirement plan.

EXECUTOR/TRIX DUTIES

In many cases the executor/trix is the surviving spouse or life partner. If this is the case with you, then the following obligations also pertain. If not, then just make sure all the actions above are completed.

Please note that an executor/trix is held personally and legally responsible for all of these actions. This is not a job that should be taken lightly. The duties of the executor/trix primarily fall into the following categories:

- Paying all outstanding bills, including taxes to the IRS
- Tallying and securing all assets in the estate until they are ready to be distributed among the rightful heirs
- Supervising the settlement procedures and managing the estate during this process
- Distributing all the assets to the designated beneficiaries at the appropriate time

LEGAL CHECKLIST: EXECUTOR/TRIX

♦ Your first job as executor/trix is to locate the will or trust and all assets, including life insurance policies, retirement, bank, and brokerage accounts, and stocks and bonds. If no will can be found, then call the deceased's attorney, if there is one, to see if he or she has a copy of a will. If nothing else, an attorney may know if one was ever written. If no will is found, the estate passes by what is known as *intestate succession*, which means that the assets in the estate will be distributed by a formula determined by law. In this case, there will be a court-appointed administrator.

Once the will is located, it must be submitted to the probate court, where it must be authenticated. This procedure can be done by the executor/trix, or it can be handed over to the attorney in charge. When the will is validated, then the executor/trix is officially appointed by a set of papers known as *letters testamentary*. These are the official documents that legally empower the executor/trix to take action on behalf of the estate.

♦ The executor/trix must protect the estate. This means that heirs are not allowed to remove any of the assets that have been left to them until the probate court has granted final approval for distribution.

♦ During the probate procedure, the executor/trix must keep careful track of all expenses as well as income (receipts, statements, etc.) that the estate pays out and receives.

♦ If the surviving spouse has not already obtained certified copies of the death certificate, you should obtain at least 15 copies.

♦ Notify all the insurance companies of the death, including life, disability, auto, and homeowner's insurance companies. Notify all the banks, brokerage firms, mutual fund companies, retirement plans and plan administrators, and any other institution where the decedent had accounts or deeds, or even accounts that were in both spouses' names. This includes the Veterans Administration if the decedent was a veteran.

♦ Often individual bank accounts in the decedent's name will be changed first to the name of the executor/trix, even if the executor/trix is not the spouse, so that the executor/trix can access funds if needed. If a *joint tenancy with right of survivorship (JTWROS)* is involved, that money and title of the account will go directly to the surviving spouse or partner. For example, Jane and John have a bank account held in JTWROS. If John was to die, Jane would get the account immediately. However, if John had an account in his name alone, and John's brother was executor of John's will, the account would first be transferred to his brother's name as executor while the estate was being settled, even if John left everything to Jane. The account would be transferred to Jane's name upon settlement.

♦ Before any accounts are closed down, please make sure that the financial needs of the surviving spouse are going to be met. It is best to clear it with the attorney before closing down any existing accounts.

♦ Make a complete inventory of the safety deposit box. After probate is completed, the executor/trix will distribute the contents according to the will. If the key cannot be located and the surviving spouse's name is not on the box, you won't be able to open it without a court order, although some states permit access to look for such estate-planning documents as wills and trusts. Most states don't seal the boxes anymore, but the bank can make access difficult. If the box is held in the trust, the trustee will have access. Without the key, you will always end up paying the bank sixty dollars or more to "drill" the box open. (Don't make those you leave behind go through all this. Leave the key and instructions

with your other easy-to-find documents for your kids or whoever is going to be the executor/trix or trustee of your own
estate.)

If the estate is to be distributed through a trust, it does not have to
go through probate court, and the trustee named in the trust will carry
out the actions designated in the trust.

DEATH'S TOLL

What lives on after you die? The legacy of your work, your kind and
generous acts, and the people you love, who will suffer the emotional
toll, and possibly the financial toll, of your passing for a long, long time.
How can you help? The care with which you prepare for your own
death is a supreme act of love toward those you will one day leave
behind. It can help your survivors a great deal emotionally, for dealing
with chaos after a loss makes the loss itself more painful and frighten-
ing. It can also help your survivors a great deal financially, because
with careful estate planning, you may save your loved ones thousands
of dollars in probate fees, estate taxes, and attorneys' fees. Won't you
take the actions necessary to protect the people you love, emotionally
and financially? Will you please do it right away? Seeing to it that the
people you love will always be safe is an expansive action, and once
you've done so, you'll be the richer for it, closer to clarity, and all the
more ready to receive all that you can, for the rest of your life.

CHAPTER 13

STARTING OVER

It may feel like small comfort to you now, but sooner or later every single one of us will be faced with the prospect of starting over. At a time in your life when you believe that everything is going great, something happens—a death, an illness, a breakup, a divorce—that leaves you emotionally and perhaps financially exhausted. And starting over from a place of loss is even harder than starting for the first time. When you were just starting out in your adult life, you were equipped with hope, dreams, expectations, and strength. All of these are stripped from you when you're starting with feelings of loss and emptiness. Will any of us be spared the painful test of starting over, one way or another, one day or another? Unfortunately, I don't think so. This test seems to me utterly universal.

As a financial planner, I can never leave emotions out of a client's financial picture. For example, if someone is terrified of the stock market, I could never, in good conscience, put their money in the market, for it would leave them feeling powerless and afraid. If someone believed with all their heart that the only way they would feel safe was by owning an expensive life insurance policy, then I would have to take that into account as well. I know, too, when someone comes to see me about how to start over, that I will be faced with a weak emotional pulse—and a weak financial pulse. If you are starting over, you already know that you must replenish your strength in order to go on. It is also a treacherous time financially, and you must be very, very careful with your money.

Facing the "what"s and "what-if"s of starting over requires immense courage.

> *What if I can't make it? I've never handled money before.*
> *I've never had to work before. What if I can't pay my bills?*
> *My husband left me with just a small settlement, and it's all I*
>   *have. What should I do with the money?*
> *What if the insurance money doesn't last?*
> *What do I do now?*

Even though your own questions may be different, the common denominator in these situations is fear—fear of not making it, fear of failure, fear of tomorrow—and these fears come at a time of life when you are at your most vulnerable. That's the bad news. The good news is that, even though you might not believe it, I have seen men and women in this very predicament who were ready to give up instead rise up and create for themselves, possibly for the first time, a new life they learned to love. A life they can call their own. How did they get there from here? By drawing on the faith and courage that reside in each and every one of us.

W E N D Y ' S   S T O R Y

> *I remember thinking at the time, If this is a test, okay, I will take it.*
>
> *It started, I guess, when I was diagnosed with Lyme disease, a serious and recurrent case, which was unbelievably debilitating. My husband, Alex, and I were frightened, yes, but it didn't seem like a major thing. I could still work, we kept telling ourselves, and we'd be okay. Then Alex's factory went*

bankrupt. He had worked there his whole life and now, suddenly, there was no more life insurance, no pension, no death benefits—his whole career erased, and our future, too. I was the office manager of a small company, but we didn't have a pension plan—and now neither did my husband. I thought it couldn't get any worse, but it did.

The epitome of health—active, fit, health-conscious—my husband had a heart attack five years ago. He was fifty. We had been married twenty-five years. We live in the country, and the hospital was a couple of hours away. It was a nightmare. Alex was in the hospital for almost five months, and his stay was a series of mistakes—one thing led to another, kidney failure, his lungs. I did everything I could to be there all the time, so bills—for the motel, for gas—were piling up on my credit card. I would drive home as often as I could to take care of things at the office. I still had my job. We thought he was going to get better, and we were really worried about the bills, the costs building up, like those national debt numbers you see just climbing. The main thing was that I stayed with him. At the time, money wasn't even an issue. We knew we'd be okay.

Then, one afternoon when I was at work, the call came—Come to the hospital at once. I had left Alex just that morning and he had seemed fine, but by the time I got to the hospital it was too late. I could not believe it; he was not supposed to die, that was not what they said was going to happen. I didn't even get to say good-bye. I went to the hospital and then went back home in shock, all alone and devastated. A few weeks later, the bills started pouring in, which did not make matters any better; all together the bills were over $80,000 more than our insurance, catastrophic care, would pay. The funeral was expensive, plus there were the credit card bills; before this happened I had never had a credit card bill I couldn't pay.

The hospital said they could set up a payment plan, but I

didn't have the money, so they sent me to see a social worker. She said that I should file for bankruptcy, quit my job, and get disability for the Lyme disease. But I couldn't, the thought of it horrified me; we had worked so long and hard for what we had. It would seem like cheating everyone out of what they were owed. I thought if I gave up now, I would give up on everything, that I would never have anything, and then what? I felt crazed and scared, but I was determined to make Alex proud of me. I went back to work and took on two extra bookkeeping jobs. My doctor said, You can't do this, you'll overtax yourself, don't worry, it will be okay; then he patted me on the head. I got so angry. I said, You come and live in my shoes. Don't send me home and tell me everything will be okay, because it won't unless I keep on going.

I was still working the three jobs when my parents died, within months of each other, and that was hard because we were a really, really close family. I felt utterly alone, and I was. I finally understood what was meant by the saying that the only friend you will always have is God. I just knew I could not give up, not now. I kept up the three jobs. I paid off as much as I could, but it was never enough, and the finance charges kept building. I kept thinking, I have to get this paid, just get it all over with. Finally I went to the bank, because I decided to refinance my house, which was the last thing I wanted to do—I love it, it's over a hundred years old, and it's the only thing I have. They gave me a loan for $45,000. That helped a lot. There's one small hospital bill I'm still paying, but they are okay about it, and now I am working only two jobs, which makes it easier. I have a little more time for myself, and I can see my friends again. Now that I feel I can breathe again financially, I'm beginning to think about the future, and I have started putting fifty dollars away each month, sometimes more, in a mutual fund. That was a turning point. Now I feel as if there is hope again. People keep say-

ing how courageous I am, but I realized long ago that courage is a choice. You choose. If you keep thinking there isn't anything you can do, then there won't be, and I didn't want to get to that point. I reaffirm this thought in many different ways, many times every single day: Yes, I can; I'm so tired; No, I am not; What if I can't make my house payment; Yes, I can.

You can't replace people, bring them back, but the things you do should at least honor them and yourself. If you simply give up because you don't have the initiative, you're not honoring anyone. If only for the love of yourself, you have to do it. My husband wouldn't have wanted me to give up. You either give up or you go on. I chose to go on.

After a loss, we rejoin the world of the living.

By opening herself up, Wendy, against the greatest possible odds, is starting over. She is close to owning her house outright again, her debt is nearly gone, and she has honored her past. She is building up her nest egg, honoring her future. Her thoughts, words, and actions have begun to make her life easier, when instead, had she taken different actions, she could have been left destitute—emotionally and financially. She met her suffering with grace, clarity, and, yes, courage. By any financial measure, Wendy is creating what she needs, and by following her course, she will have more than enough. By the measure of the soul, she has been immensely rich all along.

YOU FIRST

When you look back upon this time, you will see that, during the months after a loss, in many ways you were simply going through the motions of life.

I can't tell you how many times I have sat across from someone who has just suffered a loss and must start over. I would review his or her situation and say, "Okay, we have to do thus and such, and then we will do this and that and finally this." My clients would agree with me, acting as if they totally understood what I was saying, and then I would take the necessary actions based on our conversation. What would inevitably happen is that six months to a year later, these same clients would come back and say, "Can you tell me why we did what we did with the money?" It became obvious to me that they had not heard a word I had said during the early stages of their grief. It was as if they had been present in body but not in mind. I would explain the reasons for the actions we took again, and this time, my clients would finally get it.

Many of us emerge from a divorce or a death with some assets, which we must protect, perhaps for the first time in our lives. After seeing the ways in which people tend to jeopardize these assets in their grief, their anger, their exhaustion, or their confusion, I have come up with a rule that has never once failed a client of mine:

THE ESSENTIAL LAW OF MONEY AFTER A LOSS

Take no action with your money other than keeping it safe and sound for at least six months to a year after a loss.

You have just been through a hard time, with the legalities and expenses of divorce, or the hard tasks you've had to take on after a death. You are not equipped now—emotionally or financially—to make the big decisions that have to be made about investing your money yourself or entrusting it to someone else.

If your money is in a secure place, a place that has made you feel safe and comfortable up until now, I want you to leave it there and to wait to take any action with your money until your emotional equilibrium is restored, along with your sound judgment. If you feel your money is not currently safe, make those financial changes that will get your money to a safe place and then do nothing else for the time being.

If you are not sure whether or not your money is invested safely, seek the advice of a financial advisor, one who comes highly recommended by a friend who has money under management with that person. If you have no friend who can recommend someone, what you want for now is a fee-based planner, one who does not sell products of any kind. When you go to see this advisor, you may want to take a friend or relative with you for support. The first thing you should say is, "I am not going to buy anything for at least one year; I just want to make sure that the money I have is safe and sound. I want to put any money that is not safe now into a money market fund or treasuries and that is all. No new purchases of any kind are to be made on my behalf."

Do not let your money be a burden or cause you needless worry at this time. Live your life, nurture and replenish yourself, but when you're just starting over, leave your money alone.

This sounds like easy advice, doesn't it? Maybe. But you will have to be vigilant to adhere to it, for you will be surprised at how many people might come knocking at your door to offer to "help" you with your money.

YOUR SUDDENLY ATTENTIVE ADVISOR

How many times did the advisor or broker your spouse was using to manage your joint money ever talk to you before your world fell apart?

What will happen is that a financial advisor builds a relationship with one of you. Seldom does the advisor take the time to talk to both of you equally. Understandably, it's more convenient for him or her to have a single contact. A separation or death gives an advisor the opportunity to establish a new rapport with the spouse who previously was merely a name on joint documents. Believe me, this opportunity is not lost on the advisor. Remember, this person is very aware of what is going on not only with your money but also in your personal life. If there is to be a divorce, and therefore a dividing of the assets, the advisor is going to be one of the first to know what you each will be left with. If there is a death, the total picture of your finances is right at his or her disposal. So do not be surprised if you get a cozy call from an advisor with whom you have never really had a relationship to ask you to come in and see him or her to go over what to do with the money in your portfolio. Stand back. You're not ready. Not for six months to a year.

WHEN LOYALTY IS NOT A VIRTUE

Just because your late spouse or ex-spouse was using a certain advisor does not mean that the same advisor is right for you. First you have to face this situation and know that this is your life, and everyone in it from this point on must be someone with whom you feel safe and comfortable. Ask yourself these questions:

- ◆ Why was it that you never had a relationship with this particular person to begin with?
- ◆ If you did have a relationship with him/her, did you like and trust the relationship?
- ◆ Did you feel as if he/she had your best interests and concerns at heart, or just those of your spouse/partner?

Bide your time. These questions will answer themselves in due course.

ONLY THE LONELY

It's not only burglars who read the obituaries. Cold callers, hungry brokers, needy financial types all look to the papers to see if they can expand their business. A sympathetic call when you are feeling vulnerable is a self-interested call—and you are not the "self" in question here. Please say that you are grieving now and ask that solicitors who appear out of the blue call back in a year. They won't.

INSURANCE PROCEEDS

If you are entitled to any life insurance proceeds, regardless of the amount, take the payment in full, even if the insurance company tries to persuade you to take it in installments, or offers to invest it or hold on to it for safekeeping. Most insurance proceeds are tax-free, so you will not incur any penalties by taking them in a lump-sum payment. You may need to deposit some cash into a checking account right away to cover immediate expenses. Then put the rest into a money market account or anywhere you know it will be safe. Leave the money there until you are more emotionally stable, so that you can intelligently decide what to do with it—six months to one year later. This account will also serve as a place to access funds if you need them for your living expenses.

TAKING STOCK

Over the next few months, try to make as few changes in your life as possible, but begin asking yourself some essential questions. How do you feel about where you are living? Are you frightened by the amount of money it takes just to live? Are there easy areas in which you could cut back? In time, clarity will set in, and you will know what you must do, however painful, whether it's selling the house, taking a job or a second job, or cutting back on what you can do for your children. In time, you will be able to do it.

People first, then money. When you are the one starting over, the "people" in the first law of money probably refers to you, even if you're the kind of person who is always taking care of everybody else. Let me be the one to remind you to grant yourself the time to recover, to assess this new beginning, to grasp the terms and necessities of your new life. So much of fear is simply not knowing. It's my hope that the information in this chapter diminishes some of your anxiety and encourages you to turn to the future, not with fear but with hope and courage. Take your good memories with you, and treasure your past even as you create a new tomorrow. Treasure your money, this legacy from your past, too, so that it can sustain you well in the new life I know you will create.

PART IV

BUYING A HOME

C H A P T E R   1 4

SEEKING SHELTER

It's the age-old dream: owning a place of one's own. For most of us, home is all-important—a place to feel safe and comfortable today, a place for security tomorrow. Large or small, new or old, one day the house we live in will be ours scot-free. Even if that "one day" is thirty years from now, the dream is well worth going after. Unfortunately, many of us pursue the dream before we're financially ready, or we chase after it in an overly ambitious way so that the house we buy ends up owning us. Others among us assume the dream is out of reach—when it may not be. If you harbor the dream of owning the perfect house, here is what you need to know in order to achieve it.

STARTING OUT

In 1973, I was living in my first grown-up home, a two-bedroom apartment I shared with a friend. We were paying $220 a month for this great place, and I loved it. It was a brown shingled house divided into two apartments, and we lived in the one on the ground floor. The dining room opened, through two big glass doors, onto a little porch not visible from the street. I used to love to lie there and soak up the sun, and I felt I could easily live in that apartment my whole life. One night, my roommate's brother came to visit, and we got to talking about a house he had bought a few years before. I thought, Wow, that must really be something, owning your own home. But thinking how expensive it must be, I didn't pay much attention, until I heard him say that his mortgage payment was only $153 a month. All of a sudden I sat up and said, "Wait a minute. Are you telling me that you own a house twice the size of this apartment and all you're paying is one hundred fifty-three dollars a month, while we're paying two hundred twenty dollars a month just to rent?" "Yup," he said. "And that one hundred fifty-three dollars includes insurance and property taxes."

Granted, this was a long time ago, when real estate in some areas of California was acknowledged—even then—to be dirt cheap. Back then, if one had the down payment, it would have been absolutely crazy to do anything other than own a home—all the more so with the benefit of hindsight. Today, many of us still believe the conventional wisdom that was true a generation ago, that real estate is the best investment around. But the fact is, this isn't necessarily true anymore. There are important factors to consider before you even begin to look to buy. Beyond the calculations of what you can afford for a down payment and a monthly mortgage, you must take into account the recent price fluctuations of real estate in your particular area, the price of rentals, your job stability with respect to income and location, the possibility that your living-space requirements are going to grow or shrink in the near future, your physical ability to maintain a house, and the current interest rates for mortgages. All of these factors must be weighed against renting before you take a single step toward buying.

PLAYING THE REAL ESTATE MARKET

In many areas of the country, the recent past has seen one of the largest surges in residential real estate prices in history. If this holds true in the area in which you want to buy, consider the possibility that perhaps you are better off renting until the real estate market cools, as it will sooner or later, than buying at the height of the market. If, on the other hand, real estate has recently been stable in your area but is beginning to inch up in value, you might want to act as fast as you can, while houses are still fairly priced. How do you know when the real estate market is too high, ready to take off, or about to decline?

This is a very difficult question to answer for certain, but you can definitely get a sense of what's happening with prices in your area. The best way to do this would be to call many—at least five—local real estate agents and ask them directly. Are houses selling within a few days or weeks of being placed on the market? Are the buyers paying more than the sellers are asking? Are more people than usual putting their houses on the market in the hopes of selling high? If the answer to all of these questions is yes, then you are in a booming market. A broker can also tell you just how much the real estate market has been going up over the past few years. This information is usually available in your local newspaper, as well, and you can learn a lot simply by reading the real estate ads and articles.

What does this information mean to you? Well, if you are seeing increases in real estate prices of 2 to 5 percent over a year ago, that's not a big deal; real estate prices in your area are just plodding along, keeping their value, holding steady. If you want to buy and the numbers work, you can probably pick up a house for what you would like to pay for it, maybe a little less. If you see that prices have declined from where they were a year ago, this should indicate that you might be able to pick up a great deal. Go in way under the asking price, knowing that you have the upper hand—and knowing too, no matter how good a deal you think you got, that a year from now, you probably could get a better one. When, on the other hand, you start seeing increases of 20 to 30 percent from a year ago, you know that you are dealing with a booming real estate market and that if you buy now you are going to pay a pretty penny. This doesn't mean that the market cannot go higher still, for of course it can, but at least be aware that if you want to proceed, it is going to cost you. Once you've determined that now is the time for you to buy, the next step is to figure out what you can afford. But first, a word of caution.

THE SIREN SONG OF THE
REAL ESTATE SECTION

Once the idea of owning a piece of real estate gets in your blood, watch out. It can overtake you. It is at this moment that most people make their first big mistake. Before they calculate what they can afford, they idly look at ads in the Sunday papers, noting the prices of houses with enticing descriptions. Then they take Sunday-afternoon drives in the areas that they want to live in, looking for houses with For Sale signs. They jot down the phone numbers of the real estate agents listed on the signs. Then they place a few calls just out of curiosity, to learn the asking prices of the houses. Before they know it—and before they've worked out their own numbers—they've made a date with a few realtors just to take a look at what's on the market. This is the usual sequence—and if you allow yourself to follow it, it can end up being one big trap.

The first question the real estate agent will ask you is how much you want to spend. Because you haven't actually taken the time (and don't even quite know how) to figure out what you can afford, you offer as your answer the approximate amount of the house that you called about in the first place. Even as you're saying it, it sounds like a lot to you, but perhaps you're too embarrassed to say so, and certainly you don't want the agent to think you can't afford something nice. So you think, Well, I'm only looking anyway, and what harm does it do to see what's out there? You are about to tempt fate, and before long could find yourself in one of the following three scenarios:

♦ You fall in love with a home that carries a hefty price tag. Even though it costs more than your gut feeling tells you is affordable, your eager sales agent will try to figure out a way to make it work financially for you. Even if you summon the courage to say you don't have the standard 20 percent to put down, don't be surprised if the agent finds a creative way for you to make the deal work anyway.

♦ Let's say this agent has spent days with you, calls you all the time to give you updates on houses you've seen or to tell you about a house newly on the market, or sends you notes of greeting, just to check in. You start to feel guilty about having wasted this person's time, and feel you must come through in the end and buy something. This guilt can get you in over your head.

♦ Even if you resist the domestic temptations put before you at the outset, you have peered into the expensive forbidden garden. It will not be easy to get those gorgeous homes out of your head. If you go to see houses priced in your realistic price range, nothing will look as good. You will be constantly comparing what you can really afford to houses you've seen and fallen in love with. You will ask to go back one more time to look at that beautiful house you saw when you first set out. On this visit, you'll spend a little more time imagining yourself there—whether or not the house is compatible with your financial reality. With the aid of a little creative financing, you think, Well, maybe I can do this after all . . . but can you?

How Much Can You Afford to Put Down?

Before you make a single call or take down one phone number on a house that looks inviting, take a look at your finances.

First, figure out how much money you have to put down.

Conventional wisdom has it that when purchasing a primary residence, the down payment should be 20 percent of the sale price. If a house is selling for $250,000, for example, then the financial institutions that might finance the mortgage will expect you to come up with $50,000 ($250,000 multiplicd by .20). So let's work backward.

How much cash do you have available to you right now to use toward your down payment? This money might come from:

- Savings accounts
- Stocks, bonds, or mutual funds outside your retirement accounts
- Money market funds
- Treasury bills, bonds, or notes
- Financial gifts you are about to receive
- Certificates of deposit that will mature shortly
- Funds you have in credit unions
- Money in your checking account
- Annual bonus

Now total the money presently available to you, or that you know will be available when it comes time to buy the house. Multiply that amount by 5 to figure out how much of a house this down payment will buy for you if you want to stick with the 20-percent-down rule. If you had $20,000 to put down, for instance, you would multiply $20,000 by 5, which will give you $100,000. This is the *most* you can spend on a house if you want to go with a traditional down payment of 20 percent. If you have $50,000 to put down, multiply $50,000 by 5 and you know you will be able to buy a house for $250,000. Remember, though, we're just talking about a down payment here; we have yet to figure out if you can afford the mortgage. We'll get to that in a bit, but first things first.

Let's say that after you add up everything, you have only $10,000. You know, then, that the most you can spend on a house is $50,000, and there is not even a doghouse in your area that sells for that price. You have two choices. First, decide whether there are any other sources upon which you could draw:

- ◆ A loan against your 401(k)
- ◆ A withdrawal of $10,000 from your IRA (which is permitted in order to buy a first home)
- ◆ A loan or gift from your parents or a friend

Now add any of these possible amounts to the $10,000 you already have. Let's suppose you can add $10,000 from a withdrawal against your IRA (factor in that you will have to pay income taxes on that money in the year of withdrawal; only the 10 percent penalty for early withdrawal is waived), plus a $5000 gift from your parents to help you out. Now you have a total of $25,000. Multiply that by 5 and you can purchase a house, using the conventional down-payment formula, for $125,000.

Let's say that there are still no homes available in the area for $125,000, but you're determined to own a house. Your other option would be to put down less than 20 percent as a down payment. In some cases, the lender (the bank) will give you a mortgage even if you have as little as 3 percent to put down. But this is another potential trap; pay less now and you might find yourself paying more later. If you buy a home and put down less than 20 percent of the final sale price, you will have to pay an extra insurance premium known as PMI, or private mortgage insurance.

PRIVATE MORTGAGE INSURANCE (PMI)

Private mortgage insurance, or *PMI,* can be a great moneymaking scheme—at least it is for many banks, so you must take care. If you pay less than the standard down payment, even 2 percent less, you will pay for it—with PMI.

Simply put, mortgage insurance protects the mortgage lender against financial loss if a homeowner stops making mortgage payments. Lenders require insurance on low down-payment loans for protection in the event that the homeowner fails to make his or her payments. When a homeowner fails to make mortgage payments, a default occurs and the home goes into foreclosure. Both the homeowner and the mortgage insurer lose in a foreclosure. The homeowner loses the house and all of the money put into it. The mortgage insurer will then have to pay the lender's claim on the defaulted loan.

It is crucial that the family buying the home can really afford it—not only at the time it is purchased but also throughout the time period of the loan.

THE COST OF PMI

The cost of private mortgage insurance premiums will vary, depending on the price of the home and what kind of mortgage you have. PMI for a fixed mortgage will cost you about one-tenth of one percent less than PMI for an adjustable-rate mortgage. In general, PMI premiums usually run about .6 percent of the loan amount the first year and drop to about .5 percent in the following years. When you buy a home with less than 20 percent down, you have to take into consideration whether you can afford your monthly payments with the additional cost of PMI. Also you need to factor in that the bank will want you to pay one full year of PMI premiums up front. For instance, let's say you're putting down less than 20 percent of the purchase price of your property and are getting a loan from the bank for $200,000. Your lender is going to require you to carry PMI. Your PMI premium would be about $1200 ($200,000 multiplied by .006) for the first year. Besides the fact that you will have to pay $100 a month for PMI on top of your mortgage payments, as a sort of security deposit you're going to have to come up with an extra $1200 up front when you actually buy the house.

Here is a table for different loan amounts, showing the approximate PMI premium that will be due all at once when you buy the house, along with the additional amount that will be added to your monthly mortgage payment:

ON A FIXED MORTGAGE AMOUNT OF	PMI WILL BE ABOUT
$100,000	$600 up front and $50 a month
$150,000	$900 up front and $75 a month
$200,000	$1200 up front and $100 a month
$250,000	$1500 up front and $125 a month

NO PMI? DON'T BE TOO SURE

Let's say you go to a bank and apply for a loan with only 10 percent down, and they never mention the fact that you have to pay PMI. You think, What a deal, because this particular bank is not charging you PMI—which means a savings to you of over a $100 a month. Not so fast. If the bank is not charging you that extra premium, most likely it's because they have hidden that extra cost in the interest rate on the loan. For instance, let's say that on a $200,000 loan, the interest rate they are charging is 7.2 percent for a fixed mortgage with no PMI costs. However, right down the block, another bank is offering a fixed-rate loan for 6.7 percent interest with PMI. The first bank has simply added the cost of the PMI into the interest rate. Now you might be thinking, Well, it doesn't matter, since they average out to be the same. Wrong. You see, once you lock in at the 7.2 percent rate, you will pay that for the life of the loan. The same is true for the 6.7 percent rate, but in this case, the PMI premiums will go down after the first year and eventually stop.

PMI: THE DURATION OF PAYMENT

What is important for you to know about PMI is that it does not apply for the duration of the loan. As soon as you have built up 20 percent *equity* in the house, PMI payments are no longer required by the lender. Equity is the fair market value of the property minus the balance of the loan. So in the scenario above, if you take the loan without PMI premiums you will in essence be paying that higher interest rate—with its built-in PMI cost—for the life of the loan. Tricky. This is why I want you to remember that if ever you are going to buy a house with less than 20 percent down, and the lender says they do not require PMI payments, make sure you check their interest rates against banks that do charge PMI. I bet you will discover that they are at least one-half of a percent higher.

Your PMI policy, however, will not just stop all by itself. If you have 20 percent or more equity in the house, it is up to you to notify the lender that it is time to cancel your policy. Some lenders will cooperate readily with this request, and some will make it more difficult. Here is what I suggest: Before you sign any papers in connection with the loan, ascertain that your bank will allow your PMI policy to be canceled.

Then ask the lender to put in writing that they will stop charging you for PMI when you reach the 20-percent-in-equity mark. Even with such a letter, remember that you are the one who must initiate canceling your PMI, because your lender has no incentive to do so.

DON'T FORGET TO GET YOUR MONEY BACK

An important reminder: Upon canceling the policy, you should also receive the first year's up-front payment, which you paid at the time you bought the house.

REQUIRED DOCUMENTS

Most lenders are going to want to see certain documentation before they will cancel your policy. The main document they'll want to see will be an up-to-date appraisal of the house proving that you do in fact have 20 percent equity. They will want further proof, such as a market analysis, that this 20 percent equity is stable. For example, if you happen to live in an area where real estate prices have just boomed, bringing up your equity in the house very quickly, they may not feel so secure in taking away the PMI insurance; from their point of view, prices could fall just as quickly as they rose. Also, they may have a stipulation that they will not allow the PMI policy to be canceled before two years have passed, so check that fact out as well. Otherwise, they may use rapid price fluctuations or first-time home ownership as reasons to decline a cancellation request. Make sure, too, that you keep your credit history squeaky clean for at least two to three years before you apply to cancel your PMI policy, and that you make all your mortgage payments on time (no late fees), or the lender can cite these as reasons to keep you paying your PMI premiums.

Over all, putting less than 20 percent down allows more people to get into the real estate game, possibly for the first time—but don't get too excited yet, because having the money to put down is just one of the hurdles to overcome.

BEYOND THE DOWN PAYMENT

Many people become so focused on the down payment, they fail to look at the substantial costs beyond it, as if the down payment will, so to speak, slide them right into home base. Please don't make that mistake. Instead, think about the money you'll need months and years beyond the down payment, to make certain that a house won't be all you have.

ALAN'S STORY

At first, it seemed like all our dreams were coming true. I was offered a position as an associate professor at a New York col-

lege. My wife, Helen, and I were very excited; we had spent all our lives in the South, but this was the big time—New York City! The salary was higher, too, which was a good thing, given the higher cost of living in New York. But Helen would be able to find work fairly easily, since she's in hospital administration, and the school would help us find an affordable apartment, so we'd manage fine. In January, we sold our cars, got rid of some of our furniture, and packed up the rest. Helen had found a good job at a city hospital, and we made our move.

Helen and I and our two sons settled into a two-bedroom apartment. But the adjustment to a much smaller space was harder on the boys than we'd expected; they felt cramped and would grow stir-crazy. Helen and I both liked our jobs, though, and wanted to stay in the area, but we agreed that we needed a house. We began looking in the suburbs—the real estate agents would meet us at the train station and drive us around—and finally we found a house we liked. We had almost enough in savings for the down payment, but we finessed that a bit and paid a little less down. We got a mortgage, and we were thrilled, because the mortgage payment was about what we'd been paying in rent. We went through the whole closing thing, which was surreal—we just kept writing checks to strangers—hired some movers, and moved. It was like a movie on fast forward.

Settling in felt great. Helen and I were unpacking the kitchen things and watching our sons running around in a backyard again. We moved in the autumn, and the leaves were turning beautiful colors—we'd never had that in the South. The kids liked their public school, and everything seemed like it was going to work out fine. We hired a teenager from the neighborhood to bring the kids home from their after-school program and stay with them until one of us got home, which went off without a hitch most of the time, *although once in a while Helen or I had to leave work early. We were both commuting to the city, and we hadn't quite figured the commuting cost into our calculations (actually, we hadn't calculated much beyond what we could put down and the mortgage payments), but, okay, we could basically afford the commute. For the first few weeks we walked to the train, which was only a few blocks from where we dropped the kids at school. But when the weather started to get colder, that walk plus the distance to the local shopping strip became more difficult. Anyway, how do you live in the suburbs without a car? So we bought a used car, which meant more money going out every month. Also moving twice in less than a year was really expensive, and we were pretty strapped. So we got another Visa card, figuring we just needed a little time to catch up.*

In the meantime, we needed to replace the dishwasher; then we bought a dining-room table and chairs from a secondhand shop. We got the boys ice hockey equipment for Christmas, plus we paid for Helen's mother to fly up for the holidays. Everything was adding up: oil bills, which we hadn't had to pay at the apartment, really high electricity, and garbage pickup. I kept feeling that we were falling more and more behind. Here we were, both making more money than we had before, living in a house no bigger than the one we had down south, but suddenly we're $12,000 in debt to the credit card companies.

So we're paying the mortgage and everything else, but barely. I mean, if the refrigerator goes, which it very well might, we'll sink. I didn't anticipate all these costs beyond the initial biggies, and now I don't see a way out.

If you're like most of us, you will start out trying not to buy more house than you can afford, but your thoughts will tell you one thing, your words will tell others something else, and your actions will head you in a different direction altogether. When you are considering any major purchase, our law of financial harmony, which requires the unity of your thoughts, words, and actions, must come into play. Otherwise, your mind will come up with all kinds of excuses to make it okay for you to spend more than you know you should. Excuses like these:

"With the money we'll get back in taxes, the house will actually cost us much less than renting did."

You do get a nice deduction on your taxes for the interest on your mortgage, it's true, but remember, this is a once-a-year deduction—money you don't pay in taxes, but money you don't necessarily see in cash, either. It will not put additional money in your pocket throughout the year, and therefore will not alter what you can afford in real terms at the time of your purchase. Your future tax break should not be a factor when calculating affordable monthly payments.

"As we get older, we'll be making more money, and it will become easier to meet those payments."

The future of your job and your income is not solely up to you. If you work on Wall Street and the market heads south, it is possible you could be out of a job before you know it. If you are working for a corporation, they may suddenly downsize, plunging your once-bright future into darkness. Even if you are self-employed, changes in the economy can affect you and your income drastically. Financial developments overseas may increasingly affect us all. Never gamble on what is to come.

"We'll just cut back on everything else in order to afford this house."

Even though you may want that perfect home so much that you're willing to make sacrifices to own it, do not underestimate how very difficult it is to cut out other ways in which you might want to spend your money—travel, hobbies, your children, even renovating the house.

Given everything else you will want to do with your life, spending more than you can easily afford on housing will be enjoyable for only a short period of time. The hardest part of owning a house comes long after the down payment has been made. The hardest part is being able to afford the payments month in, month out, for the next fifteen to thirty years, while still enjoying a full, rich life doing the things that you love. I've seen plenty of clients who were house rich, cash poor, and miserable.

CRUNCHING THE NUMBERS

After you've figured out how much house you can afford based on the amount of money you have for the down payment, you now must make sure you can afford the monthly mortgage payment, as well as the property taxes, the insurance, and, if your down payment is less than 20 percent, the PMI premium. Remember, too, that if you borrowed money for the down payment from your 401(k) or any other sources, you will have to calculate paying that money back into your monthly costs.

Start with the amount of money you have for the down payment. Subtracting that figure from the total cost of the house will give you the amount of the mortgage you will need.

For example, if you can afford a house of $250,000, and you are able to put 20 percent down ($250,000 minus $50,000 equals $200,000), you will need a mortgage of $200,000. If you're working with a real estate agent, ask him or her to figure out what your mortgage payment would be for a 15-year mortgage and for a 30-year mortgage, given the current interest rate. You can also try SmartCalc on the Web at http://www.financenter.com/calcs.html or use the chart below as a quick reference guide. Find the going interest rate to the nearest half of a percent, and then find the closest mortgage amount and go down the chart to find the amount of the monthly payment.

For example, on a 15-year, $200,000 mortgage at a 6.5 percent interest rate, the monthly payment would be $1742; the monthly payments for a 30-year mortgage would be $1264.

15-Year Mortgage

	$100m	$150m	$200m	$250m	$300m	$350m	$400m
6%	$844	1266	1688	2110	2532	2953	3375
6.5%	$871	1307	1742	2178	2613	3049	3484
7%	$899	1348	1798	2247	2696	3146	3595
7.5%	$927	1391	1854	2318	2781	3245	3708
8%	$956	1433	1911	2389	2867	3345	3823

30-Year Mortgage

	$100m	$150m	$200m	$250m	$300m	$350m	$400m
6%	$600	899	1199	1499	1799	2098	2398
6.5%	$632	948	1264	1580	1896	2212	2528
7%	$665	998	1331	1663	1996	2329	2661
7.5%	$699	1049	1398	1748	2098	2447	2797
8%	$734	1101	1468	1834	2201	2568	2935

Once you calculate your monthly mortgage cost, add about $100 a month to that figure for homeowner's insurance. Please note that the cost of insurance varies from state to state and depends on the price of the house, as well as the kind of coverage you apply for. Place a call to a local insurance agent and ask approximately what it would cost to have an insurance policy for the house that you are thinking of buying.

Write that figure here: $_____

Next, call your county tax assessor's office to find out what percentage of the price of a home they charge for property taxes. It will be anywhere from 1 to 3 percent of the sales price. Your real estate agent could also provide this figure to you.

Write that figure here: _____%

Multiply that percentage by the sales price of the house. If your sales price was $250,000 and the property tax for your county is 1.75 percent, then $250,000 multiplied by .0175, or $4375, will be your yearly property tax bill. Divide that figure by 12 ($4375 divided by 12 is $365) to determine how much it will cost you per month for property taxes.

Write that figure here: $_____

Add your monthly mortgage payment, your insurance cost, and your monthly property tax to determine the total cost of your monthly payments. In the above scenario, based on a 30-year mortgage, you would add $1264 for the mortgage, plus $100 for the insurance, plus $365 for the property taxes, for a total of $1729. Please note: If you put less than 20 percent down, remember to add PMI into this calculation as well.

Here's a worksheet for you to fill in:

Take the price of the house	$_____
Multiplied by the percentage of sales price	
your county charges for property taxes	
	×_____%
Equals yearly property taxes	$_____
Divide by 12	÷_____
Add $100 for home insurance	+ $100
Add mortgage payment	+_____
Add PMI premium	
(mortgage balance x .006÷12)	+_____
Total monthly payment	$_____

Now let's see if you can afford this monthly payment. First, add up your current net income from all sources:

Take-home pay	$_____
Social Security payments	$_____
Interest and dividends	$_____
Miscellaneous	$_____
Total	$_____

**Subtract your total monthly payment from
your total monthly income:** $_____

That is the most basic calculation of the impact your new home
will have on your monthly earnings.

Now let's go one step further so you can really see what your financial
life will look like if you were to buy this home. Figure roughly your
monthly and seasonal bills to calculate how much more it will cost
you to live in this house than it does for you to live where you are now.
Estimate as best you can the following monthly costs. Be as accurate as
possible. Call service providers in the area; see if your realtor can provide you with information. If you're guessing, better to err on the high
side than to underestimate.

Utilities, gas, oil	$_____
Firewood, if there's a fireplace	$_____
Pool maintenance, if there's a pool	$_____
Extra gasoline, if you'll have a longer drive to work	$_____
Gardener, landscaping costs	$_____
Garbage removal	$_____
Water treatment or drinking-water delivery	$_____
Other	$_____

**Total up all these costs and subtract the figure
from your remaining monthly net:** $_____

If you still have money left over, then you can afford to buy this
house. Welcome to the dream.

BYPASSING THE CONVENTIONAL ADVICE

Other advisors might tell you that it's not necessary to go through all this trouble to see if you can afford a house. Just go to the bank and see if you can prequalify for a loan, they'll say. Let the bank do the work for you, and then you will know for sure. The problem I have with this advice is that every single person who has lost a home to foreclosure or bankruptcy originally qualified for a bank loan. Got the loan, moved in—and then something went wrong.

The conventional formula used by the bank tells you that your housing should cost 28 to 36 percent of your gross income. When I bought my first home, the formula at the time was 25 percent of gross income. Now that real estate prices have skyrocketed in many areas, that percentage is edging up to keep up with the prices, to allow more and more people to qualify for a mortgage. There is a huge difference between 25 percent of your gross income and 36 percent of your gross income. Let's say that you make $50,000 a year. Years ago, in order to qualify for a mortgage, the equation would have said that you could not spend more than $12,500 (25 percent) a year on mortgage payments, property taxes, and insurance. By today's formula, you could spend $18,000 a year (36 percent) on those same items and still qualify for the loan. That's a difference of $5500 a year, or $458 a month. And $458 a month is enough money to seriously affect the quality of your life.

In my opinion, this formula simply does not hold up. Gross income is almost irrelevant. Most of us never see anything close to our gross income—and certainly don't see as much of our gross income as we did years ago, what with 401(k) contributions and the high cost of medical insurance, to name two factors. Even though tax brackets have fallen, we pay more in taxes today than we used to, because there are fewer write-offs available to us. When I bought my first house, you could deduct from your income taxes sales tax, car interest payments, and the interest paid on credit cards. One by one, those hefty deductions were taken away from us. In addition, even a few decades ago, most people did not spend money to send their children to private schools for a primary and secondary education, and college costs were a fraction of what they are today. Relatively speaking, cars cost much less than they do now, never mind the upkeep. In short, you cannot adhere to a single formula when you are gauging how much housing you can afford. The object here is not just being able to buy a home. The object is to keep the home you buy forever.

FALLING IN LOVE . . . AND KEEPING YOUR HEAD

There's something about the prospect of owning a home that makes otherwise rational people giddy with longing. Your relationship with your house will be an important and long-term one, so it's important not to "marry" it in the throes of early passion. Rather, get to know it well first. Go back time and again before you say "I'll take it." Visit it at different times of day to see where the sun hits, what it feels like in the morning, afternoon, and night. Go on weekdays as well as weekends. See it with your kids, so you can feel and hear what it will be like to live there together. Walk around the house, drive by it, and listen. See if you can hear the neighbors, their children, or barking dogs. Talk to your neighbor's neighbor and ask them if your shared neighbor is loud. Do the kids blast music? Ask about break-ins or robberies in the area. It is important that you do not simply take the seller's word at face value. Neighbors will be more candid and objective, and they are the people whom you will be living among for a long time to come. I have known many people who bought a home, loved it, but ended up selling, finally unable to tolerate noisy neighbors. And make sure that you like the area. The grocery store, dry cleaner, restaurants, movie theaters, schools—the places that you are going to frequent. For instance, if there is a school nearby, you may have a herd of kids hanging out on your block for hours after school and on breaks. Drive around at rush hour, check out access to the freeways, and time how long it will take you to get to work every day. Look, too, at the surrounding areas, what would happen in case of a major rain, floods, etc. Make sure the whole package works.

Now turn your attention to the house itself, not just the view from the pretty bay window you're falling in love with, but everything about the house. Don't be shy. Flush the toilets, test the water pressure. Turn on the hot water in the kitchen and bathrooms and see how long it takes to become hot; it should take only a few seconds. Check to make sure that each and every appliance works. Find out how old the water heater, furnace and air conditioners, refrigerator, washer, dryer, dishwasher, and stove are. Most appliances last about seven to ten years before they need to be replaced. If any of the appliances are under warranty, find out if the sellers have the paperwork; would they mind leaving it for you if you buy the house? Look at the placement of electrical sockets and make sure that they all work. Check to see if the house has an up-to-date electrical system or if it's still wired with older circuitry. If you plan to put in anything that is going to require more electrical amperage, make sure that the current electrical system can handle it. And turn on everything at once to see whether you blow a fuse or the circuit breaker trips. Make sure you ask when the roof was last replaced, and visit the house after a heavy rain to see if there are any leaks. A roof is a huge expense. And take one more good look: Does this house have everything that you want? I have a friend who fell in love with a town house that she saw, simply because of the fireplace. It was absolutely beautiful, and that was that, she bought the house. After she moved in, she realized that she didn't have much of a backyard or a deck, and what good's a beautiful fireplace all summer? Look at the house and really make sure that it has everything you need. You will find the perfect house if you just take your time.

LISTENING TO YOUR REAL ESTATE AGENT, LISTENING TO YOURSELF

When you find the perfect house, the next step is to make an offer to buy it. Your inclination will be to ask your real estate agent for advice. However, you must remember that despite all appearances to the contrary "your" real estate agent doesn't really work for you but for the seller. The bottom line: The agent is paid by the seller.

A realtor makes a commission from the sale of the house. Typically that commission is 6 percent. If there is a real estate agent who represents the seller and another who represents you, usually they will split the commission. Regardless of how the agents divide the pie, it's the seller who pays the commission, which comes out of the sale price of the house. If the sellers get $200,000 for their home, for example, $12,000 of that comes off the top and goes to the agents involved in the sale.

As the buyer, you of course want to get the best possible price, but you must understand that the better the deal you get, the worse the deal for the agent. You pay less; they earn less. You pay more; they earn more. In short, the agent's best interests are the seller's best interests as well. This is an important fact to keep in mind. When it comes time to make an offer, stick with the figure you want to offer without worrying that you are insulting the seller or the agent.

So without talking to your agent, think about what you are truly prepared to pay for this house. Do not lose courage here, for often we begin to feel we are going to lose the house if we don't offer the right price. If you do end up losing it, trust me, it is a blessing in disguise. Back in 1976, I found what I thought was the perfect house, and I put in a bid on it. Someone else bid more, and I lost it. I was terribly upset, until a week later when I was driving around the Oakland Hills and saw a sign for an open house. I went in and fell in love all over again, only this time the house was less expensive and was situated on much more property. That's the house that I live in to this day, and every so often I still think how glad I am I that I didn't get the other house. If you try and do not get what you want, just move on; there are many, many houses out there.

LAW OF MONEY

If you are not overly attached to what you want, you will attain it.

Come from a place of plenty when looking for a house, not from a diminished place. Set the price in your head, check it out with your heart, and then tell the agent what you want to offer. If the agent says he cannot make an offer at that price, ask him why not. Chances are he will say he has been instructed not to put in a bid under a certain price. Depending on what that price is, you may feel okay about changing your bid. If, however, you feel that this is simply a sales tactic, just walk away, let it go, don't engage on that level; if it is meant to be yours, it will come back to you.

Years ago, I used to love to go along with friends who were looking to buy a house. One Sunday I accompanied two of my friends who were both looking, and before long we saw a home that was offered for sale by the owner. When we went in, my friend Woody absolutely fell in love with the house. We had already done the numbers, so Woody knew exactly how much she could afford to spend. We asked the owner how much he was asking for the house, and he named a figure that was $30,000 more than Woody could afford. She looked at him and said, "Too bad. If you would sell it for thirty thousand dollars less, I would take it on the spot." He apologized, but declined, so we left. As we were about to get into our car, the owner came running out of the house. "Wait a minute," he said. "Okay, okay, I'll accept your offer." So Woody bought the house she fell in love with at first sight.

About a month later we went out again with Paula, another friend, who was still looking for her dream home. Once again we came across a home that was for sale by the owner, but this time we had to make an appointment to see it. We made a date that was five days away. During those five days, Paula drove by the house a thousand times, and she was becoming more and more attached to it. "If the insides are anything like I imagine them," she said, "I've found my dream house." Sure enough, the house was adorable inside and out. Now the only thing left was to make a deal. The owner was asking more than Paula could afford to pay. Remembering what had happened with Woody a few weeks earlier, she said, "Too bad. If you would sell it for twenty thousand dollars less, I would buy it on the spot." With that she thanked him, we said our good-byes, and we left. We got into the car, and as I put the key into the ignition, Paula said, "Wait!" "Wait for what?" I asked. "He's going to come running out of the house—watch!" she said. We sat in his driveway for a few minutes, and then I said, "Uh, Paula, I don't think this is going to happen." She got a sad look on her face and said, "God, I wanted that house so much. How come he didn't come running out after us like that other guy did with Woody?" The answer to that question was that Paula was too attached to getting the house; Woody was not. When Woody walked out, she never imagined that the owner would come running after her. She liked the house but knew what she could spend, and that was that. Paula, on the other hand, had spent days driving around, falling in love with this house, before she ever set foot in it. Whether he was consciously aware of it or not, I would bet that the seller could feel it. As most overly attached buyers do, Paula ended up going back to him and paying full price for the house—she paid the price of wanting something too dearly.

IT DOESN'T HURT TO ASK

Sometimes you really want to buy, and the seller really wants to sell to you, but you're still thousands of dollars apart. For whatever reason—

be it that he owes money on the mortgage or needs money to buy his new home—the seller is unable to come down in price. Sometimes in these situations, you can enlist the help of your real estate agent to chip in some money. An agent's 6 percent commission is not fixed in stone. Often, to bring a deal to completion, the agent will cut a percentage point or more from his commission. With real estate prices in many areas astronomical, 1 percent can mean a nice savings for the buyer. If you are a buyer and the seller refuses to come down to your top offering price, ask the real estate agent if he will throw in some of his commission to make it happen. It doesn't happen every time, but sometimes, under the right circumstances, you can get lucky.

THE INSPECTION

My friend Woody took a risk when she made her offer—and had it accepted—after seeing her dream house just once. What if the house harbored some hidden structural damage or was being devoured by termites invisible to an untrained eye? What if it contained dangerous levels of asbestos or flaking lead-based paint? For this reason, an engineer's inspection is essential. In the best-case scenario, you would bring in an expert to inspect the house for structural soundness, pest problems, environmental risks, and the like before you made your offer. That way, your offer could take into account any expensive repairs you'd need to undertake once the house was yours, which could end up serving as a bargaining tool.

Unfortunately, in most cases you will likely be worried about someone buying the house out from under you while you are taking the time to conduct your inspection. Which means that in most cases, you will have your inspection conducted after your offer's been accepted and before the seller's attorney sends the contract to your attorney. Check in the Yellow Pages or ask friends or a real estate attorney to recommend a certified building inspector.

THE CONTRACT OF SALE

Now is the time to negotiate the terms of the contract of sale. In some parts of the country (New York, for example) it is customary to retain a real estate attorney to do this for you; in other parts, a real estate agent is all you need. This contract sets forth the terms of the transaction, including a description of the property, the purchase price, the down payment, the closing schedule, whether or not the deal is conditional upon your obtaining mortgage financing, and the seller's representations concerning the property. Typically, the seller's attorney draws up this contract, but in some jurisdictions a real estate broker can draw up this agreement as well. Be sure you understand your rights and obligations before signing. Don't be afraid to ask your attorney or realtor to explain whatever you don't clearly understand.

CITY HOUSE/COUNTRY HOUSE

These chapters will give you a basic understanding of what is involved in buying a house, but for many—especially those who live in urban areas—a home of your own more likely will mean a *cooperative apartment* or a *condominium* than a ranch or split-level with a yard and picket fence. When you buy a cooperative apartment, or what's commonly known as a *co-op,* you are purchasing shares of a cooperative corporation that owns the building; thus, strictly speaking, you don't actually own your apartment, you own shares of the corporation allocated to your apartment, together with a lease that allows you to occupy the apartment. When you buy a condominium unit, just as when you buy a house, you are purchasing a piece of real estate—albeit one that's part of a larger building or development.

Much of the information and considerations of these chapters apply equally whether you are buying a house or a co-op or condo. However, there are some important distinctions. First, interest rates are generally higher for financing the purchase of a co-op or condo.

From the lender's standpoint, there's considered to be more risk involved, since these are not freestanding units but units contained within a larger building, the operation and maintenance of which can affect the value of the individual units. Second, because they are situated within a building, the inspection prior to signing a contract should focus not only on the unit to be purchased but on the financial and physical condition of the building overall. Third, with a co-op or condo, your monthly costs also include *maintenance charges* or *common charges,* respectively, in addition to your monthly mortgage payments. There may even be assessments to be paid monthly, if the building or any of its systems is undergoing repair or restoration. Some of these costs may be tax-deductible for the co-op or condo owner, but these additional monthly charges should be factored in when you crunch your numbers to determine what you can afford.

CHAPTER 15

THE MORTGAGE MENU

GETTING THE BEST MORTGAGE

You find the perfect house, and before you know it, your offer has been accepted. Unless you have prequalified for a loan, your next step is to find someone who will lend you the money to close the deal. You can find a mortgage for yourself or you can enlist the help of a *mortgage broker.* A mortgage broker is someone who will find you the best loan to finance your home and make the process as easy as possible.

How do you find a good mortgage broker? Chances are that there will be at least one real estate agent—maybe two—involved when you buy your home. An agent will very likely recommend a mortgage broker to help you get a loan. You see, once your offer has been accepted by the seller, the agent switches hats, so to speak, and begins to work on your behalf, in order to make sure the deal goes through—and that the commission does, too. So the agent has a vested interest in helping you get your mortgage.

There is a tremendous difference between a mortgage and a good mortgage. This is why it is so important that you learn how mortgages work, so you know all the right questions to ask. If there is no agent involved or the agent doesn't know a broker, ask your homeowner friends for recommendations.

Why get a mortgage broker? A good mortgage broker can offer you a variety of loans from many different lenders. They're usually very up-to-date on the nuances of each lender and what each particular lender is looking for in order to qualify people for loans. Also, the mortgage broker will put together and present your entire loan package, so that you get through all the paperwork and documentation that will be required with as little hassle as possible. Many people wonder if it is more expensive to use a mortgage broker than simply to go to a bank and do it themselves. The answer is no. Either way, you are going to have to pay *points* (unless you choose a mortgage with a higher interest rate; but more on this later) as well as the *closing costs*. Since the fees are essentially the same, the differences start to come in with what a mortgage broker can offer you compared to what a bank can. The best words to describe the differences are choice and convenience.

If you investigate the bank options yourself, you are limited to the number of banks you've contacted, which will likely be only a few and in any case not very convenient. It is not a bad idea first to check out rates or deals for yourself; you can find a list of interest rates that are currently being offered by various banks in the real estate section of your local newspaper. The Internet can be another great source of information, and applying on-line for mortgages is getting more and more common. Once you have gathered your information, you can compare your notes to what your mortgage broker or loan officer is quoting you. The whole process of approval, start to finish, should not take more than three weeks. If it does, then something is wrong. Either your broker or loan officer is not doing his job or there is some other problem, but after three weeks find out why you've not yet been given an answer.

You can find a licensed mortgage broker by asking for referrals among friends who've gone through the process, or by checking with the state licensing board or a consumer affairs bureau. Usually brokers' fees are paid by the lending institution, but you'll need to verify fee arrangements ahead of time. I do recommend reputable mortgage brokers, but I also recommend that my clients know and understand the mortgage process. As complex as it seems, it is comprehensible. Please read the sections below before you begin to look, and then again before you buy.

MORTGAGE: THE MENU OF CHOICES

This part of the decision-making process is probably the hardest. Years ago, the only option available to most people was a 30-year fixed-rate mortgage. But now there are more choices available. Some factors you will want to consider:

♦ How long are you planning to live in this house?
♦ Are interest rates at the time of purchase high, medium, or low?
♦ Are interest rates projected to go higher, go lower, or remain stable?
♦ Will you struggle to make the mortgage payment or make it with ease?
♦ Are you approaching retirement, or do you still have more than fifteen years to go?

The answers to these questions will play a big part as to what kind of loan you should get in the first place. So please keep them in mind as you read through this section.

There are hundreds of variations when it comes to a mortgage. However, the primary types of mortgages that you will be considering are as follows:

1. Fixed-rate mortgage
2. Adjustable-rate mortgage (ARM), also known as a variable mortgage

3. A fixed and variable combined mortgage
4. Federal Housing Administration (FHA) mortgage

FIXED-RATE MORTGAGES

Fixed-rate mortgages are one of the two most popular types. This mortgage is just what it sounds like. The interest rate is fixed for the entire life of the loan. Since the interest rate is fixed, so are your monthly payments. This means that you know from the start how much your monthly payments are going to be—they will never change. Each mortgage payment is made up of interest and principal. In the first years, the greatest percentage of your mortgage payments is made up of interest, with very little going to pay off your principal, because lenders always want their interest paid first. So these early years of a mortgage always offer you the greatest deductions with respect to your income tax, since the interest portion of your mortgage payment is tax-deductible.

Just to give you an idea, on a 30-year, $150,000 mortgage at 7 percent, the payments would be $997 per month.

The first year, 13 percent of your payment goes to principal; 87 percent goes to interest.

The tenth year, 25 percent of your payment goes to principal; 75 percent goes to interest.

The twentieth year, 50 percent of your payment goes to principal; 50 percent goes to interest.

The twenty-fifth year, 70 percent of your payment goes to principal; 30 percent goes to interest.

The thirtieth year, 99.5 percent of your payment goes to principal; .5 percent goes to interest.

The period of time that you will have to pay back your loan can vary. For years, the most conventional time frame was 30 years. A surprisingly unknown fact among home buyers even today is that you can get fixed mortgages for almost any time frame: 10, 15, 20, or 30 years. The time frame for the payback period makes a difference in two ways:

1. *The longer the length of the loan, the lower the monthly payments.*

    Monthly payments for a 30-year mortgage are lower than monthly payments for a 15-year mortgage, which are lower than those for a 10-year mortgage.

2. *The longer the length of the loan, the higher the actual interest rate.*

    The interest rate will be higher for a 30-year mortgage than for a 15-year mortgage. The longer the loan, the more you will pay in interest in the long run.

    Overall, you will end up paying far more for a 30-year loan than you will for a 15-year loan, and you will pay more for a 15-year loan than you will for a 10-year loan.

See pages 259–61 for a detailed comparison of 15- and 30-year mortgages.

Fixed mortgages are best utilized:

- When interest rates are low and you expect to stay in the house for more than 5 to 7 years.
- If interest rates are currently low and you are approaching or are in your retirement years and are or will be living on a fixed income. Whenever you have a fixed income, it is preferable to have fixed expenses whenever possible.

ADJUSTABLE-RATE MORTGAGES

An *adjustable-rate mortgage (ARM)* is the opposite of a fixed-rate mortgage. Rather than being fixed for the entire length of the loan, the interest rate of an ARM can adjust either up or down over the length of the loan. To entice you to go the ARM route, a bank usually starts the loan at a lower rate than comparable fixed-rate mortgages, so that, at least in the first year, your monthly payments will be less than they will be later on. This can be appealing for cash-strapped home buyers. After your initial entry interest rate, which is set for 1 to 3 years, depending on the terms of your loan, the interest rate will adjust. In most cases, it will adjust upward, and when that happens: ouch.

In fairness, back in the eighties and early nineties, when interest rates were high and then came down, ARMs adjusted downward, so they were a big boon for many borrowers, but as of the writing of this book, interest rates are extremely low, so in years to come they are more likely to go up or remain right around where they are, rather than go down.

Regardless of what happens to interest rates, with an ARM, the lender cannot raise your interest rate more than a set percentage each year, usually around 2 percent from your starting rate; this annual limit is what is known as your *yearly cap*. What is more, over the lifetime of the loan your mortgage interest cannot be raised more than 6 or 7 percent above the initial starting rate; this is known as your *lifetime ceiling cap*. Many such loans have not only a lifetime cap but a floor as well.

Let's say you get a 1-year ARM that starts at a 6 percent interest rate with a 2 percent yearly cap and a 6 percent lifetime cap, with a minimum interest rate of 5 percent. What this means is that for your first year your interest rate is fixed at 6 percent. After the first year, the most that your new interest rate can be raised is 2 percent. So in this case, that would mean the most you would have to pay the second year would be 8 percent. The year after that, the most it can be raised is another 2 percent, to 10 percent, and so on. However, the lender cannot raise you above your lifetime cap, which in this case is 12 percent, so from the get-go, you know the worst-case scenario. Keep in mind, too, that the lowest your interest rate on this particular ARM can go is 5 percent, even if interest rates drop to 3 percent. So ARMs have an upside limit, a downside limit, and a yearly limit.

KEEPING THE LENDER HONEST

What keeps the lender from raising your loan that 2 percent every year till they hit the lifetime cap?

There are many limits to what the lender can and cannot do with respect to the interest rate they charge you. The lender cannot indiscriminately bump your interest rate up every 6 months just because they want to make money. Instead, the increases are tied to a certain percentage above a designated index. This percentage is known as a *margin*. Margins can be anywhere from 1 to 3 percent over the index. Depending on the terms of your loan, your lender can change your initial interest rates after the starter term of the ARM is up, anywhere from 1 to 3 years. From that point on a lender can usually make changes every 6 months or once a year.

The interest rate changes are governed by an *index*. You see, there is a difference between your yearly cap and the actual rate that the lender can charge you. The yearly cap simply tells you the maximum to which your increase can climb each year, regardless of the index that it is attached to, but that does not mean your rate is allowed to go up by that full amount. If it were, the lenders would automatically increase your interest rate by that yearly cap till your loan reached its lifetime cap—and borrowers would have caught on long ago.

Let's say that your particular loan is attached to the U.S. Treasury bill index, and your margin is 1.5 percent above the index rate. (Note that this index has nothing to do with your lender; it is an index set by the going interest rates issued on Treasury bills by the government.) If the current T-bill index is at 5.5 percent, the most that the lender could charge you that year would be 7 percent (5.5 percent plus 1.5 percent). It's important to consider, too, that even though the Treasury bill index will be the same for all lenders, the margin varies from lender to lender. If the T-bill index was 5.5 percent, and the margin on a loan from a different lender was 3 percent, then this particular lender could charge you 8.5 percent that year on your interest, as long as that 8.5 percent fell within your yearly cap amount.

Bottom line: With an ARM, get the lowest margin over the index you can.

Please note: An ARM with a margin that is *too* low can create a situation known as *negative amortization.* When negative amortization occurs, the monthly payments do not cover the full amount of principal and interest, so the amount of principal that you owe actually *increases.* This means that, over time, you could actually end up owing more than your original mortgage amount.

Do all lenders use the same index?

The indexes that lenders use to govern your loan are usually any of the following:

♦ 6-month U.S. Treasury bill index
♦ Federal Cost of Funds index
♦ 11th District Cost of Funds index (COFI)
♦ 1-year Treasury Constant Maturity Series
♦ LIBOR index (the London Interbank Offer Rate)

Which index your lender uses will be important to you because some indexes move up or down faster than others. The 6-month Treasury bill index may move up and down faster than the COFI, for example.

When interest rates are high and projected to come down, you want your loan to be attached to an index whose fluctuations are more rapid, so that you can take advantage of the decrease in rates. The opposite is true if interest rates are currently low. In this case, you'd want to be attached to a less volatile index, so that you can enjoy your current low rate for as long as possible.

Obviously, you want the index that will give you the lowest average rate over the life of the loan. However, since we don't have a crystal ball to tell us which direction interest rates will take in the future, I always take into consideration what different indexes have done over the past years to help me make my decision. As of the writing of this book, the most popular and best-performing indexes that are connected to an ARM are as follows:

♦ Coming in in first place has been the 6-month Treasury bill index.

♦ Second place has been the 1-year Treasury Constant Maturity Series, followed closely by the COFI index.

Bottom line: If you pick the right index, you will save yourself lots of money over the life of the loan.

If one bank is offering a lower starter rate on an ARM, is that always the right way to go?

In addition to the index, the margin, the lifetime cap, and the yearly cap, there is one last element that you have to investigate before you sign on with an ARM: How often can the lender make these regulated adjustments? Remember, in most cases, after the initial starter period is up, the lender can make adjustments either once a year or every six months, and in the long run there can be a big difference between the two.

The adjustment period is, in my opinion, more important than the starter interest. In a rising-interest-rate environment, an ARM that offers you a lower starter interest rate that could change every six months could end up costing you more than an

ARM with a higher initial interest rate that adjusts only once a year. So don't get lured into the lowest rate to start, for that is exactly what the lenders are hoping you will do. What happens after that starter rate is up and how quickly it can happen is what you really want to focus on.

In an interest rate environment that is currently low, you would want the longest possible time limits between changes; a yearly change would be much more advantageous than a change every six months. This would offer you the most protection against rising interest rates. However, if interest rates are high and projected to go down, then the best strategy would be to get an ARM with six-month adjustment periods, rather than yearly ones.

GUIDELINES

Questions to ask before signing up for an ARM:

1. What is the term of your initial interest rate? Will it remain in effect for one, two, or three years?
2. What is the yearly cap?
3. What is the lifetime cap?
4. What is the lowest the rate can go?
5. Which index is the rate attached to?
6. What is the margin that the lender can charge, based on that index?
7. After the initial period is up, at what intervals can the lender make changes? Every six months, or once a year?
8. Does the ARM you are signing up for have negative amortization?
9. Does it have a prepayment penalty—that is, a penalty incurred for paying off your loan early?

Make sure you get the answers to each of these questions, then go back and reread this section again to make sure you understand how the loan really works.

ARMs are best utilized:

- ♦ By people who know that they are going to stay in their home for a maximum of 5 to 7 years.
- ♦ When interest rates are high and projected to come down.
- ♦ When your cash flow is currently tight but you expect it to increase as time goes on.

Bottom line: Whether you should choose an ARM over a fixed mortgage will ultimately depend on what interest rates end up doing during the time you are living in your home. Try to do a few projections using various interest rate scenarios. If you are computer-literate, there are many programs on the Internet that will help you analyze the different possibilities. A good site is SmartCalc, at smartcalc.com. Make sure you run the numbers, or have someone else do them for you. Make sure, too, that you work out the numbers in a worst-case scenario and think about what would happen if that scenario came true.

FIXED AND VARIABLE COMBINED

A few years ago, a new kind of mortgage—a fusion of a fixed mortgage and an ARM—popped onto the scene. Known by the formidable names of *Five Twenty-five* (5/25) and *Seven Twenty-three* (7/23), these mortgages need not be formidable at all. They're available in two forms: convertible and nonconvertible.

A convertible 5/25 or 7/23 is what I think of as the fixed-fixed version. For the first 5 or 7 years, the rate is fixed. After that, for the next 25 or 23 years, your interest rate is adjusted just once, and then converts to another fixed rate for the time remaining on the loan. A nonconvertible 5/25 or 7/23 works in the opposite way. For the first 5 or 7 years, the rate is fixed, but after that it converts to an ARM for the remaining 25 or 23 years.

If you look closely, you will see that in both the 5/25 and the 7/23, the numbers add up to 30. In essence, these mortgages are amortized over 30 years. In both cases, you choose whether to have your initial interest rate fixed for 5 or 7 years, and then for the remaining 25 or 23 years—depending on whether you chose convertible or nonconvertible—you will automatically convert to a new fixed or variable rate. As you can see, these mortgages follow a two-step process, which is why they are also sometimes called *two-step mortgages.*

As with traditional ARMs, the adjustment after the initial time frame of 5 or 7 years is tied to an index, and usually the lender adds a margin of 1 to 3 percent on to that index as well. So the new rate is not an arbitrary one.

Fixed-and-variables are best utilized:

♦ If you doubt that you will be staying in your home for more than 5 to 7 years—and many of us do move often these days. The interest rate can be at least one full point less than that of a traditional 30-year fixed mortgage, and that can save you a heap of money in the long run.

Let me give you an example. Let's say that your mortgage will be $200,000. The interest rates for a 30-year fixed mortgage are at 7 percent, and the starting fixed rate for the 5/25 is 6.5 percent. That is just half a percent less. Your payments on the fixed mortgage would be $1331 a month over the next 5 years, for a total of $79,860. Your payments on the 5/25 would be $1264 a month over the next 5 years, for a total of $75,840. That is a savings of $4020 over those 5 years. If you sold the house after that time, it would have been well worth your while to have had a two-step mortgage.

A two-step mortgage also works the same way as a traditional fixed mortgage in that the longer the time frame of the loan, the higher the interest rate. A 30-year rate will be higher than a 15-year rate. With the two-step, the rate for the initial 7 years might be a quarter of a point or so higher than that of the initial 5-year period.

Look into these mortgages if you are fairly certain that you're buying a starter home, or if you know you will want to stay there for only about 5 to 7 years.

FEDERAL HOUSING ADMINISTRATION (FHA) MORTGAGES

If you are in need of $150,000 or less for a mortgage and do not have the 20 percent you'd need for a conventional down payment, or have a bad credit history, then there is one loan that very well might solve your problems. This is an *FHA mortgage.* The initials stand for the Federal Housing Administration, a division of the government that falls under the jurisdiction of HUD (Housing and Urban Development).

It is the norm with FHA mortgages that you do not have to put down 20 percent of the purchase price. In fact, FHA mortgages let you put down as little as 3 percent. Better yet, in order for you to qualify for an FHA loan, your past credit history may not hurt you as much as it would with a conventional lender. In many cases, the FHA will help you when no other lender will.

In the same way that a conventional lender will require that you carry PMI if you pay less than 20 percent down, the FHA will require that the loan be insured, although in this case, you will carry insurance issued by the government.

DIFFERENCE BETWEEN FHA LOANS AND A CONVENTIONAL LOAN QUALIFICATION

There are two basic formulas commonly used by lenders to determine whether you qualify for the loan for which you are applying. These formulas are called *qualifying ratios* because they estimate the amount of money you should spend on mortgage payments relative to your income and other expenses. As I said earlier, I do not put much faith in these formulas to determine whether you can truly afford the house in the long run, but they are nevertheless the formulas that the lender will use. While the following ratios may vary from lender to lender, and while each application is handled on an individual basis, the guidelines remain just that—guidelines. When you compare the FHA loan to a conventional loan, you will see that the FHA guidelines are in general more lenient. Let's compare the two:

Generally speaking, to qualify for conventional loans, housing expenses should not exceed 26 to 28 percent of your gross monthly income.

For FHA loans, the ratio is 29 percent of gross monthly income. Monthly housing costs include the *mortgage principal, interest, taxes,* and *insurance*—often abbreviated as *PITI.*

For example, if your gross monthly income is $3000, with a conventional loan the most of that $3000 you could spend on PITI would be 28 percent ($3000 multiplied by .28 equals $840).

Also taken into consideration when you apply for a conventional loan are any long-term debt obligations you have, defined as financial obligations or expenses that extend 11 months or more into the future, such as a car loan. For a conventional loan, your total monthly costs, including PITI and all other long-term debt, should be no greater than 33 to 36 percent of your gross monthly income. Using the above example, $3000 multiplied by .36 equals $1080. So the total of your monthly housing expenses plus any long-term debts each month cannot exceed $1080.

For FHA loans, the ratios are higher. The maximum percentage for your PITI is 29 percent. Twenty-nine percent of $3000 would mean that you could spend up to $870 a month on PITI, $30 more a month than with a conventional loan. In addition, the maximum allowable monthly housing expense and long-term debt ratio for an FHA mortgage is 41 percent, compared to the 36 percent of gross monthly income for a conventional loan. This means that on that $3000 you could be spending up to $1230 a month on your monthly housing and long-term debt compared to $1080 for a conventional loan. That's $150 more a month, which can make a big difference.

Loan Amounts Vary

When looking into an FHA loan, it is essential that you investigate the rules governing FHA loans in the county where you are buying your home. Just as different banks have different loan rates, different counties have maximum amounts that they will lend out, amounts that can change each year. As of 2000, the FHA loan maximum is around $160,000. But depending on the county and the local median prices of real estate, this average amount can be adjusted. You can find the exact amount available in your county on the Web under http://www.hud.gov/fha/sfh/sfhhicos.html. Or to get in touch with the FHA office nearest you, please call directory assistance and ask for the number of your local FHA office. You can also find the office nearest you on the Web under http://www.hud.gov/local.html.

FHAs are best utilized:

- By people with a bad credit history.
- By people with very little money to put down.

In my opinion, the government rarely gives us as good a deal as the private sector does, so if you have 20 percent to put down or need a larger mortgage amount, conventional loans are the best way to go. However, FHA loans are a fabulous way for those who are starting over, or for those who have had a hard time getting up and running. If you have claimed bankruptcy, you will have difficulty, at least for a number of years, qualifying for and obtaining a mortgage. If you have bad credit history, you will also have a hard time. This is where an FHA loan can help out.

Let me qualify this. You cannot simply get a mortgage even if you are a bad credit risk today, nor should you. The FHA is going to make sure that you can meet their lending guidelines, just as a regular lender will. However, they will not take into consideration your past problems or credit history in the same way a regular lender would. So if you are solemnly turning over a new leaf, this approach may be the break that you need.

THE LENGTH OF A LOAN

In deciding which kind of mortgage you should apply for, you will also have to decide whether you are going to apply for a 15- or 30-year mortgage. There are other durations as well—a 10-year mortgage, a 40-year mortgage—but the two most popular are the 15 and the 30, so that is what we will focus on here. What's the difference between these two? Simply put, with a 15-year mortgage, your house will be paid off in 15 years rather than 30, and you will have an interest rate that is about one half of a percent less than what you would have with a 30-year mortgage. Potential downside: Because the time frame is shorter, you will have to pay a few hundred dollars more a month.

Twenty-five years ago, when I bought the house that I live in now, I didn't know that a 15-year mortgage existed. I was buying a home, I was told to get a 30-year mortgage, and what did I know? Nothing, so I did what I was told. It wasn't until I had already owned my home for 10 years, with 20 years left to pay on it, that I learned that if I had gotten a 15-year mortgage to start with, I would have had only 5 years remaining on my mortgage. Yes, you may be thinking, but it's a lot more expensive to have a 15-year mortgage; I probably couldn't have afforded it. Not true! In many cases the difference could be as little as $150 a month, and in most cases it's not more than $300 or $400. For instance, my mortgage at the time was for $48,000. The difference between a 15-year and a 30-year mortgage was only $115 a month. If I had known that for $115 more a month, I could own my home outright in just fifteen years, I would have found a way to make it work.

Not only that, but with a 15-year mortgage you will save a tremendous amount of money overall. Let's say that you have a 30-year, $150,000 mortgage at 7 percent. Your monthly payments are $998 a month. Over 30 years, you will have paid $359,280 for that mortgage ($998 multiplied by 360 equals $359,280). A 15-year mortgage would cost you about a half a percent less in interest, which is to say that $150,000 for 15 years at 6.5 percent would be $1307 a month, $309 more a month. However, in 15 years, you would have paid a total of $235,260, or $124,020 less than you would have with your 30-year mortgage. That's a lot of money.

Below is a chart so you can see the difference in monthly dollar amounts between a 15-year and a 30-year. Also included are the total overall dollar amounts of a 15-year mortgage versus a 30.

Mortgage Amount	15-Year/6.5%	30-Year/7%	Monthly Difference	Total Savings of 15-year Loan over 30-Year Loan
$50,000	436	333	103	$41,400
$100,000	871	665	206	$82,620
$150,000	1307	998	309	$124,020
$200,000	1742	1331	411	$165,600
$250,000	2178	1663	515	$206,640
$300,000	2613	1996	617	$248,220
$400,000	3484	2661	823	$330,840
$500,000	4356	3327	1029	$413,640

Note: Loans for $227,150 or more are considered jumbo loans and are usually one half of a percent more than the going interest rate for loans under that amount. The chart above is for illustration purposes only and assumes that on loan amounts over $227,150, the going jumbo rates would be 7 percent for a 15-year loan and 7.5 percent for a 30-year loan.

Why don't more people take out 15-year loans? My guess is that many of us think first of what we can comfortably afford today, and think, too, that over the years we'll make more money, and then if we want we can pay the mortgage off faster later. The problem with this approach is that very few of us are disciplined enough, even if we start to earn more, to put more money monthly into our payments.

In my opinion, a 30-year mortgage can be a waste of good money. If I still haven't convinced you, consider this: with a 7 percent, 30-year mortgage, after 15 years of paying month in and month out, you would still owe roughly 75 percent of your original balance. If you had gotten a 15-year mortgage, you'd own the house outright.

THE POINTS OF A LOAN

All mortgages, whether fixed or adjustable, no matter the duration, carry with them what are known as *points*. Points are what the lender charges you up front for lending you the money. One point is equal to one percentage of the loan amount. For instance, a $150,000 mortgage with one point would cost you an up-front charge of $1500 ($150,000 multiplied by .01). On a loan carrying 2 points, you would pay $3000 ($150,000 multiplied by .02). As you can see, points can add up to quite a bit of money, and usually this money is due in cash at the time of the closing, when the house transfers from the old owner to you, or else the lender will let you add the points on to the mortgage and let you pay them over the life of the loan—which can cost you more in the end, so be careful.

Let's say that you have decided that you want to go with a 15-year fixed mortgage, and the going rate is 6.5 percent. The lender may offer you an interest rate of 6.8 percent with no points, 6.5 percent with one point, 6.25 percent with 2 points, or 6 percent with 3 points. If, in other words, you are willing to pay more up front in points for your loan, the bank is willing to lower your interest rate over the life of your mortgage. If you want, you can also "buy down your mortgage"—that is, you offer to pay more in points in exchange for an interest rate that's lower still. For example, you might offer to pay the bank 4 or 5 points if they'll give you an interest rate of 5.5 percent. Lenders will negotiate, so do not be afraid to ask. Please be careful, however, when it comes to ARMs, because it may well be a waste of money to pay points to buy down the initial rate, since the starting rate is in effect for a short time.

When presented with these choices, the majority of us will be tempted to go for the 6.8 percent with no points, because most of us will be totally strapped for money after coming up with the down payment. And as we just saw, a point or two of the mortgage amount can add up to a lot of money.

Even so, keep in mind that if you are able somehow to come up with the cash, your points are tax-deductible in the year of closing. You need to sit down with a calculator and figure out which way is the best for you to go in the long run. Take into consideration how long you really plan to keep the house and the difference in monthly payments. Again, there is a good program on the Internet under SmartCalc that can help you decide on the best way to go.

Here's an example: Let's say that you're taking out a mortgage for $150,000. Your choice is an interest rate of 6.8 percent with no points, 6.5 percent with 1 point, or 6.25 percent with 2 points. Which way should you go?

First, figure out how much it will cost you up front:

$150,000 at no points is zero.
$150,000 at 1 point is $1500.
$150,000 at 2 points is $3000.

Next, look at the monthly payments:

$150,000 at 6.8 percent over 15 years is $1332 a month, or $239,760 over the life of the loan.

$150,000 at 6.5 percent over 15 years is $1307 a month, or $235,260 over the life of the loan.

$150,000 at 6.25 percent over 15 years is $1286 a month, or $231,480 over the life of the loan.

Now add in the points for each of these totals:

$239,760 plus zero in points equals $239,760.
$235,260 plus $1500 in points equals $236,760.
$231,480 plus $3000 in points equals $234,480.

As you can see, if you are going to stay in the house for the entire fifteen years, it is worth paying more in points to get a lower interest rate. Remember, too, that not only will you pay less over the life of the loan but also that those points, if paid in cash, are deductible from your taxes in the year of the closing, so you really end up saving that much more. If you were in the 28 percent tax bracket, for example, you would have to add in the tax savings as well. So in the case of the 2 points, or $3000, this would save you $840 on your taxes, compared to a tax savings of only $420 if you paid only one point.

CHOOSING YOUR INTEREST RATE

The last decision you will have to make about your mortgage is whether you want to pay more for the loan and have a lower interest rate, or pay less for the loan and have a higher interest rate.

This is my basic advice: If interest rates are currently low and not expected to go any lower, if you need the tax write-off and have the money for closing costs, and if you know you are going to stay in this house for the long term, go for the lowest interest rate possible, or try, if you can find the money somewhere, to buy down the loan.

If, on the other hand, interest rates are high and projected to come down, go for the zero-pointer, for you can always refinance and get the better rate with points later on.

Bottom line: Run the numbers every way you can to see which of the loans available to you is the best option. Your broker can help you with this or, again, turn to SmartCalc on the Internet. Remember, it's not that *the bank* is granting you a loan. *You* are taking out a loan. Even though millions of us do it every year, buying a home is a big, big step, and most home buyers meekly do what they're told. It takes courage here to take charge, but it's worth it financially, and making the soundest decision, for yourself, will grant you true pride of home-ownership.

YOUR HOME AND YOUR FUTURE

TAKING TITLE

If you are buying the house with another person, then the way in which you take title—that is, the way ownership is recorded on the deed—will be very important. There are four main ways that people take title to a house: *joint tenancy with right of survivorship, tenants in common, tenancy by the entirety,* and *community property.*

JOINT TENANCY WITH RIGHT OF SURVIVORSHIP (JTWROS)

This is the way in which most married couples or partners take title to their house; however, marriage is not a prerequisite in order for you to be able to take title in this form (as it is with community property or tenancy by the entirety). When taking title in JTWROS, the parties involved are considered to have equal ownership of the entire property. In the event that one of them dies, regardless of the beneficiary instructions of the deceased's will or trust, the surviving spouse or partner automatically receives ownership of the deceased person's half of the house. One great part of titles that are held in JTWROS is that the deceased person's half passes directly to the survivor or survivors without having to go through the probate court procedure (and the probate court expense). The deceased's half will also receive a step-up in cost basis for tax purposes. This means that if husband and wife buy a house for $200,000, that $200,000 is considered the cost basis in the property for tax purposes. Since they both own the house, that cost basis gets divided equally between the two of them. In essence, they each are considered to have a $100,000 cost basis in the property. Years later, the house is worth $500,000, let's say, and the husband dies. The new cost basis will be half the value of the house when he died. If it is valued at $500,000, then his half at the time of his death is worth $250,000. You see, the wife still has a $100,000 cost basis for her half, but now that she has received a step-up in basis on her husband's half, to $250,000, her new cost basis is $350,000. This is important for tax purposes. If she sold the house now for $500,000, she would not owe anything in capital gains tax. The reason she does not owe any capital gains tax is that, according to the new tax laws passed in 1997, for a single person the first $250,000, and for a married couple the first $500,000, of a gain from a sale of a primary residence is exempt from taxes.

Bottom line: This is an incredibly efficient way to own property together and to have it change hands upon a death.

TENANTS IN COMMON (TIC)

This is the way to take title if you want to make sure that upon your death, your portion of the house goes to your designated beneficiaries as governed by your revocable trust or will, and not to the person or people who own the property with you. Property under TIC ownership can be owned by two or more people. When you own real estate under this title, you really own only a designated percentage of the property. Unlike joint tenancy, where in essence you each own the entire house, with TIC, your partner could own 60 percent and you could own 40 percent. You also could sell your 40 percent anytime your heart desires, and to whomever you desire. When you take title under TIC, the beneficiary or beneficiaries to whom you leave your portion via your will will have to go through the probate court procedure to take ownership of their share of the property. If you're in a second marriage, say, and want to leave your share of the house you're living in to your children from your first marriage, TIC is a way to pass your share to your children through a will or trust.

TENANCY BY THE ENTIRETY

Not available in all states, and available only for married couples, this is one of my favorite ways for married couples to take title. Just as in JTWROS, husband and wife own the property entirely, with the other automatically inheriting it upon a death, but with this form of ownership there is an added bonus. As long as the couple stays married, the house will be protected against claims from any creditors. So if you have a husband who is out of control when it comes to his credit cards and decides to default on the money that he owes, his creditors cannot come against the house and put a lien or claim on any of your marital property held in this way. If you ever sell the house, or get separated or divorced, or if one spouse consents to let the creditors go after the other, well, now we have another story, because the creditors will descend on you. In the meantime, holding title in this way is your best protection against creditors.

COMMUNITY PROPERTY

This form of ownership is available only for married couples and only in the following states: Arizona, California, Idaho, Louisiana, Nevada,

New Mexico, Texas, Washington, and Wisconsin. Ownership under community property works in much the same way as it does with JTWROS, except that the surviving spouse gets a step-up in basis on the *entire* piece of property. To compare community property owner-ship to the example we constructed under JTWROS, in this case the surviving spouse would get a step-up in cost basis on the entire prop-erty. Her cost basis would be $500,000 rather than $350,000. She could then sell this property for up to $750,000 before she would have to pay taxes—not bad.

CLOSING COSTS

Okay, you've made it this far. In order for the house you're buying to become truly yours on paper, you have to go through a few more financial acrobatics and come up with some more money. In addition to the down payment, you are also going to have to come up with money for *closing costs,* or costs that you have to pay to close the deal on your home. I have to tell you, these are not cheap. When you go to the closing, you will be told to bring your checkbook, because you will be writing quite a few more checks before you are the proud (and per-haps exhausted) owner of your home. It's true that sometimes many of these costs can be absorbed right into the balance of the loan, but one way or another you are paying for them. On average, closing costs run approximately 2 to 4 percent of the cost of the house. This per-centage may vary, depending on where you live.

Closing costs include the *loan application fee* (if not already paid), *lender's points, prepaid homeowner's insurance,* an *appraisal fee, lawyer's fees, recording fees, title search and insurance, tax adjust-ments, agent commissions,* and *private mortgage insurance* (if you are putting less than 20 percent down), among other expenses. By law, your lender, within 3 days of your application for a loan, is to supply you with what is known as a good-faith estimate, which should give you a good idea as to what these closing costs are going to add up to. If you do not get one, call the lender and ask for it. Here is a list of the approximate upper limits of closing costs and fees that you can expect:

- *Loan application fee.* This should cost about $375. This is the fee the lender charges you simply to apply for the loan.
- *Credit report.* The lender will run a report to make sure that you have good credit when it comes to paying your bills, which should cost about $75.
- *Appraisal fee.* Your house must be appraised independently, so that the lender can make sure that the amount of the mortgage is in keeping with the true value of the house. This costs about $300.
- *Title search and insurance.* The lender wants to make sure that the title to the home you are about to buy is free and clear of any liens from the previous owner, and wants to be insured against any future problems that could arise. Title insurance runs about $300.
- *Lender's points.* This is the charge that the lender imposes in connection with the loan. On a mortgage of $150,000 with 1 point, the figure would be $1500.
- *Processing fee.* This is a fee that the lender charges to process your application—and, yes, you are reading this right—there is one charge for you to apply for a loan and another for them to process this loan. This fee will run about $150.
- *Preparation fee.* Don't faint, but the lender also gets money to prepare all the paperwork that is required; the preparation fee is about $150.
- *Prepayment of interest.* Depending on the time of the month you buy this house, you will have to come up with an amount of money to prepay the interest on your mortgage until the loan closes. Assuming a $150,000 mortgage at 6.5 percent and 15 days of prepaid interest, that will come to about $400.

All of these sums add up to a whopping $3250—so far! And that may not be the end of it. You may also have to pay something toward *transfer taxes, mortgage taxes, recording fees, real estate tax escrow, insurance escrow, inspection fees, attorney's fees, real estate broker's fees,* and other fees that usually fall under the category of *junk fees.*

When all is said and done, the closing costs on a mortgage of $150,000 can add up to about $5000. Make sure that you have your lender outline in great detail what they think every one of these items is going to cost you. Factor these costs, too, into your overall financial picture.

CAUTION

As I mentioned earlier, many people will find themselves wrapping some of the closing costs into the mortgage itself. For instance, if you had a $150,000 mortgage, the lender might suggest that you let your $5000 of closing costs be tacked on to the mortgage and that you pay it out monthly. Sounds like a great idea, but if you do that, you have just increased your $5000 in closing costs to $11,520. How? Well, let's say you have a 30-year mortgage at 6.5 percent and you plan to keep the house for all 30 years. That extra $5000 adds about $32 a month on to your payments, which over 30 years adds up to $11,520. Another way to look at it is that if you invested that $32 a month over the next 30 years at 8 percent, you would have $47,692. Either way you look at it, there's a lot of money at stake. If you have the cash, pay for closing costs up front, especially if you plan to stay in the house for the entire life of the mortgage. If, however, you plan to stay there for only 5 years, I don't have a problem with financing your closing costs.

SOMETHING TO PONDER

Think about this. You put your money in the bank, they pay you 4 percent or less on it, then they turn around and lend out your money to a home buyer for 7 percent. Then they turn around again and sell that loan in the secondary market to one of three major investors. Maybe over the years you've heard the names Fannie Mae or Freddie Mac in connection with home loans, and have wondered who they are and what they have to do with your loan. Well, the two primary investors in home loans are the Federal National Mortgage Association (Fannie Mae), and the Federal Home Loan Mortgage Corporation (Freddie Mac). These agencies purchase and sell residential mortgages in the secondary market, which means they buy the value of your loan from your bank. The reason that Fannie Mae and Freddie Mac do this is to help keep money available in local banks to lend out for home mortgages across the country. There is one more agency that you may have heard of: the Government National Mortgage Association (Ginnie Mae). They work a little differently from Freddie and Fannie but essentially accomplish the same goal. Ginnie Mae does not actually buy the mortgages from banks, it simply adds the guarantee of the full faith and credit of the U.S. government to mortgage securities issued by private lenders.

Where do Fannie, Freddie, and Ginnie get the money to buy the loans from the bank? From investors like you. They sell bondlike instruments in the market that will guarantee you a certain percentage rate for a specific period of time. Fascinating, isn't it, that on some level we all are financing our own real estate transactions—and paying big bucks to do so?

YOUR HOME AND YOUR FUTURE

Most of this chapter has been devoted to what you need to know in order to make wise decisions when it comes to buying and financing your home, which is the investment most of us hold closest to our hearts. But there are still lessons to learn, even after you become a homeowner. To my mind, the most important of these is how best to use your home to secure your retirement years. Your home can prove to be one of your greatest financial and emotional friends, if you learn how to make it work for you. Whether you're starting over, whether your working years are ending (perhaps sooner than you expected), or whether you just haven't planned as well as you should have, if you happen to own a home and you'd like to remain in it for a long time, I want you to consider as your first priority paying off your mortgage in full, as quickly as you can.

Many of us have been told for years that you would never want to pay off your mortgage, not only because it is the best tax deduction you will ever have but also because you could be investing that extra money and getting real growth on it, rather than having it simply remain as equity in your house. Both these points are valid, especially when you have more than enough money to meet your monthly expenses and have the money to do all that your little heart desires.

However, if you are barely making it and every penny counts, these points do not apply. When you have to start over or simply make up for lost time, tax deductions are not going to be what saves you in the long run. And think about this: As time goes on, the interest deductions for your mortgage will diminish as, in the later years of your mortgage, more and more of your monthly payment is going to pay off the principal. When this happens, the mortgage ends up offering you less in tax deductions. What's more, if you are in a situation where you do not have much income and feel that you have very little money to last you forever, then taxes aren't a problem one way or the other, right? With respect to investments geared toward growth, rather than good money just sitting in your home, well, some of us would rather be safe than sorry. True, growth investments such as stocks can go up, but they can also go down. The bottom line is this: If you are in a situation where you are having trouble meeting your monthly expenses, one of the best alternatives available to you, if you possibly can, is to pay off your mortgage right now.

Let's say that your mortgage was originally a 30-year, 7 percent fixed-rate mortgage for $150,000, with payments of $998 a month. You have been paying off this mortgage for about 10 years, which leaves 20 years to go. Even after all these years, the balance remaining on your mortgage is $128,718. You're happy living where you are, and you really don't want to move or have to sell your home just to make ends meet, but you're having a hard time, you're barely squeaking by. You have four choices: You can go back to work; you can make sure that the money you do have is making the highest safe return possible; you can reduce your expenses; or you can do a combination of any or all of the above.

The first option is always a possibility but not always a reality. Depending on your skills, your health, your desire, your ambition, the current job market, and your age, sometimes going back to work may not be as easy as it sounds. Plus you just may not want to, and even if you do go back to work for now, there may come a day when you're not able to work. Remember, there is a big difference between having to work and wanting to work.

In the second place, when you are approaching or are in your retirement years and have very little money, it is essential to place what you have in investments that are safe and sound. In reality, all that you have saved will, most likely, be required to generate the income that you use to pay your bills, so you cannot take the risk and invest it for growth. Investments that give a nice secure dividend or interest rate will be your best bet. But secure investments cannot do a lot to give you a significant increase in income. For instance, let's say that you had $200,000 invested in your money market account, paying you 5 percent interest, and you change that to a Treasury note paying you 5.8 percent. The difference would be $1600 a year. Granted, that's $133 dollars more a month, which can help, but it won't pay the mortgage.

Your third option is to reduce your expenses. If your largest monthly expense is your mortgage payment, getting rid of it would certainly free up a good portion of your available income. If you still have time before retirement and are able to send in more money every single month, please make sure that you do so, so that your mortgage will be paid off in full by the time you retire—one of the richest feelings there is. If you think money is going to be tight when you retire, if you want to continue to live in your home, and you do not have any current credit card debt, I urge you to start paying down that mortgage right now. To find out how to be home free by retirement, call your lender and ask them to give you the extra monthly amount that will be needed to have your house paid off in X number of years, X being the number of years until you retire.

If you are facing retirement and don't have years to pay off your mortgage, here is what I would suggest.

THE COURAGE TO OWN YOUR HOME

If you have retirement savings inside and outside of retirement accounts, you probably plan to use those savings, along with your Social Security payments, to generate the income to help you pay for the mortgage and your other monthly expenses. However, if you have enough money available to you to pay off that mortgage in full right now, then I must tell you that is the best thing you could do to increase your cash flow. Let me show you why, assuming this money is not in a retirement account and that there will not be a heavy tax burden to liquidate it.

Let's assume that you have a mortgage balance of $128,718 with a monthly payment of $998, and you have 20 years remaining on the loan. Let's also say that you have $200,000 in a money market fund earning 5 percent, but that is essentially all you have besides a little sum of money in a retirement account; you will get Social Security; you do not have a pension; and let's also assume that you are single, so your tax bracket is 15 percent. We are not going to take into consideration the income taxes owed on the money earned in the money market account or the income taxes saved on the interest for the mortgage, for in many ways they cancel each other out. Your tax savings on the mortgage would be $1366 and the taxes owed on the interest would be $1500, so we'll call it a wash.

Most people do not like to touch the cash they have in reserve, because money in the bank makes us feel safe. But sometimes you jeopardize your safety by holding on to what you have rather than using it wisely. So let's say this is true for you, that you feel safe with that $200,000 in your money market account, for you know that with its 5 percent interest rate, it generates about $10,000 a year, or about $833 a month before taxes. You take that $833 a month and add $165 from your Social Security check, and you have enough to meet your mortgage payment of $998 a month. Not bad. But think about this.

What if instead you took $128,718 out of your money market fund and paid off your mortgage in full? That would leave you with $71,282 in cash, which at 5 percent would still give you income of $297 a month. Even though your income from the interest would drop from $833 to $297 a month, your monthly expenses would have dropped by $998, since you no longer have a mortgage payment. The result will make all the difference, once you think about it.

Perhaps you're thinking that having only $71,000 in cash to your name does not make you feel safe. It is important that you remember that this money has not disappeared but is in your home. And it may be safer there than in your accounts. For instance, let's say that as you get older, something happens and you have to go into a nursing home. If you do not have nursing home insurance, you would have to spend almost all of your cash before Medicaid would pay for you. However, many states consider your house an exempt asset when it comes to qualifying for Medicaid, regardless of the equity you have in it. So in many states you could have your home paid for in full and still qualify for Medicaid.

Another scenario: You want the security of knowing you will have access to cash sometime in the future, should you need it. You can put your home to work for you by applying for an equity line of credit. The time to do this, however, is preferably when you still are working and have an income, for it is hard to qualify for a loan when you do not have money coming in. If you do get an equity line of credit, make sure you get one where you can write checks when you need the money, not one where they give you a lump sum of cash. What we want here is a source for emergency cash only; if you never have to use those funds, it shouldn't cost you anything. It is only when you need money and write a check against that line of credit that you start paying interest on the money you used. If you do this, then in case of an emergency you have access to some extra cash and you do not have to feel afraid. Also, chances are good that any payments for whatever money you do use from the line of credit will be far less than your mortgage payments were.

Look for an equity line of credit with no points and no up-front fees except an appraisal fee (approximately $300) to verify the value of your home.

After retirement, your house can also be put to work for you with a *reverse mortgage.* A reverse mortgage is a kind of mortgage loan available to senior citizens who own their home outright. It is a safe and easy way to turn your home equity into cash. A reverse mortgage is unlike a home equity loan in that you do not have to make monthly payments; rather, a reverse mortgage pays you. More important, you do not have to repay the loan for as long as you live in your house. Your beneficiaries repay the loan, plus interest and any finance charges, when you die, or you repay it when you sell the house. It's a great way to keep your home and draw income from it at the same time. A reverse mortgage can make all the difference for many people. I have covered this subject in detail in my books *You've Earned It, Don't Lose It* and *The Road to Wealth,* or you can read about it at www.reversemortgage.org on the Internet.

HOME FREE

In the long run, if money is expected to be tight, the sooner you pay off your mortgage the better off you will be. The other aspect to doing so is that nothing will make you feel more secure than owning your house outright—knowing that you have a place to live that no one can take away from you. All my elderly clients have said that it was the best thing they ever did. For that matter, many of my younger clients worked hard to pay off their mortgages early as well, for the emotional payoff that comes from owning their home outright.

When you're younger, is it better to invest that extra money for growth rather than use it to pay off your mortgage early? It depends. If the idea of owning your house outright makes you feel safe and powerful, then that's the way for you to go. If you have the discipline and the tenacity to invest your money for growth, follow through on your instinct with focus and determination. I have found that the people who follow a course toward wealth and financial freedom have the courage to be rich, the courage to plan for tomorrow.

PART V

THINKING AHEAD

CHAPTER 17

THE COURAGE TO CREATE YOUR FINANCIAL DESTINY

Think of the lengths we go to keep our lives safe. We want recommendations when we hire baby-sitters for our children; we buy the best locks we can to keep our houses secure. We insure what we own; we practice preventive medical care. We even make sure that a beloved pet who has to be tended to while we go on vacation will be sent to a clean, cheery kennel. Yet what do we do to safeguard our money? Surprisingly little. Can you tell me how your 401(k) money is invested and how much it is earning? Can you tell me what the load is on any mutual fund you may have? Are you absolutely certain that you are doing the right thing with your money? If you have a financial advisor, are you confident that you have picked the right person to whom to entrust your financial future, and do you know much he or she is earning from your money every year?

If it is your intention to be the master of your financial destiny, you must begin paying more attention to your money. Not all financial advertisements or advisors have your best interests at heart, so you must learn the difference between the myths that you are being told and sold, and the reality of how money works. It is never too soon to begin, it's true, but it's also true that it's never too late to start.

LAW OF MONEY

If you expect your money to take care of you, you must take care of your money.

There are only three ways to make money. One is to go out and work for it. However, few among us can work forever, and there will likely come a time in our lives when working for a paycheck may not be an option. The second way to make money is to inherit it or to win the lottery. Again, not something that we all can count on. The third way, and the only one that is available to all of us for an unlimited amount of time, is to invest what we earn during our working years wisely, so that the money we work so hard for goes to work for us.

True richness begins when the money you earn begins to earn money itself.

MONEY MARKET FUNDS

Who should pay attention? Everyone, whatever your age. It is key that you know what to do with your cash, how to build a foundation of liquidity, and how to avoid becoming a target of salespeople when you have money just sitting in an account.

When I first started working in the money business, most people simply kept all their money in a passbook savings account at a bank. They were happy with the 5 percent a year that their savings earned, and felt safe because, in most cases, their money was insured. The other bank account that everyone had was a checking account. This was where everyone kept the money to pay the monthly bills. Checking accounts did not pay any interest—and in most cases, you would have to pay the bank a monthly service fee just to be able to write those checks.

Then, brokerage firms and mutual fund companies saw an opening in banking and began to market a more aggressive way to bank money, by combining a savings and checking account in one account known as a *money market fund*. A money market fund was simply a mutual fund that offered investors stability and a higher interest rate than passbook or checking accounts, and in many cases, at a cost far less than the monthly expense of having a checking account.

For instance, if back then you had had $20,000 in your savings account at your bank earning 5 percent, you would have earned $1000 a year in interest. If you also kept $1000 or more in your checking account to pay bills, not only did you not make any interest on that $1000 but you paid $10 a month in service fees, so your checking account cost you $120 a year.

When money markets really started to hit the scene, in 1980 and '81, interest rates were unusually high. If you had had that $20,000 in a money market fund, you would have earned 18 percent a year, or a total of $3600, compared to the $1000 you'd have earned in your savings account. The fee that most firms charged back then for a money market fund was around $100 a year. But remember, many of these funds also served as checking accounts for people who wrote just a few checks a month. Compared to the $120 a year the banks charged, this was still $20 less. Add to this the $1000 in our example that you always kept in your checking account that did not earn a penny of interest; in a money market fund, you would have seen interest on that money, too, to the tune of $180 a year back then. That alone would more than cover the $100-a-year fee to enjoy this account. In the end, between the $1000 interest that you earned on your passbook savings account and the $120 cost of your checking account, you would have netted $880 on your $21,000. If you had opened a money market fund with both your checking and passbook accounts in one place at 18 percent interest, you would have earned $3780 that year, minus the $100 fee to have the account, so you would have netted $3680. That would have been $2800 more in just one year.

Even though interest rates paid for money market funds today are about one-quarter (4.5 percent) of what they were in the early eighties, the principle still holds true. Most savings accounts today no longer pay 4.5 percent or 5 percent as they did years ago; these days, they are paying about 2 percent. Consider, too, the hidden charges of banking— service charges for your checking accounts, fees for ATM withdrawals, and so on—and then ask yourself whether a money market fund is the right kind of account for you to have. I'd be willing to bet it is.

Questions you need to ask yourself: The money that you want to keep liquid, safe, and sound—is it earning only 2 or 3 percent in interest? Could it be earning more? How about your checking account? Are you still paying $10 a month for checks and not earning any interest on that money? If the answer to these questions is yes, or if you don't even know for sure, then you need to put the law of money into effect: What are you doing for your money? What you can do right now is to start checking out money market funds.

To find the funds paying the best interest rates, check a financial magazine such as *Kiplinger's, Money,* or *Smart Money.* Every month they list the best-performing money market funds in the United States, along with phone numbers. You can also find this information on the Internet at www.suzeorman.com, www.smartmoney.com, or www.kiplinger.com. I feel, too, that you can never go wrong with getting yourself a Schwab One money market fund at Charles Schwab, a major discount-brokerage firm with locations throughout the country. (In fact, that is where my mom and I have our money market accounts.) If you have $25,000 or more that you want to keep safe and sound, Charles Schwab has an account called the Value Advantage, which pays about one half of a percent more than other Schwab money market accounts.

Money market accounts usually offer both checks and a debit card.

The debit card is different from a credit card. It works like a check, in that as soon as you use it the money is taken out of your account. Rather than getting a bill at the end of the month (as you would with a credit card), you simply get a statement every month, showing you the balance in your account and detailing the interest that your money has earned, the checks you wrote that month, and money you spent using your debit card. Debit cards are particularly useful when you're traveling internationally. For instance, if you are in a foreign country without access to an ATM, or you simply need more cash than your ATM card will allow you to withdraw, you can go into any bank, present your debit card, and get as much money as you want, based on what you have in your account. Obviously this also works here in the United States. Your debit card can serve as an ATM card as well, enabling you to make withdrawals from your account at any cash machine. This way, you do not have to carry a lot of cash or go to the trouble of getting, and possibly losing, traveler's checks when you travel. Instead, your money could be sitting in your account earning interest, ready to be accessed anytime you want.

THE BEST USES FOR MONEY MARKET FUNDS

People will often ask me, "Suze, I have some money I'll need a few years down the road, but in the meantime, what's the best way for me to invest it?" They're saving to buy a house in two years, let's say, or their child is going to college next year, or they want to buy a car in six months, or they know they'll need a new roof in about a year. Whatever the case, they want to make the most of their money in the interim. When I suggest a money market fund, they always look at me and say, "No, you don't understand. I want to make the most I can on these funds until I need the money, and money market funds only pay around four and a half percent." With that, before I say another word, I ask them to take this little test.

I ask them how much money they have to invest right now. Maybe $10,000 is the answer. Then I ask them to choose between two investment options. In the first, I can guarantee an 80 percent return on the money the first year, but it will lose 40 percent in the second year. In the second option, I will guarantee a 5 percent return on the money the first year, and in the second year it will earn 5 percent again—pretty much the way a money market fund works.

Almost without fail, they choose the first option, for if they think they earn 80 percent the first year and only lose 40 percent the second that will still be a 40 percent gain, which is still more than the 10 percent total gain in the second example. Right? Wrong. An 80 percent gain on $10,000 is $8000, for a total of $18,000 that first year. The second year the loss is 40 percent of that $18,000, or $7200. $18,000 minus $7200 is $10,800. With the second option, 5 percent of $10,000 is $500, for a total of $10,500 after the first year. And in the second year 5 percent of $10,500 is $525, for a total of $11,025. This example tends to illustrate for people that sometimes if you just plod along steadily you can still come out ahead—much like the fable of the tortoise and the hare. This doesn't mean you should always just plod along with all of your money, not by any means. But when you have a limited time frame in which to invest, such as a year or less, then you really have only a couple of safe choices, and those are money market funds or Treasury bills (more on these later in this section).

GUIDELINE

Money you know you will need within the next six months to two years belongs in a money market fund.

"SAFE AND SOUND" MONEY

After you have taken care of the money you know you're going to need in the not-too-distant future, the next eventuality you need to plan for is the unexpected. The goal of creating emergency funds is to make you feel safe, and this money, too, belongs in an investment such as a money market fund. Some will feel safe with $100 in a "safe and sound" account; others will need to have $10,000 or more. Conventional wisdom says one should have three to six months' worth of living expenses set aside in a safe place, and, for the most part, I agree with this. But there is no set formula for "safe and sound" money, because your relationship with your money is personal and unique to you. So you need to ask yourself this question: How much money do I want to have safe and sound for an emergency?

Write down the first number that pops into your head. $_____

Okay, that's your figure. Either put that sum of money away in a money market fund right now, or if you do not have that money available to you at this point, you must begin to create it. (This is assuming that you have already paid off all credit card debt.)

Let's say that you wrote down $5000, and you have nothing to start with. The next time you pay your bills, and every month thereafter, I want you to write a check for at least $50 to deposit into an account to work toward that goal. The sooner you get to this goal, the sooner you can go on to creating even more. Again, as soon as you have enough, try to keep this money making the most interest it can, for it will help you reach your goal that much sooner. For instance, let's say that you are able to put away $100 a month. This $100 a month put into an account earning 5 percent interest will take only 3.7 years to grow to $5000. If instead you kept the money in an account earning only 2 percent, it would take you three months longer to reach that goal.

The reason I want you to have this "safe and sound" money? Because when you feel safe, you feel powerful, and power, remember, attracts money. The safer you feel, the more powerful you are, the more money will come your way.

THE RISKS INVOLVED IN A
MONEY MARKET FUND

Once you have accumulated a nice sum of money, you must make sure that it stays secure. You see, one danger of having more than five or ten thousand dollars in an account is that it is possible—probable, in fact—that you will receive a call from someone representing the bank or brokerage firm where the money is kept, offering to help you invest it so that you can get a better rate of return. Many banks now have in-house brokerage services to help their clients invest. Obviously the bank or brokerage firm will make more money in the long run if you invest it in certain ways rather than others. So these companies keep an eye on accounts with a consistent stash of cash, in the hope that if they call you, you will be open to listening to their ideas. Please be careful if this happens. Just keep in mind, and say so, that your goal with these funds is to keep them safe and sound in case of an emergency.

M A R G A R E T ' S   S T O R Y

When I was eighteen and going to college, my dad got me a checking account at his bank, which was great—my own checks, with my own name on them. That was that, I never thought about it again. Banks are there to take care of your money, right?

When my dad died about two years ago, he left me forty thousand dollars, which was the most money I'd ever seen. I'm single now, I work at a magazine and don't make that much money, so I thought this would be a great nest egg; I would just keep it forever. I don't know anything about money. I just wanted to keep it in the bank, so I opened a savings account at the same bank, my dad's bank.

The money had been in there for about five months when

I got a call from a man who said he was representing the bank. He was concerned, he said, that I had so much money sitting in a savings account when it could be working harder for me and earning more. He asked if I wanted to come in and talk to him, so I did. I remember thinking how nice it was for the bank to be so concerned and to offer this service. He said that he could put the money into mutual funds, where it would grow at a great rate and be totally safe, and also that it wouldn't cost me a penny, that there weren't any commissions or fees. I said, Great, let's do it.

About six months later, I was out with a friend, and started to tell him about what had happened and all my bank was doing for free. He said that was impossible, that nobody can guarantee a great return and nobody does this stuff for free. So we went and called the bank, but the guy didn't work there anymore. The man I got instead looked up my investments in the computer and said he would never have put my money in those mutual funds. The first guy had put all the money into these two funds that I now learned were loaded funds, with a 5 percent commission. They were speculative small-cap funds, whatever that means, but I learned it meant that my money wasn't safe at all. In fact, I had lost six thousand dollars by then, and I got out of those funds that very day.

Margaret was lucky. A friend tipped her off that she had not done the right thing, but far too many of us do not have such knowledgeable friends. It may also be true that the people we have helping us might not know themselves what is right, even if they have our best interests at heart. Or it may be that they care more about their commissions than they do about our future. Whatever the case, when your money is at stake, it is your responsibility to know and understand exactly where it is; why it is where it is; what it is costing you to be there; and what the return on your investment is amounting to.

At thirty, Margaret was well advised—even by her unscrupulous advisor—to invest some of her nest egg for growth, though she was ill advised to invest it all, as well as on how to invest it. This is not a morality tale to keep you from investing, which is the last thing I'd want to do. It is a morality tale to compel you to invest wisely and well.

INVESTING FOR YOUR FUTURE

Once you have your "safe and sound" money, you have also acquired the habit of creating money, systematically, month after month. Now it is time to put that money to work for your future.

Very simply, over the course of your lifetime, a lot of people are going to try to tell you many things about many different kinds of investments. It is going to be your job to know if these investment recommendations are good for you, bad for you, or merely good for the people who are trying to sell them to you. There are a handful of investment options that come up time and again. Regardless of how your bottom-line numbers read, I want you to understand each one of them inside and out, because sooner or later, someone is going to dangle them like sugarplums before your eyes: annuities, bonds, bond funds, stocks, mutual funds, spiders, gold, gold funds, real estate, and IRAs. I'll address some of these investment options in the coming pages.

There is a reality inherent in most investments, and a myth, and I want you to understand the difference in each case. And you must also know and understand what is in the investment for you—and for the person selling you the investment.

KEVIN AND SUZE'S STORY

Recently I was on a plane, sitting next to a wonderful man named Kevin, who was telling me all about his youngest son,

*who had just become a financial planner for a small finan-
cial outfit in their hometown. Kevin went on to tell me how
he had turned over all his and his wife's money to their son,
and how safe they felt, since they knew that they could trust
their son not to take them for commissions. When I asked
what kind of investments he had put them into, I felt sick to
my stomach. All of their money had been put into a variable
annuity. In my opinion, Kevin's son hadn't made the wisest
investment choices for his parents' money. Not even close.*

*I tried to be gentle as I explained to Kevin what was
involved in this investment. But first, I tried even harder to
explain the investment from his son's point of view, because
his son, I knew without a doubt from talking to Kevin, would
never have knowingly done anything in the world to hurt his
parents.*

*You see, when you become a broker, you are learning the
business from the ground up, and what you are learning is
what your brokerage firm teaches you. And what is that? They
are teaching you how to sell investments that make the most
money for the firm but don't always make the most sense for
the investor. All investments presented in a certain way can
seem perfectly suited for a particular investor, even if they
don't in the real world. Most brokers are not bad people. I
know; I worked with many wonderful people at Merrill Lynch
and Prudential-Bache, and by no means is this to suggest that
every broker—and every investment he or she advises—will
work against your best interests. Investing your money wisely
and well will, indeed, make you rich. It is, however, a
reminder that, bottom line, you and you alone are responsible for your money and your investments.*

CHAPTER 18

MAKING SENSE
OF INVESTMENTS

What do we think, say, and do with our money? Too often, we base our thoughts, phrase our words, and take action based on myths that have been passed down from parent to child, financial advisor to client, real estate agent to home buyer, car salesman or insurance agent to consumer; from colleague to colleague, neighbor to neighbor, or friend to friend. The problem is that when financial reality hits—perhaps in our forties, fifties, or even later—these financial myths explode, making us wish that we had been paying closer attention to our own financial reality all along.

Things are going to be different in this century from the way they were in the previous century. Most likely, you are not going to have a benevolent employer to take care of you throughout your working life and provide a pension that protects your retirement as well. What will happen to Social Security, and the promise of that system, is anyone's guess—although the people who are guessing don't, for the most part, have high hopes that the system will protect you in the way you wish it would. If you have an employer now, this employer is probably asking you to help fund your own retirement, or to fund it yourself entirely. If you are self-employed, as more and more of us are today, you already know that you must fund your own retirement. Statistically, you are projected to live longer in this century, too. Tomorrow, in other words, is becoming much more urgent for all of us. And for many of us, tomorrow may be closer than we think.

So the question that presents itself is: How are you going to live tomorrow? It is a question that we all must answer today.

ANNUITIES

This is the great blanket investment to cover you when you're about to retire or are retired, right? Not so fast. Even though this is an investment that many financial advisors love to sell you, and one that lots of people, regardless of age, love to buy, more myths surround it than almost any other investment I know about. In some cases, annuities make sense, and in others they do not, but sooner or later someone will try to peddle you some, so I want you to read this section very carefully. Getting into an investment is easy. Getting out is a different matter entirely.

GRACE'S STORY

When my father died, everything was left to my mom in an insurance policy. He left her $56,000, which was pretty much all she had. So my brother, my mom, and I went to a financial advisor, who put her into an annuity with something called a ten-year-certain period of time. He said this would give her the highest possible monthly income. The advisor was really persuasive on this point, so we went ahead.

Shortly thereafter, my mom started feeling really unwell, and it turned out she had cancer. The doctors couldn't tell exactly how long she had, but they thought it would be a matter of months. My mom died two months later, and of course *she left the money to my brother and me, and again we had to sort everything out. We decided we didn't want the annuity anymore, since we didn't need the monthly income, so we called the advisor again. This time he wasn't so congenial. He said that if we cashed it in, we would get only $38,000. This was just two months later! Our so-called investment had gone down by 32 percent! We found out where some of that money went when my brother read the fine print more carefully. The advisor had made a commission of $3000. But the more upsetting part was why he had put Mom into an investment that lost so much money. We still don't understand it.*

Grace is right not to understand, for investing her mother's money in an annuity makes no sense from her standpoint. From the broker's standpoint, however, it made a great deal of sense. Let's define an annuity, and how various ones work, and then I will explain when they make sense and when they do not.

WHAT IS AN ANNUITY?

An *annuity* (regardless of what kind of an annuity it is) is a contract, or policy, between you as the policyholder and an insurance company, which invests on your behalf. The minimum investment in most annuities is usually around $5000.

WHERE DO YOU BUY AN ANNUITY?

In the same way that a bank sells you an investment called a certificate of deposit, the United States government sells you an investment called a Treasury bill/note/bond, a city sells you an investment called a municipal bond, or a corporation sells you an investment called a corporate bond, an *insurance company* can sell you an investment called an annuity. As with these other investments, you can buy an annuity through a brokerage firm or discount-brokerage firm, and in some cases through banks and mutual fund companies.

COMMISSIONS/FEES

The difference between the annuity and a CD or Treasury note is that, in most cases, annuities carry the highest commission percentage, which is why brokers love them so. Usually the fee that the person "earns" by selling you an annuity is around 5 to 6 percent of the amount of money you invested. In some cases it can be lower, and in others higher still.

OWNER

The person who purchases the contract, or policy, is known as the *owner.* This person can make any changes (of beneficiary, of the amount of the distribution) he wants, anytime he wants—he owns the policy. Two people or more can own a policy as well, as co-owners. If you want, you can also name a successor owner, someone you designate to step in as owner of the policy in the event of your death or, in some cases, an incapacity.

DEATH BENEFIT/ANNUITANT

In order for an annuity to qualify as a legitimate insurance contract—which is what allows it to enjoy certain tax advantages—someone has to be insured. This person is known as the *annuitant.* The annuitant has no power whatsoever over the money, unless, as is often the case, the owner and the annuitant are the same person. There is no additional death benefit involved with an annuity, which makes it very different from other life insurance policies that you may be familiar with.

The annuitant becomes important if one day you choose to *annu-itize* your annuity (see page 300), which means to get a monthly income for life, for the amount of income that you can receive will be determined by the annuitant's age. In other words, if I bought an annuity and named my mom as the annuitant, she would qualify for much more money each month than I would if I named myself the annuitant. This is because the monthly payments are partly based on the annuitant's life expectancy. The older the annuitant, the shorter their life expectancy, the shorter the amount of time the insurance company will have to pay out those monthly payments, and so the larger each payment will be.

THE BENEFICIARY

The *beneficiary* is the person or people to whom you, as owner, will leave the remaining money in the annuity when you die. The owner decides how much to leave each beneficiary. The beneficiary and the annuitant cannot be the same person, but the owner and the beneficiary can. For instance, if I wanted to, I could own the policy, have my mother be the annuitant, and name myself as beneficiary. More commonly, however, the owner and the annuitant are the same person, and a different person(s) is named the beneficiary.

NONQUALIFIED/QUALIFIED ANNUITIES

If you are investing with money that you have already paid taxes on, then you will be buying what's known as a *nonqualified annuity*. If you're investing with pretax money, then you will be buying what's known as a *qualified annuity*. Usually this happens when you buy an annuity within your IRA or retirement plan at work, or when you transfer your 401(k) or 403(b) retirement plans into an annuity.

DEFERRAL OF INCOME TAX

With the exception of an *immediate annuity,* annuities defer
income taxes owed on all interest earnings or gains on your original
deposit until the money is withdrawn either by the annuitant or the
beneficiaries. In essence, they work for you as a tax shelter—that's
perhaps the biggest draw. The true advantage of this is that your tax
money is allowed to stay in the account earning interest, or growing
for you, rather than sitting in the coffers of the IRS. If you're in a qualified annuity, you will owe ordinary income taxes on any and all of
the money when you withdraw it. If you are in a nonqualified annuity, you will generally pay ordinary income taxes only on the earnings
you withdraw above the amount of your original deposit. Nonqualified annuities are taxed on a *LIFO* method, which means *last in, first
out.* So any interest or gains that your fund has earned are considered
to have been put into your account last, and therefore this is the
money that has to come out first—and it is taxable income. Once
you have withdrawn your earnings, then you can withdraw your original deposit without incurring any additional taxes. If you happen to
die with money in a nonqualified annuity, your beneficiaries will also
have to pay income taxes on any earnings when they withdraw
those funds.

SURRENDER PERIOD

Most annuities have what is known as a *surrender period,* or set
amount of time during which you have to keep the majority of your
money in the contract. Most surrender periods last 5 to 10 years. Most
contracts will allow you to withdraw at least 10 percent a year of the
accumulated value of the account without a surrender charge, even
during the surrender period. If you take out more than that 10 percent, you will have to pay a surrender charge on the amount that you
have withdrawn in excess of 10 percent. That surrender charge usu-

ally starts at around 7 percent of the amount of the withdrawal and drops to zero by the time the surrender period is up.

Let's say you are 60 years of age and put $50,000 into a nonqualified annuity that is paying you an annual return of 5 percent for the next 5 years. At the end of the third year, your annuity is worth $57,881. You need $7000. You can withdraw 10 percent of the $57,881, or $5788, without any penalty whatsoever. The additional $1212 you need will cost you approximately $60, based on a surrender charge of 5 percent. Please note that you will owe ordinary income tax on that $7000.

AGE LIMITATIONS

In order to take advantage of the tax deferral, the government slaps on a few restrictions, the primary one being that in most cases you have to be 59½ to withdraw funds—otherwise you face a penalty of 10 percent of the value of what you withdraw above your original deposit, in addition to the surrender charge.

So, in the example above, if you were 40 rather than 60 years old and needed $7000, you would have to pay to the IRS a 10 percent early withdrawal penalty—or $700—plus ordinary income tax on that money.

DIFFERENT KINDS OF ANNUITIES

Today, for all practical purposes, the main kinds of annuities fall under the following categories:

- ◆ Single-premium deferred annuity
- ◆ Immediate annuity
- ◆ Variable annuity
- ◆ Index annuity
- ◆ Tax-sheltered annuity

SINGLE-PREMIUM DEFERRED
ANNUITY (SPDA)

One of the most popular annuities is the *single-premium deferred annuity.* This annuity got its name because it requires the deposit of a *single premium,* or lump sum, in the policy, and all taxes on the earnings are postponed, or *deferred,* until money is withdrawn. An SPDA is a contract between you and an insurance company that guarantees you a specific interest rate for a specified period of time, which can vary from 1 to 7 years. In most cases the longer the guarantee, the lower the interest rate. This type of annuity is most easily compared to a certificate of deposit at a bank. In both cases, you get a guaranteed interest rate for a prescribed period of time. In an annuity you incur surrender charges if you take your money out, and in a CD you'll be faced with a 3- to 6-month interest penalty if you withdraw money before the time period is up. The difference, however, is that with a certificate of deposit, you will be paying taxes each year on the interest you have earned, even if you don't withdraw it. With the SPDA, you will not pay taxes until you withdraw the money.

Let's say you are 60 years of age, are in the 28 percent tax bracket, and have $50,000 to invest. You do not need to live off the interest on this money now, nor do you expect to have to for many years to come. But you want to know this money is safe and sound. Two options available to you are buying a CD or an annuity. Both investments are paying 5 percent interest. Which one should you do? Assuming both investments paid you that 5 percent for the next 10 years, you would have a total of $81,445 with the annuity and only $71,214 with the CD. This is because you had to pay taxes yearly on the interest that the CD was earning, even though you were not using it. This comes into play when you want to start taking income from your investments. You see, $81,445 generates $4072 a year of income at 5 percent, while $71,214 generates only $3560 a year. Don't think that just a few dollars a month during retirement won't matter, for it very well may.

Who Might Want to Buy an SPDA?

People who want to let their money grow risk-free while deferring income taxes, with the main goal being to use the investment to generate income later in life.

SINGLE-PREMIUM IMMEDIATE ANNUITY (SPIA)

An *immediate annuity* is a contract with an insurance company that guarantees the annuitant an immediate fixed income for the rest of his or her life, and, in some cases, continuing—to the beneficiary—for a certain period after the annuitant's death. For this promise, however, you must sign over all the money you have deposited in the annuity to the insurance company with full knowledge that you will never be able to touch it again, apart from receiving the monthly income. There are tax advantages to a policy like this, in that each monthly payment is considered a partial return of principal, so that a portion of your payment is not taxed. In addition to the interest your funds are earning, the return of some of your principal enables the company to pay you a higher monthly income than you could probably get elsewhere on a guaranteed basis.

Annuitization

The amount of income you will receive is based on your age, the current interest rates, and the maximum amount of time you have chosen for the company to pay out that stream of income, even if you were to die. The income options range from the highest monthly amounts of *life only*, to lower amounts known as *life plus five* or *ten years certain*. Here's how they work.

Life Only

If you were to choose *life only,* the company would pay you a certain amount of money every month, starting immediately, for the rest of your life. These fixed payments would continue like clockwork for as long as you are alive, even if you were to live another hundred years. You cannot outlive the income stream of an annuity, no matter what option you chose. If, however, you opted for life only, and you died the month after you had started to receive this income, too bad—the payments stop, and your beneficiaries get nothing. The reason that this option gives you the highest monthly income is that they know that once you die, they're off the hook. These monthly payments are determined by a number of factors, including your age, your medical history, and the current interest rate environment. An insurance company can usually project your life expectancy with a fair amount of accuracy. If they're wrong, and you die sooner than projected, they win bigtime. If you live to your full life expectancy, then they are within the limit of their projected figures. If you live far longer than expected, well, they figure that doesn't happen very often, so it's not a financial disaster for them.

Life Plus Five or Ten

The other option is *life plus five* or *ten years certain.* What this option means is that they will pay you your designated amount every month for as long as you live, but if you die, the annuity will continue to pay your beneficiaries for 5 or 10 years (your choice) from the contract date. In other words, they pay for the duration of your life regardless of how long that may be, but for no less than a period of 5 or 10 years from the starting date if you are not alive. If you were to die the month after you started receiving the monthly income, the company would have to keep paying your beneficiaries the same monthly amount for 5 or 10 years, depending on which time period you chose.

Remember, once you have chosen an option and started receiving your income, the amount is fixed for the rest of your life and/or for the rest of the time your beneficiaries would receive the income as well. Even if interest rates skyrocket, your fixed income is just that, fixed. This annuity contract is one that can most easily be compared with a monthly pension from a corporation.

Who Might Want to Buy an SPIA?

- Those looking for a guaranteed monthly income with some tax benefits
- Those who have no beneficiaries to whom to leave their money
- Those who immediately need a higher income than a straight interest-bearing investment can provide
- Those who want to take advantage of a high-interest-rate environment. The perfect time to have purchased an immediate annuity, for example, with respect to interest rates, would have been in the eighties, when interest rates were high, not in the late nineties, when interest rates were relatively low.

Caution

Please note than an SPIA is my least favorite of all annuities. Purchasing an SPIA, especially in today's low-interest-rate environment, is not something I recommend. If interest rates go up—and as of this writing I do not think they can go down much farther—you are stuck at these low rates for the rest of your life.

The process that we just described, receiving monthly income from an annuity, is known as *annuitization,* or *annuitizing your annuity.* What I want you to know is that you do not have to buy an immediate annuity in order to get monthly income from an annuity. You can do so by simply withdrawing money each and every month, from an SPDA, for instance. This way you are not locked into an interest rate and can have access to your money as well as leave it to your beneficiaries.

If for some reason you want to annuitize your annuity (and I cannot imagine why you would), what you need to know is that, by definition, all annuities can be annuitized at any time, but please be careful, for some companies are better at facilitating the process than others. How much a company will pay you monthly will depend on the actuarial factors and the interest rates that a company uses, so shop around if you ever plan to annuitize. It might make sense to switch from one insurance company to another, especially if the surrender charges have expired. This is formally known as a *1035 exchange.*

VARIABLE ANNUITY

With mutual funds gaining such ground in the recent past, receiving billions of investors' dollars, insurance companies wanted to get into the act. So they created what they called a *variable annuity.* A variable annuity is also a contract with an insurance company for a specific period of time, but when you deposit money into a variable annuity, the money is used most often to purchase various mutual funds within the insurance contract. A variable annuity can have many funds for you to choose from, or just a few, depending on the company. The main draw of a variable annuity is that you enjoy the so-called privilege of tax deferral. Even if you buy and sell a different mutual fund every day, you will not have to pay taxes on your gains until you actually withdraw money from the annuity. This gives the appearance of being a great benefit of the variable annuity, especially if you've had large gains in a mutual fund not held in a variable annuity that you wanted to sell but haven't sold because you'd have to pay so much in taxes. If you had invested in the same mutual fund within a variable annuity, you could sell it and not pay any taxes until you withdrew money. Another so-called advantage is that even if you invested

100 percent of your money in a risky mutual fund within a variable annuity, you are guaranteed never to get back less than you originally deposited or the current value of the account, whichever is greater. In a regular mutual fund, there is no such guarantee. Now, before you go and cash everything in to purchase a variable annuity, I ask you to read ahead to the section called "Annuities: Myth and Reality" (page 307) to learn the downside of variable annuities.

Who Might Want to Buy a Variable Annuity?

♦ Someone who likes to buy and sell mutual funds often
♦ Someone who is in a very high tax bracket now but plans to be in a much lower tax bracket at retirement

INDEX ANNUITY

In their struggle to keep up with mutual funds, the insurance industry introduced another kind of annuity in the mid-nineties, the *index annuity*. This new product was to compete with the wildly popular index funds, mutual funds that tracked the indexes, such as the Standard & Poor's 500 index. The Standard & Poor's 500 index is made up of five hundred stocks that are actually more a gauge of what the entire stock market is doing than the traditional Dow Jones Industrial Average that we hear about every day. The reason this is true is that the Dow Jones average is calculated from only thirty stocks, not as realistic an overview as five hundred stocks provide. To participate in this index trend, insurance companies created the index annuity. Even I have to admit that when this investment first came out I liked the concept a lot—for the right investors. Today index annuities are not as attractive as they once were but are still worth knowing about.

Here's how they work. Like all annuities, an index annuity is a contract with an insurance company for a specific period of time. The surrender period on an index annuity is usually about 7 to 10 years. The index annuity tracks an index such as the Standard & Poor's 500 index, and your return on your money will usually be a percentage of what that particular index did for your corresponding investment year. For instance, let's say your index annuity happens to track the S&P 500 index. If the S&P 500 index goes up, you would get a set percentage up to a maximum of what the yearly return of the index was for that year. In this case, let's say that your index annuity will give you 50 percent of what the S&P index returned, up to a maximum of 10 percent. You invest $20,000 on March 15. By March 15 of the next year, the S&P index has increased 30 percent. According to the terms of your annuity, they have to give you 50 percent of that increase, up to a maximum of 10 percent. Since 50 percent of 30 percent is 15 percent, which is 5 percent higher than the preset yearly maximum of 10 percent, you will get credited with 10 percent of your original deposit, or in this case $2000. If the S&P index had gone up only 15 percent for the year, you would be entitled to 7.5 percent on your investment (.5 multiplied by 15 percent equals 7.5 percent).

Why, you might ask, do you get only a percentage of what the index returns? Wouldn't it be better simply to invest in a straight index fund and get 100 percent of the return? For some people, it would be better, but for others who do not want to take any risks at all, this index annuity might be a better option. Here's why. When you invest in a regular index fund, you claim 100 percent of the upside—and 100 percent of any downward swerves as well. For instance, let's say you invested $20,000 in a good no-load S&P index fund. The first year it went up 10 percent, bringing your investment up to $22,000. The next year it went down 20 percent, leaving you with only $17,600, or $2400 less than what you started with. That may make you too nervous. In many index annuities, you do not participate in any downside risk. To follow the same example, if you invested $20,000 in a particular index annuity, and the market went up 10 percent, you would end up with $21,000 for that year (50 percent of 10 percent is 5 percent, or $1000). Within this particular index annuity, your money can only go up; it cannot go down. So the next year, when the market went down 20 percent, you would not participate in that downside activity, and you would still have $21,000 in your account. That's why the index annuity does not credit you with 100 percent of the return. It is set in reserve to protect you from the downside. Consider, too, one last safety feature. If you invest in an index annuity and the market goes down every single year, it won't matter to you. Because in an index annuity, the insurance company usually guarantees that after your surrender period is over, you will get at least 110 percent of what you originally put in. If you put in $20,000, the worst-case scenario would leave you, after 7 years, with $22,000, or about a 1.4 percent minimum guaranteed yearly return on your investment no matter what happens in the market.

Bottom line: If you are willing to give up some upside potential, you can also protect yourself totally against downside risk with an index annuity.

Who Should Invest in an Index Annuity?

♦ Anyone who wants to invest in the market but is afraid of losing money

TAX-SHELTERED ANNUITY (TSA)

Last but not least is the *tax-sheltered annuity* that many schoolteachers and hospital workers are offered in their retirement plan. The TSA really falls more into the category of retirement plan, since money is invested in a TSA on a monthly basis, unlike other annuities, where the money is deposited in a lump sum. Also, with a TSA, all the money is qualified money, or money that has not yet had the taxes paid on it. For our purposes, the TSA is, in most cases, a fine investment. If you have a TSA in your retirement account, just make sure that the funds are performing in a satisfactory way.

ANNUITIES: MYTH AND REALITY

Now it's time to learn the pitfalls and disadvantages of annuities.

MYTH: It's great to own annuities within a retirement account.

REALITY: What you need to know is that even though there are exceptions, holding an annuity within a retirement account is a concept I have never agreed with. With the exception of the Roth IRA and the nondeductible IRA, retirement plans—such as the traditional IRA; 401(k), 403(b), SEP-IRA, KEOGHs, SIMPLEs—are tax-sheltered vehicles funded with pretax dollars. In other words, you fund these plans with pretax dollars, and taxes on these funds, along with the growth of these funds, are deferred until the money is actually withdrawn.

Annuities, remember, can be funded with posttax *or* pretax dollars. So let's say that you have some money sitting in your money market account that you want to shelter from further taxes. One way to do it would be to deposit your money into an annuity. Until you withdraw it, all your growth and interest is sheltered. In other words, an annuity offers you the same tax-deferring benefits as a retirement account. So you tell me: What sense does it make to hold a tax-shelter vehicle like an annuity in an already tax-sheltered account? Very little sense.

Are there exceptions? Yes. Apart from a TSA, the only two reasons to purchase an annuity in a retirement plan are these:

1. You are under the age of 59½, you need access to the funds in your traditional IRA, and you do not want to pay the 10 percent penalty. By purchasing an annuity within your traditional IRA, there is a way that you can get around that 10 percent penalty. (This process is explained at length in *The 9 Steps to Financial Freedom.*)
2. You are approaching retirement age and you want to invest in the market but are afraid of losing money. You are willing

to take a smaller profit if you are guaranteed never to lose a penny. Since the index annuity accomplishes this goal, even if it is within your IRA, it can still make sense.

Otherwise, let's examine why an annuity held in a retirement account isn't a sound investment. We'll use my old favorite, the variable annuity, as an example to start with. As we noted above, a variable annuity is, by definition, nothing more than a bunch of mutual funds held by an insurance company so that you can enjoy tax deferral on the growth of your money, whether it's held in a retirement account or not. For the privilege of having your taxes deferred, the insurance company charges you many fees, as well as the potential surrender charge. These charges come on top of the management fees and other expenses that each mutual fund charges. In most cases, the fees for the insurance companies alone will amount to about 1.5 to 2 percent each year, right out of your pocket. Now, whether this makes sense even outside a retirement account is something that you have to decide, but within a retirement account, if you ask me, this is way too hefty a price to pay for a privilege that is inherent in your retirement account. Remember, all retirement accounts are tax-deferred, regardless of where your money in the account is invested.

Let's look at this a little more closely. Let's say that you have two IRAs, with $25,000 in each. One is invested in a variable annuity, where you divided all your money equally among five mutual funds. The other $25,000 is in an IRA invested directly in the same five mutual funds, but not in a variable annuity. Let's say over the next 15 years the mutual funds averaged a yearly return of 8.5 percent. How much do you have in each IRA account after those 15 years?

In the first one, invested with the variable annuity, you have $68,976, whereas in the second one, invested directly into those same mutual funds, you have $84,994. That is $16,018 more. Why? The variable annuity charges about 1.5 percent a year in fees that you do not have to pay if you invest in the mutual funds directly.

Furthermore, a variable annuity has surrender charges, so even if you want to move your money out of the variable annuity and into those mutual funds directly, it will cost you to do so for those first 7 to 10 years.

Another consideration is that some annuities carry what is known as a *state premium tax*. This tax varies from state to state, but it is levied on the amount you originally deposited into the annuity and must be paid either when you surrender the annuity or when you annuitize the annuity. The tax can vary from .25 percent if the money was in a qualified plan such as an IRA, all the way up to 2.5 percent if it was in an annuity outside of a retirement plan. Unfortunately, this tax is seldom disclosed before one buys an annuity. In fact, most agents who sell annuities do not even know of its existence. But it exists, and in most cases it is another unnecessary fee that cuts into your overall return.

Below is a quick comparison showing you how a variable annuity on its own duplicates many of the characteristics of a traditional IRA account.

	Traditional IRA	Variable Annuity Within an IRA
Tax deferral	yes	yes
Pre-age-59½ tax penalty	yes	yes
Age 70½ mandatory withdrawal	yes	yes
Surrender charges	no	yes
State premium tax	no	yes
Mortality charges	no	yes

(Note: This chart is not applicable to annuities held in Roth IRAs.)

MYTH: A variable annuity not in an IRA is a great way to invest in the market and not have to worry about taxes every time you buy or sell.

REALITY: It will not save you taxes in the long run, which defeats the purpose for most people who buy annuities. With a variable annuity, it is true that every time you buy or sell a mutual fund, you do not pay taxes. It is also true that if the mutual funds you are invested in through the variable annuity pay a distribution at the end of the year (known as a capital gains distribution), you do not pay taxes on those distributions. However, this is where the advantages end and the disadvantages begin.

In a variable annuity, you pay taxes when you withdraw your money. At what rate? Your withdrawal is subject to ordinary income taxes. If you had held your money in a mutual fund for 12 months or more, you would have to pay only the capital gains rate, and in some cases, that rate could be quite low. By purchasing a variable annuity, you give up the right to pay capital gains tax rates, as you opt for ordinary income tax rates instead.

Okay, you think, that's no big deal. Maybe you plan to leave the money to your kids and never take it out of the annuity, so you won't have to worry about this tax problem. But you've now passed this tax problem down to your kids, because when they take the money out of the variable annuity, they will have to pay income taxes on any of the growth of your funds, plus the additional fees and the state premium tax cutting into your return. If you had simply purchased good mutual funds not in a variable annuity and left them to your kids via your will or trust, they would receive what is called a *step-up in cost basis* on the value of those funds, based on their worth the day you died. If they then sold those funds after they inherited them and before there was a further upward swing, they would not owe a penny in income taxes.

Here's an example. You put $25,000 into a variable annuity, and by the time you die, your money has grown to $125,000. Your kids inherit the money and withdraw it. They will owe income taxes on the $100,000 in earnings, along with any state premium taxes, if applicable.

Let's say you put that same $25,000 into some great tax-efficient mutual funds, and when you die, your kids inherit the money and withdraw it. If it was worth $125,000 on that day, then that amount is their new cost basis for tax purposes. If they were to turn around and sell this investment for $125,000, since there was no gain, they would not owe one penny in income taxes. This step-up in cost basis applies to inherited investments such as mutual funds, real estate, or stocks—but not annuities, traditional IRAs, or retirement plans.

If you're thinking about buying a variable annuity because end-of-year taxes are a concern and you do not want to get hit with capital gains distributions from mutual funds, think again. You could instead buy mutual funds that are tax-efficient, which means they do not make end-of-the-year capital gains distributions. You could also buy investments that duplicate certain index mutual funds, known as *SPDR*s (*"spiders"*), that are sold on the American Stock Exchange, where again, you won't run into end-of-the-year distributions. Or you could buy individual stocks and avoid the problem that way.

As for postponing taxes on your buying and selling of mutual funds—another reason you might be considering a variable annuity—the reality is that most people tend to hold on to their mutual funds, stocks, and so on for long periods of time. Very few of us buy and sell very often. Most of us buy and hold, and buy more and hold. So for most of us, the tax implications are not so dire. If you do sell and you have held your investment for at least a year, the most you are going to pay is the capital gains tax rate, which is 20 percent. Not so bad. Remember, however, when you take your money out of a variable annuity you are going to pay ordinary income taxes on the amount that you withdraw. But remember also that with regular mutual funds, you will owe taxes only if you sell. Outside of possible end-of-year distributions, you will not pay taxes if you do not sell the mutual fund. It is the same as owning a home. Maybe you purchased the home for $100,000 and now it is worth $300,000. You do not owe a penny in income tax if you don't sell that house, no matter how much it appreciates. Thus, if you are not, most likely, going to owe taxes for quite a while, and when you do, it will probably be at the capital gains rate versus ordinary income tax rates for the variable annuity, then just what is the variable annuity sheltering you from?

All for the desire not to pay taxes, which you very likely wouldn't have had to pay anyway, you lock up your money in a variable annuity where you cannot access it without surrender charges for a number of years—does this make sense to you? What's more, if you are under age 59½ and need to withdraw all or some of your earnings, you will pay a 10 percent penalty tax to the IRS. Also, when you do close out the account for whatever reason, in some states a state premium tax of about 2 percent of your original deposit will also be owed. Does this make sense? No, it does not.

MYTH: It is impossible to lose money in a variable annuity.

REALITY: That depends. Remember that an annuity shelters your money from immediate taxation, because it is considered an insurance product. For it to qualify as such, there has to be someone who is insured—the annuitant. Most variable annuities carry what is called a *mortality fee,* which usually runs you 1.3 percent a year, or $13 for every $1000 that you invest. This mortality fee supposedly protects you against losing any of your money. You see, the way a variable annuity works is that when the annuitant dies, the owner will get back at least the amount of the original deposit or the account value at the time of death, whichever is greater; this is what this fee covers. So in theory you do not get back less than you put in. However, in most cases the owner and the annuitant are the same person. This means that while you are alive if you need this money or want to withdraw it completely and close the account, and your balance at the time happens to be less than what you originally deposited, guess what? You are out of luck, and yes, you will have lost money. The only way you are guaranteed to get back at least 100 percent of what you deposited is when the annuitant dies. If you are the annuitant, a lot of good this guarantee—for which you have been paying dearly—will do you. It could, however, help your family out after you have gone. If, for example, you withdrew money from the variable annuity at a time when you had less in it than you originally deposited, but you didn't close the account completely, upon your death, if you are the annuitant, your beneficiaries would at least get the amount that would have brought you back to even.

Let's illustrate this with an example. You deposit $25,000 into a variable annuity. You are the owner and the annuitant. Sometime later, you need this money. When you go to cash it, the account is worth only $19,000. You take out $18,000, leaving $1000 in the annuity. Two weeks later, you die. Your beneficiaries will get $7000. Remember, you have been paying that mortality fee of 1.3 percent a year to guarantee that on your death your beneficiaries get 100 percent of your original deposit or whatever the account is currently worth, whichever is greater. In this case, your original deposit of $25,000 is higher. Since you withdrew $18,000, the insurance company upon your death owes your beneficiaries that additional $7000 ($25,000 minus $18,000 equals $7000).

Did this help you while you were alive? No. Did you get to deduct the loss from your taxes or use it to offset a gain? No. And what if you hadn't died right away? How long did that extra money have to sit in the account, possibly not doing so well? Perhaps for a long, long time, even as the extra charges and fees continued to accrue. Is that extra mortality charge worth it to protect what you have? I don't think so.

UNDOING THE POSSIBLE DAMAGE

If you already have variable annuities and now decide that this isn't what you want, what do you do?

1. If the annuity is inside a retirement account: Unless you have a variable annuity that is an outstanding performer, as soon as the surrender charges expire, I most likely would say to cash them in and buy instead into some solid, well-rated, no-load mutual funds. If your returns have been horrible, even if the surrender charge is still in force, you might want to take the hit in order to get a better return. Another possibility, if the surrender charge is still in effect, is simply to withdraw the 10 percent you are allowed to take out without the surrender penalty, and transfer those funds into a good, no-load mutual fund. You can do that every year until the surrender charges are up. Since the money is already sheltered within a retirement plan, you will not have to worry about tax implications.

It is entirely probable that you can buy the same funds that you are currently invested in with the variable annuity. Discount brokerage firms like Charles Schwab offer many mutual funds for you to choose from, so you could probably duplicate what you had in your annuity if you wanted without much difficulty at all. Remember, the fees that the mutual funds charge for managing the account will always be the same, whether you are in or outside of a variable annuity. It is the fees from the insurance company that you will be getting rid of—and rightfully so.

2. If the annuity is outside of your retirement plan: Everything noted in point 1 applies here, but there are additional rules to take into consideration before you do anything, such as those regarding penalties for withdrawals prior to the age of 59½, taxation on the money when withdrawn, as well as the state premium tax (if applicable) if you were to surrender the account altogether. Because all these rules—the main reasons why I do not like variable annuities to begin with—have to be taken into account, I would advise you please to see a fee-based financial planner who has nothing to gain from giving you honest advice so that you can give them the exact specifics of your situation. Everything from your age, the terms of the annuity you purchased, your tax bracket, how long you have owned it, to your financial goals and so on will determine the actions, if any, that should be taken with your particular contract.

ANNUITIES: WHEN TO SAY YES

Is there ever a time when an annuity does make sense?

Yes. We have seen when TSAs and sometimes index annuities make sense, but there is also one other circumstance. If your goal is to have income during retirement years and you do not want to take *any risk* with this money, and you want to avoid paying taxes now, but you are still not in a high enough tax bracket for municipal bonds to make sense, and last, you feel that you will be in an even lower tax bracket when you retire, then I do have to say that a single-premium deferred annuity is great regardless of your age.

Let's follow this scenario. At age 50, you deposit $25,000 into an SPDA, and over the next 15 years it pays you an average of 5 percent on your money. Tax-deferred, your money will grow to $51,973. Now you are 65 and need income. Simply start taking the interest from the $51,973. At a 5 percent interest rate, that would be $2599 a year of income to you on which you would owe taxes.

If instead you had kept that money in a bank's certificate of deposit, and you were in the 15 percent tax bracket, over the same 15 years, you would have accumulated only $46,674.62. The income at 5 percent interest would be only $2334, on which you would also owe taxes.

If you put your money in an SPDA, and it performed as it did in our example, this would mean $265 a year more in income to you than if you had invested in the CD. Remember, every penny counts, especially during your retirement years. When you take into account how much money you really did invest and the real rate of return of your money earned over the long haul, the difference could be significant.

BOTTOM LINE ON ANNUITIES

As we've seen, there is much to know about this one investment that so often is presented to us as if we would never want to invest our money anywhere else. There are reasons why they sometimes make sense, but there are many more reasons why they do not. Please be careful; even though this is an investment that most likely will not devastate you, it is not, in most cases, an investment that will give you the biggest bang for your buck. When in doubt, get a second or a third opinion. Make sure the people you are getting the second or third opinion from know at the outset that they will not be selling you anything, that you are just asking for advice. Remove any sales motivation from the transaction. And take the time to look around to see whether you can do better.

If you already own an annuity, please don't react to the information in this chapter in a panic. Your particular situation might be precisely right for owning one, or your particular annuity might be performing fabulously. I myself still have clients invested in annuities—inside and outside of their retirement accounts, because it makes perfect sense for them. Don't automatically assume you're in a terrible investment until you've thoroughly checked it out. Rather, feel confident that you now have the information to do so.

CHAPTER 19

SEEKING SAFETY IN BONDS

We've heard the phrase all our lives: *stocks and bonds*. Yet with the stock market fever and low interest rates of the past decade, the subject of bonds has receded. Perhaps it's not as sexy as the idea of the dizzying stock market heights and lows, but as you have seen, what goes up can also come down. The years 2000 and 2001 were a sobering reminder of this principle. No doubt we'll see its like again.

If you're in your twenties and thirties, I urge you to invest in the market for growth and to use as your approach the method known as dollar cost averaging. This subject is covered at length in *The 9 Steps to Financial Freedom*, *The Road to Wealth,* and elsewhere, and you can read any of the financial magazines every month to find really great, highly rated, no-load mutual funds in which to invest. Other excellent resources can be found at www.suzeorman.com. The sooner you start, the richer you will be, even by investing sums as small as twenty-five dollars a month.

If you're older and playing catch-up, take your emotional pulse to see how squeamish the idea of risk makes you. You may want to chance the market with some of your money; you may not. But I want you to read about bonds in any case, because one day slow and steady income and stability is what you want to feel safest and most secure. And when you feel safe, you are powerful.

If you're a baby boomer in, say, your mid-forties, or older, I also want you to read the pages that follow. As you get closer to retirement, many of you will want to know increasingly not only that your money is safe but also that it will provide you with income you can count on. It may be, too, that your money has grown so much in the market that you want to pull out some of those gains, for safekeeping. Investing in bonds has the potential to fulfill all these needs.

What, exactly, are bonds? Which bonds are best? Is it better to invest in individual bonds or bond funds? Knowing the answers to these questions might help you to address some serious questions about your future.

HOW BONDS WORK

A bond falls under a category of investments known as *debt investments.* This is because a bond is created when a corporation, municipality, the U.S. government, or an agency of the government is in need of some money and is willing to go into debt to borrow that money to meet its needs. In many cases, it borrows money from people like you or me. When you lend any of these entities your money, you have purchased what is known as a *bond.* For that bond, the issuer will give you a guaranteed fixed interest rate for a fixed period of time. Depending on the bond, that interest is paid to you monthly, quarterly, semi-annually, or annually. At the end of the time period, or on the maturity date of the bond, the issuer will return to you the original amount of money that you gave to them.

There are many different kinds of bonds, but for our purposes, we'll focus on three primary kinds: *corporate, municipal,* and *Treasury.* There are variations on these themes, but they're all offshoots of these three categories of bonds.

CORPORATE BONDS

When you take out a bond with a corporation, it is known as a *corporate bond*.

TAXATION: Corporate bonds are taxable on the state and federal levels.

YIELD: The yield is usually a little higher with corporate bonds than with other types of bonds, for in theory there is more risk of default with a private entity such as a corporation than with government issuers. However, if you pick a good, solid corporation highly rated by Standard & Poor's or Moody's, it might be worth the supposed extra risk.

MATURITY: A corporate bond can vary in length from 5 to 30 or even 100 years.

MUNICIPAL BONDS

When you take out a bond with a state, county, or local agency, it is known as a *municipal bond*.

TAXATION: Generally, all municipal bonds are tax-free on the federal income tax level. In order to avoid state income tax as well, you have to purchase a municipal bond from your state. For instance, if you live in California and you do not want to have to pay state or federal taxes on the interest you earn, then you would purchase a California municipal bond. If, however, you live in California and purchase a New York municipal bond, you would not have to pay taxes to the federal government on the interest, but you would owe the state of California.

YIELD: The yield is usually lower here than with other kinds of bonds, because the yield is federal tax-free. To figure out whether it's better to buy a tax-free bond or a taxable bond, given your particular tax bracket, divide the tax-free yield by the difference between your tax bracket and 100 percent. That will give you the equivalent taxable yield.

For example, if your tax bracket is 28 percent, and you are thinking about buying a municipal bond with a coupon rate (interest rate) of 4 percent, first subtract .28 from 1.00, which gives you .72. Then divide the interest rate of the bond that you are considering by .72 and that will give you the equivalent taxable yield. So 4 divided by .72 equals 5.5 percent.

If you can get a taxable bond that gives you a higher yield than 5.5 percent as opposed to a tax-free yield of 4 percent, then in this case you should buy a taxable bond.

MATURITY: Municipal bonds can vary in length from 5 to 30 years.

Municipal Bond Insurance

If you are willing to take about a quarter of a percent lower on your interest rate, then you could buy what is called *municipal bond insurance*. This insurance guarantees that you will get back your principal, no matter what. Certain bonds come with this insurance, while others do not. If you feel you'd like to have the insurance, look for a bond that offers it. The three top companies offering municipal bond insurance are the MBIA (Municipal Bond Insurance Association), AMBAC (American Municipal Bond Assurance Corporation), and FSA (Financial Security Assurance). If your broker tells you an insurer other than these three is insuring the bond on offer, be wary. These three companies are the ones to trust.

TREASURY BONDS

When you take out a bond with the government, it is known as a *Treasury bond*.

TAXATION: When you buy a Treasury, it is exempt from taxes on the state and local level. You will have to pay federal income taxes, however. This is important to keep in mind, for a Treasury paying 6 percent will give you more income after taxes than a CD paying 6 percent if you live in a state where you pay state income taxes.

YIELD: The yield on a Treasury bond is usually the lowest of all bonds with comparable maturities, for they are the safest. The Treasury bond is 100 percent guaranteed by the United States government, which means they can do one of two things if they have trouble paying you back. They can print money, or they can raise taxes. For this kind of safety you get just a little lower interest rate.

MATURITY: Treasuries of different maturities are known by different names.

♦ A Treasury *bill* is usually 90 days to 12 months in length.
♦ A Treasury *note* is usually 1 to 10 years in length.
♦ A Treasury *bond* is usually 10 to 30 years in length.

BOND PRICING

Most bonds (except for some Treasuries, such as bills and series EE, which can start as low as $50; see page 350) are issued in $1000 denominations. In bond talk, this $1000 denomination is called *par value.* Par value is always $1000. So if you buy 10 bonds when they are issued, at par, or $1000 each, you will have bought $10,000 worth of bonds. When you look at the price of a bond, it will be quoted in hundreds. In other words, you may see that a bond is trading at $102 and wonder what that means. Just add a zero to the number, and it will tell you that the bond is actually worth $1020, or $20 above par.

Because they have such short maturities, Treasury bills (one year and under) do not pay interest every 6 months and are not priced at par, or $1000 each. Nevertheless, when your T-bill matures, it will mature at par. What this means is that T-bills are sold at what is known as a discount from par and do not pay interest before maturity. The difference between the purchase price of the bill and the amount that is paid at maturity (par), or when the bill is sold prior to maturity, is the interest earned on the bill. When you buy a Treasury bill, it might cost you $4800, and when it matures 9 months later, you might get back $5000. That $200 would be considered your interest. By the way, the year in which you receive your money back with a T-bill is the year that you will owe taxes on that money. So if you bought a T-bill in 2001 and it did not mature until the year 2002, you would not owe taxes on that $200 until the year 2002. When people buy large amounts of Treasury bills they take this into consideration, because it may make a big difference with respect to taxes.

COUPON RATE

All bonds (except some inflation-adjusted bonds offered by the Treasury and also savings bonds) have a fixed interest rate attached to them, known as a *coupon rate*. When a bond is first issued, for example, it might be issued with an interest rate, or coupon rate, of 6 percent. This would mean that if you bought the bond at par, or at $1000, then you would get $60 of interest each year on every bond that you bought ($1000 multiplied by .06 equals $60). If you had bought 10 bonds you would get interest of $600 (10 multiplied by $60) a year on your $10,000 investment.

MATURITY DATE

All bonds are assigned a *maturity date* when issued. The maturity date is the time when the issuer returns the money they owe to investors who are holding bonds with that particular maturity date. For instance, let's say you're offered a $1000 bond with a maturity date of June 1, 2011. This means that it will mature for par, or $1000, on that date. Let's say that you bought 10 bonds at par in June 2001, for a total investment of $10,000, with a coupon rate of 6 percent, paying every 6 months—that's $600 a year in interest.

This would mean that you would get $300 in interest on this bond every 6 months for 10 years. If you never sold it, in June of 2011 this bond would mature and you would get back your $10,000.

The month in which the bond matures is also the month from which your interest payments are dated. So if the bond is maturing in June 2011, you will receive your interest payments every June and December. Many bonds make interest payments every 6 months, but note that others operate on different payment schedules.

WHY DO DIFFERENT BONDS OFFER DIFFERENT INTEREST RATES?

The interest rate that an issuing company will offer is dependent on three things:

- The current interest rate environment
- The safety of the issuer
- The length of the bond (bond maturity)

The Current Interest Rate Environment

When you lend someone money, you want to get the highest and safest interest rate available. The issuer knows this, and knows, too, that they must offer you an interest rate that is competitive with currently available interest rates. If you could get 7 percent on a safe bond with issuer ABC, there would be no reason in the world that you would buy a bond from an identically safe issuer at 6 percent.

The Safety of the Issuer

The entity issuing the bond also knows that you, the investor, want to make sure that your money is safe. You see, when you invest in a bond, the concern is not only how much interest it's going to pay you. You also want the assurance that you'll get your money back when the bond matures. If you remember, this was an important factor some years ago with the California Orange County bonds that many people invested in. They were given a good interest rate, but the bonds defaulted, which meant investors did not get their principal back. Thus if you had a choice between two bonds, both offering 6 percent, both maturing in 10 years, but one issuer held the risk of defaulting and the other was a totally safe company with virtually no chance of defaulting, hands down you would choose the safe company. So when an issuer is not as financially sound as they should be, they then have to offer you a higher interest rate than the totally safe issuers, to entice you to take the risk. If a safe issuer is offering 6 percent, maybe a slightly more speculative issuer might be offering 6.5 percent. The more speculative the issuer, the higher the interest rate. The most speculative bonds are those known as *junk bonds,* or these days, they're also known as *high yield bonds.*

Rating Services

The best way to gauge the quality of the bonds you're considering is to consult two independent rating services: Standard & Poor's and Moody's. Both companies use a rating system based on the first three letters of the alphabet.

Standard & Poor's

Their basic ratings go from the highest quality to the lowest:

AAA, AA+, AA, AA-, A+, A, A-, BBB+, BBB, BBB-, BB+, BB, BB-, B+, B, B-, CCC, D

Moody's

Their basic ratings go from the highest quality to the lowest:

Aaa, Aa1, Aa2, Aa3, A1, A2, A3, Baa1, Baa2, Baa3, Ba1, Ba2, Ba3, B1, B2, B3, Caa, Ca, C

Please note: If you are investing in bonds for safety and income, consider only bonds that have a rating of A or above; otherwise, even though you might find a higher interest rate, you could be risking your principal. In my opinion, you should only invest in AAA, AA, or A grade bonds.

Most corporate and municipal bonds are rated, and it is important that you check these ratings. Treasuries are guaranteed by the taxing authority of the government and therefore are considered the safest bonds there are.

Your broker also can give you the ratings of bonds.

Bond Maturity

The last element that determines the interest rate is the *maturity* of the bond. The theory is that the longer the issuer is asking you to tie up your money, the more they should be willing to pay for it. However, this does not always hold true.

If the bond is issued at a time when interest rates are higher, and are projected to go down in the future, the issuer may offer higher rates for shorter maturities compared to ones they might offer for longer maturities. That's why it's important to check the coupon rate, or the yield, of bonds offered at all different maturities, for it may not pay to tie up your money for longer periods of time. For instance, if a 10-year bond is paying 5 percent and a 30-year bond is paying 5.1 percent, it's probably not worth tying up your money for 30 years, unless you really believe that interest rates are going to be considerably lower than 5 percent in 10 years.

RISK

Many people who invest in bonds do so because they want the income from the bond in order to meet their daily living expenses. The maturity of a bond is very important, for if when the bond matures the current interest rate is a lot lower than it was when you bought the bond, then when you go to buy another bond, your coupon will be less—and so will your income. This can hurt you tremendously when you are on a fixed income and you expect your income to be just that: fixed.

BARRETT'S STORY

I retired in 1990, with my Social Security and $100,000—I had hoped to have more and work longer, but it just didn't turn out that way. But our house is paid off, and we figured we'd be okay. We put the $100,000 in bonds that paid 9 percent and matured in ten years. I remember at the time that we talked about getting twenty- or thirty-year bonds, but we decided against it. As it was, back then, ten years seemed like such a long time. So for those ten years we got $9000 a year in income from our bonds, and we managed fine. They matured in 2000, and we got our $100,000 back. Boy, were we sorry then that we hadn't bought longer-maturity bonds. The best we could do with the interest rates for new bonds was to earn around 5 percent, and the maturity didn't make any difference at all. This meant that the most we were able to get was about $5000 a year. We lost $4000 a year in income, which, we figured, was about $333 a month. And have we ever felt the difference. We're getting by, but we feel the pinch every day.

If Barrett had simply purchased a longer-term maturity bond, he and his wife would not now be facing this problem. That is not to say that he would never face it, for the situation might still be the same twenty years from now—but that is still twenty years longer at $9000 a year of income over what they have now. This kind of situation is even harder to face when you take inflation into the picture. Not only has his actual income decreased but so has the buying power of the money he still has. Even at just a 1.76 percent inflation rate over 10 years, it would take $10,584 in 2001 to buy what $9000 did in 1991. To cut out another $4000 on top of it, well, that's really tough.

In short, when interest rates are low and projected to go up, it is better to buy shorter-term maturities (generally 5 years and under) over longer-term maturities (10 years and longer). When interest rates are high and projected to go down, the longer-term maturities are a far better deal than shorter-term ones.

BEWARE THE CALL FEATURE

Most issuers of bonds protect themselves with what is known as a *call feature.* This allows the issuer actually to give you your money back before the maturity date of the bond, or, in the lingo, to *call in the bond.* The call feature will tell you at what point the bond can be called in and how much the issuer has to pay you if they do call in the bond. The reason an issuer will do this is that if interest rates come down after they issue a bond, it will cut their losses to call that particular bond in, pay off all the investors, and then issue a new bond at a lower interest rate. For the investor, though, this call feature is not such a good thing.

Let's say that you bought a 30-year bond that was issued in 1991 with a coupon of 9 percent. And let's say that this bond had a call feature specifying that after the year 2002, the bond could be called in at a price of $1020 a bond. Remember, you paid par, or $1000, for the bond when you bought it. This issuer could in effect take the bond back by paying you $1020.

Beware of call features when you buy a bond, because you do not want to have to give up a good interest rate without at least knowing about it. Municipal bonds and corporate bonds can have a call feature, although Treasuries are seldom issued with call features. An exception, however, is that some Treasury bonds issued before 1985 are subject to call by the Treasury Department before their final maturity. Government agency bonds (Ginnie Maes, Freddie Macs, etc.) all are callable.

PROTECTING YOURSELF: LADDERING

It is very difficult to predict the direction interest rates will take over the long run, especially when they are low, inflation is low, and the economy is good—the climate of the late nineties, for example. Even so, things can change at any time, so you must be prepared for any eventuality. The best way to do this in the bond market is through a technique called *laddering* your maturities.

Let's say that you have $100,000 to invest in bonds in order to generate an income for yourself. Rather than taking the entire $100,000 and buying bonds that mature at the same time, let's say, in 5 years, you would instead buy a $20,000 bond that matures in 1 year, a $20,000 bond that matures in 2 years, a $20,000 bond that matures in 3 years, a $20,000 bond that matures in 4 years, and a $20,000 bond that matures in 5 years. This way, you would have $20,000 coming due every year for the next 5 years. If interest rates start to go up, you simply replace the bond that matures with a bond with a higher interest rate. If interest rates stay the same, you have nothing to lose. If interest rates start to go down, well, you still have some money that is invested for a few years at the better rate.

All successful fixed-income money managers use this laddering technique. By using this technique you really are protected, no matter what happens with interest rates. You win either way.

THE SECONDARY BOND MARKET

Even though all bonds have maturity dates, this does not mean that you have to hold on to a bond until that time; you can sell it before the maturity date. This is because after a bond is issued it can trade on the bond market, assuming there's a demand for it. When you sell your bond, you might get more or less than your purchase price of par, or $1000. The only time that your original investment is scheduled to be paid back to you in full is when the bond matures. But there are times that you can sell your bond for even more than you paid for it.

The price of a bond is directly proportional to the rise and fall of interest rates. It's like a seesaw: When interest rates go up, the price of fixed-income investments goes down, and when interest rates go down, the price of fixed-income investments goes up. A bond is considered not only a debt instrument but also a fixed-income investment. This means that the income that the bond pays can never change throughout the life of the bond. The only thing that can fluctuate is the price of the bond itself.

Let me explain how it works. Let's say you bought a bond for $1000, one that was paying 6 percent, or $60 a year in interest. Now let's say that two years later, interest rates for new bonds are 8 percent, and you want to sell your bond. Who in the world will buy your bond from you for $1000 when all it is paying is 6 percent and they can get for the same price a new bond that pays them 8 percent? No one. So since the $60 a year is fixed, the price of the bond has to come down to a level that makes that $60 a year equal in percentage to the price of a new bond. In this case it would have to come down to about $750. You see, if you were to buy a bond for $750 that paid $60 a year in interest, that would be 8 percent on your money. So you would have no problem buying that bond. The reverse is also true. If interest rates were to go down to 5 percent in the economy and you wanted to sell your bond, the price of the bond would go up so that those who buy it would average an interest rate of only 5 percent. In this case, the bond would have to go up in price to about $1200, which at 5 percent interest would pay $60 annually.

This example was merely for illustration purposes, for in reality a change in the price of a bond will always depend on three criteria: the quality of the bond, the coupon rate, and the years remaining till it matures. The longer the maturity and the lower the quality of the bond, the more a bond will move up or down in price. The closer to the maturity date and the higher the rating or quality of the bond, the less movement there will be when interest rates change.

CURRENT YIELD

In addition to knowing the coupon rate, it is also important to calculate your *current yield* at the time of purchase. Because you can buy a bond in the secondary bond market for more or less than par, or $1000 a bond in our example, what that bond will yield you will be different than what it would yield someone who bought it when it was first issued. Think about it. If you buy a bond when it is issued for $1000, and the bond pays a coupon rate of 6 percent, or $60 a year, then your coupon rate of 6 percent and your current yield are the same. If instead you buy your bond in the bond market for $1100, that bond will always have a fixed coupon rate of 6 percent, or $60 a year, but since you paid $1100 for it, in actuality your current yield really is only 5.45 percent, not 6 percent.

Let's say that you are approaching retirement and you call up your stockbroker because you want to buy a bond to keep your money safe and to generate some income. The broker says that there's a great bond he knows of that matures in 10 years with a coupon rate of 6 percent. You think to yourself, How terrific, since current interest rates are only at 4.5 percent. You say, Go ahead and buy it. What you needed to ask, and what he needed to tell you, was not only what the coupon rate was, but what the current yield would be.

The other thing that he needed to tell you was what the yield to maturity would be.

YIELD TO MATURITY

In addition to the coupon rate and the current yield, you also need to know what's called the *yield to maturity.* In other words, if you hold on to a bond until maturity, what is the actual yield, or interest, that you will have received? When you buy a bond in the open market, you have to compare how much money you're going to get back when the bond matures to how much you paid for it. Remember, when your bond matures, regardless of when you bought it, you are only going to get back par, or $1000 per bond. So if you buy a bond in the market for $1200, given that it will mature at $1000, you have to figure in the loss of $200 when calculating your true return.

PURCHASING BONDS

Bonds are purchased at full-service or discount brokerage houses and are sold with a commission attached to them. The commission is decided upon when the bond is purchased and can vary significantly from broker to broker. It is usually worth your while to call a few brokers if you are shopping for individual bonds. Do not be surprised if you find that the same bond gives you a higher yield at one brokerage house than another. Remember, if you are buying bonds on the bond market, the coupon rate is not as important to you as your current yield and your yield to maturity, both of which are based on how much you actually pay for a bond. If one broker is taking a higher commission than another on the same bond, your current yield will be less in the long run. Do your comparison shopping with this one.

TREASURIES

Bonds sold by the U.S. Treasury or the Bureau of Public Debt can be bought from a brokerage house, usually with a very small fee attached, around $25, regardless of the amount bought. Treasuries can also be bought directly from the government, with no commission, through a program called TreasuryDirect, or through auctions conducted by the U.S. Treasury, or even at banks.

TREASURYDIRECT

TreasuryDirect is a service operated by the Bureau of Public Debt that allows you to purchase securities and hold them until maturity. It is a book-entry securities system, which means that you do not get an actual bond certificate; your ownership is simply recorded on the books. You can set up a single TreasuryDirect account for all your Treasury securities and hold all your bills, notes, and bonds in it. You will receive a TreasuryDirect statement of account when your securities are issued, reinvested, or redeemed, or when changes are made to your account. TreasuryDirect principal and interest payments are made electronically by direct deposit to an account at whatever financial institution you choose. If you ask me, this is the way to go. Contact TreasuryDirect on the Web at www. publicdebt.treas.gov/sec/sect-des.htm or call (800) 943-6864.

LIQUIDITY

There are some bonds that aren't very liquid and may be a problem to sell, while others, like Treasuries, sell in the billions all the time. Make sure that the bonds that you are looking at are bonds that can be easily sold—again, a quality bond. If you buy a Treasury through Treasury-Direct and want to sell it, you can do so through SellDirect, another service of TreasuryDirect, or you will first have to transfer it to a commercial account like a brokerage firm.

BOND FUNDS

All this information may seem overwhelming, but it's really not so bad once you become familiar with the phrases and the concepts. Rather than learn the language, however, many people have discovered that there is an easier way to invest in the bond market than buying individual bonds, and that is by buying bond funds. I have to tell you, however, that I do not think this is the best way to go, especially if you have $10,000 or more to invest. I will tell you why after I explain what a bond fund is.

BOND FUNDS: A *bond fund* is simply a mutual fund that is made up entirely of bonds. Bond funds come in all shapes and sizes, just as bonds do. You can get a municipal bond fund, a municipal bond fund for the state you live in, a corporate bond fund, a bond fund made up entirely of Treasuries or high-yield junk bonds, a short-term bond fund or an intermediate-term bond fund. The list goes on and on and on.

INTEREST RATES: The interest rate with a bond fund is not fixed, the way it is on a single bond. It will fluctuate along with interest rates in the economy, although it will lag behind a bit. Bond funds pay dividends every single month, however, and investors like knowing they can rely on that check.

MATURITY: Unlike bonds themselves, bond funds do not have a maturity date. In other words, there is never a payoff date on which you will get back the amount of money you originally put in.

CAPITAL GAINS DISTRIBUTIONS

At the end of every year, all mutual funds, whether stock or bond funds, that have made gains will distribute that gain to you in cash or allow you to purchase more shares of the fund, your choice. This is known as an end-of-the-year capital gains distribution. What this means is that at the end of the calendar year, the fund offsets its gains against its losses, and if they still have gains, they pass those gains on to you. When they do, you will have to pay taxes on those gains. If you are in a municipal bond fund, do not be surprised if at the end of the year, you end up with a capital gains distribution on which you have to pay income tax, even if your main objective was to avoid taxes. When a fund distributes a capital gain, it also reduces the price of the fund by the amount of the capital gain. So you have to be careful, for if you bought into a bond fund in November at $10 a share, and they made a capital gains distribution of $1 per share, you would owe taxes on that $1. In addition, the price of your mutual fund would be reduced to $9 a share—big bummer.

SALES LOADS

Bond funds, like all mutual funds, come in a variety of types, but the three main variations are A shares, B shares, and no-load.

A SHARES

An A share bond fund (or, for that matter, any mutual fund) describes a loaded fund, or a fund that has a sales charge attached to it. Sales charges for A share funds usually run around 5 percent. This means that if you invested $10,000 into an A share fund and wanted to sell that fund two seconds later you would get back only $9500. The load or the fee that you paid to the person who sold you the fund was 5 percent or, in this case, $500. Another way to look at it is that your fund has to go up $500 in value just for you to break even. I would be hard-pressed to buy a loaded mutual fund, especially a loaded bond fund.

B SHARES

In my opinion, B share funds are the worst of the loaded funds. B shares can be sold under the premise that there is no load or fee to buy into the fund. You will be told that as long as you stay in the fund for at least 5 to 7 years, you will not have to pay a penny. If, however, you want to sell before that time, you will have to pay a surrender charge, usually starting at 5 percent the first year, dropping to 4 percent the second, 3 percent the third, 2 percent the fourth, 1 percent the fifth, and from that point on there will be no charges to come out of the fund.

I can't tell you how angry this makes me. What they always fail to tell you is that you are paying to be in that fund, whether you know it or not. You see, the broker who sold you the fund, just as in the A shares fund, most likely got a 5 percent commission, paid by the firm he works for or the fund itself, up front and in full at the time you made the purchase. The way the brokerage firm or mutual fund company gets their money back is that they charge you what is known as a *12(b)1* fee of anywhere from .5 to 1 percent a year. This fee is taken out of the return of the fund. So if your fund earns 10 percent, and your 12(b)1 fee is 1 percent, your return would be only 9 percent, because the brokerage firm or fund takes that 1 percent to pay itself. That is why your surrender charge goes down by that 1 percent each year. You see, if they paid the broker 5 percent up front, and they take 1 percent a year from your return, if you were to sell after the first year, your surrender charge would be only 4 percent. Add that to the 1 percent they already took—and they've recouped the money they paid the broker. Tricky. But you are the one paying in the long run.

Some B share funds automatically convert to A share funds after the

surrender period, but some do not, and you continue to pay that 1 percent a year for as long as you own the fund. Again, in my opinion, B
shares came about simply because brokerage firms needed to find a
way to keep your business by luring you into a loaded fund (one that
charges you a commission) under the guise of being a no-load fund
(one that does not charge you a commission). I can prove this to you.

Below is the actual return of a bond fund from a major brokerage
firm that has both A shares and B shares. Note the difference between
the return of the two. Remember that they are both managed by the
same portfolio manager, and they have identical bonds in the portfolio.
The only difference is that one is an A share and the other is a B share
fund. I have chosen this fund because it has a small 12(b)1 fee, only .75
percent, but you will see how that .75 percent shows up in the returns.

Annual Return Percentage

	YTD	2000	1999	1998	1997
A Shares	3.6%	−9.8%	5.80%	−3.0%	11.5%
B Shares	3.2%	−10.5%	5.00%	−3.7%	10.6%
Difference	.40	.70	.80	.70	.90

Trailing Return Percentage

	3-Year Average	5-Year Average
A Shares	−2.73%	2.89%
B Shares	−3.47%	2.11%
Difference	.74	.78

Source: Morningstar, 9/30/98

Take a good look and you will see that in every year the return on
the A shares is about .75 percent higher than on the B shares. And the

loss is about .75 percent less than on the B shares. Why? Because of that 12(b)1 fee that you are paying out of your own pocket! If you look in the trailing return percentage, which is what you would have averaged if your money had been in there all 3 or 5 years, you will see that the 12(b)1 fee makes about a .75 percent difference.

NO-LOAD

This is the only kind of mutual fund, especially a bond fund, to buy. *No-load* means no commission. You can buy or sell anytime you want, and it will not cost you a thing. You invest $10,000, and if two seconds later you want your money back, assuming that the market has not moved, you will get your $10,000 back in full.

A NEW TRICK OF THE TRADE

Because so many people have become aware of the value of no-load funds, brokers are trying to finagle their way into the scene—and into more money. They are beginning to sell no-load funds themselves. What they will tell you is that for a management fee of about 1.5 percent a year they will pick a portfolio—or you can pick a portfolio—of no-load funds, and they will manage them for you. In my opinion, this is just another way for brokerage firms to continue to make money at a hefty cost to investors.

WHAT GOOD IS A CAR SALESMAN
IN THE BOND MARKET?

When you go to buy a car, what does the person who sold you the car have to do with how the car drives? What does that person have to do with the car when it breaks down? Or when you sell it? The answer to these questions is *nothing*. The only thing the salesperson did was to tell you about the car and convince you to buy it.

It's the same deal with buying a mutual bond fund. The salesperson has absolutely nothing to do with the performance of the fund. He or she doesn't buy or sell bonds or make internal fund decisions, and is in fact as removed as you are from the actual performance of the fund. Are you willing to pay a load of either 5 percent or a management fee of 1.5 percent a year for that—especially when you don't have to? I don't think so.

If you want to buy a fund, simply buy a no-load fund on your own. If you don't know which one to buy, you can always fall back on index funds or get a good newsletter. One of my favorites is the Bob Brinker Marketimer letter, which you can get by calling (914) 591-2655 weekdays between 9 A.M. and 5 P.M. Eastern time. Bob is also on ABC radio for three hours every Saturday and Sunday. He's had his show for more than a decade now, and gives wonderful advice. Tune in and start learning—and if you have a question, call it in. Bob also has a Web site at http://www.bobbrinker.com.

If you're going to buy a mutual fund on your own, here are a few more things you should know.

CURRENT OFFERING PRICE

The *current offering price* is the dollar amount that people who want to buy this fund will have to pay.

NET ASSET VALUE (NAV)

All bond funds that trade as open-ended mutual funds, which means that the number of shares they can sell to people is unlimited, are valued by an *NAV,* or the *net asset value* of the fund. The NAV is the total worth of the portfolio at the end of every day, divided by the number of shares of the fund that have been issued. When you sell your shares, you will get the NAV of your fund on the day you sell it.

Please note: When there is a difference in the current offering price and the NAV of a fund, that's because the fund charges a load. If it is a true no-load fund, the NAV and the current offering price will always be the same.

For instance, let's say you look up the ABC no-load fund in the paper, and what you see is: NAV 10, current offering price 10. This means that people who bought the fund that day paid $10 a share, or the current offering price, and those people who sold the fund that day got $10 a share, or the NAV. No difference, no load.

Now look up XYZ loaded fund. What you would see is NAV 9.5, current offering price 10. This means that people who sold the fund that day got $9.50 a share, or the NAV, and those who bought paid $10 a share, or the current offering price. The 50-cents-a-share difference, or 5 percent, went to pay the broker.

PORTFOLIO MANAGER

If you buy individual bonds, you will in essence be your own *portfolio manager,* deciding which bonds to keep or sell; your broker can also guide you in that process. In a fund, there will be a professional portfolio manager who makes those decisions for you. This is the person to whom you should be more than willing to pay a management fee, because this is the person who will make you money, or lose you money. The management fee in a good bond fund should be half a percent, give or take a fraction. If it's more than this, you've got a greedy manager.

EXPENSE RATIOS

With every fund, there are charges in addition to the manager's fees—even those that don't carry 12(b)1 charges or sales charges (no-load funds). The *expense ratio* comprises all the fees the fund charges its investors. The expense ratio for a good bond fund should not be above .6 percent.

INDIVIDUAL BONDS OR BOND FUNDS

MYTH: BOND FUNDS
REALITY: BONDS

JONATHAN'S STORY

My parents were the best. I am disabled, in a wheelchair, and I can't work, but the most important thing to them was that I would always be taken care of. They worked hard all their lives, and a good part of the reason they did was that they wanted to make sure that I would have enough money to get by after they were gone. My dad died first, and then my mom, four years later. Amazingly, they left me $300,000.

I already understood that this money was meant to generate income for me and to supplement my disability insurance benefits. My parents were so proud of it because they thought it would be enough. I went to their advisor, who put me in a bond fund, and for a while, I was fine. I was getting about $2250 a month and was totally okay with that. But over time interest rates started to come down, and then I was getting $1500 a month, and then even less than that. My landlord sold the building I was living in, and that was just the beginning of it. I decided I wanted to buy myself a small *place to live so that I could never be displaced again, so I wanted to get out of the funds and put that money toward a home, but by then the money I had put in was worth only about $250,000. I didn't understand how that was possible, since I was told when I bought the funds that if interest rates were to go down, the value of the fund would go up. So now I'm stuck in the fund with less money than I had to begin with.*

You see, Jonathan's money was now carrying the other investors in the fund. Because interest rates had dropped so sharply, because, perhaps, some bonds had defaulted or the money new investors had deposited had to be invested at a lower interest rate because it was no longer a safe time to be in a bond fund, Jonathan was no longer as safe as his parents had wanted him to be. Or as safe as he would have been if he had invested strictly in bonds, where what you sign up for is what you get.

MYTH: BOND FUNDS

I have to tell you, in almost all circumstances, I have a hard time justifying bond funds over individual bonds—unless you are desperate and need the highest yield you can get and yield is more important to you than knowing that you will get your principal back in full.

Many advisors may disagree with this. They will say that you need a bond fund, especially if you do not have a lot of money, because individual bonds always carry a risk of defaulting. They will say that you need to protect yourself and diversify among a lot of bonds, which you cannot do if you don't have a lot of money with which to do so.

In theory, that sounds correct, but we are dealing with reality. So here is the reality I have seen over the years. While it is true that some bonds carry the risk of defaulting, not all bonds do, not by any means. Treasuries, for instance, are the safest possible investment you can make. If you have just a small sum of money, your investment does not have to be diversified as long as your money is safe. If you wanted, you could put 100 percent of absolutely every penny you have in a Treasury, regardless of your age, and your money would be safe from credit risk. This may not be the wisest thing to do with respect to inflation risk or to the return, but the money would be absolutely safe. So the reasoning that tells us that the only way to be safe with a small sum of money is to diversify by using a bond fund simply does not hold water, in my opinion.

People will also say, "But what if I don't want to buy a Treasury? I want to buy munis—municipal bonds—because I am in a high tax bracket and I do not want to pay taxes on that interest." If that's true, then we have to look at your money more closely. If you are in a high tax bracket, that means you are bringing in or receiving a nice income, and therefore you should have more than a small sum of money to invest in the bond market. For the purpose of this discussion, I am considering anything under $10,000 a small sum.

So in this case, I would tell you to do two things. Number one, the taxes on an investment of $10,000 or less in a taxable bond are not going to be that great. If you're in the 36 percent tax bracket, let's say, and you put $5000 in a Treasury that earns 5 percent, on the $250 you will earn in interest, $90 will go to the IRS in taxes, leaving you with $160. If you were to put that same $5000 in a municipal bond fund— let's say it paid you 3.5 percent—you would get $112 after taxes. However, in a Treasury you know you will get back all $5000 at maturity date. In a bond fund you do not have that assurance, because bond funds do not have a maturity date. It is possible you could get back more than your $5000 when you sell (which could happen if interest rates were to go down and your bond fund increased in value), but you also could get back less if interest rates started to go up, if one of the bonds in the portfolio defaulted, or if there was a rush on money and the portfolio manager had to sell before he intended—and so on. So it is highly possible, especially if you are buying your fund while interest rates are quite low (as they were at the beginning of 2001), that when you sell your bond fund you will get back less than the money that you saved in taxes. In short, this reasoning does not really hold up, either.

But maybe you are thinking, Okay, but I have a lot more money to invest than $5000, and I do not want any more taxable income—so wouldn't it make sense in my case to buy a municipal bond fund? No. First of all, if you have a lot more money to invest, you can diversify by buying individual bonds. Second, if you really want to avoid paying taxes, there's an even stronger case against staying away from the capital gains distribution of bond funds.

You see, imagine yourself in a bond fund. You put your money in when interest rates were okay, when you could have had a coupon rate of 7, 8, maybe even 9 percent. New investors are entering the fund all the time, even as rates go down. The portfolio manager has to keep buying new bonds—whether the interest rate is high or low. This affects your rate of return. If you had bought individual bonds when the interest rates were high, you would be reaping the rewards, since your interest rate is fixed.

Downside: Taxes on Municipal Bond Funds

Remember, most funds have an end-of-the-year capital gains distribution. So even if you go into a municipal bond fund with the sole intention of never having to pay taxes while you own it, you may very well find you are paying taxes at the end of the year.

Downside: Management

Some advisors might also tell you that it is worth the management fees to have a professional manager watch over all the bonds in the portfolio and decide for you what to do. That may be true, but those decisions may not always be just for your benefit. For instance, if the overall fund performance is not great, in order to beef up the annual return numbers, a portfolio manager may make decisions based on what is best for the track record of the fund—such as buying longer-term maturities or riskier bonds—rather than what is best for the actual money in the fund. The goal for the fund is to attract new investors' money. The way all funds do this is to make sure the reported returns of the fund are as high as possible. Isn't that how you choose to buy one fund over another? You bet it is.

What's more, if you decided to purchase a mutual fund, as most people do, because the returns have been good, you have to make sure that the portfolio manager who created those returns does not leave the fund to go somewhere else. Even though a new person may intend to do great things, he or she might not be able to duplicate the performance of the previous manager. I have never heard of a broker calling his clients to inform them of a portfolio manager switch. This is your money. You—and not an anonymous portfolio manager—must watch over it.

Bond Funds and Interest Rate Performance

Another reason I don't prefer bond funds to individual bonds is that even though bond fund prices are supposed to go up when interest rates go down, and vice versa, this does not always happen, which makes bond funds unpredictable, even though bonds are supposed to be the most predictable investments of all. In addition, when interest rates go down, the interest rate that you are earning in a bond fund will also decline. If you are on a fixed income, this could be disastrous. When interest rates decline, which means you are getting less money monthly, and the price of the fund does not increase or, worse, declines, then you could really be in trouble, when all you wanted was to be safe.

Buying and Selling

When you buy into a bond fund, you pay the current offering price of the fund on the day you place your order. You can tell your broker how much you want to spend, but you will not know for sure until the fund closes for that day how many shares you will actually get, since the NAV and the current offering price for the day are calculated at the end of the day's trading. Or you can tell your broker how many shares you want to buy, but the actual dollar amount that you've spent will not be available until the close of business that day. So if you place your order in the morning, when everything is just great, and then the market experiences a day of wild swings, you could end up having paid far more than you thought per share or getting far less when it translates into the yield of the fund. With a fund, you really have no idea what you will end up with at the end of the day. With an actual bond, you do.

REALITY: BONDS

If instead of a bond fund you bought individual bonds (with or without the aid of a financial advisor), then this is the upside:

- You know precisely the amount of money that you will get back at maturity date.
- You will never have to pay end-of-the-year capital gains tax.
- You will not have to worry about whether the portfolio manager leaves.
- You do not have to worry about inside fees and expenses of the fund.
- If interest rates go down, you will most likely see an honest movement to the upside.
- You will know your exact coupon rate and it will never change, even if interest rates go down.
- You will know the exact price that you are paying per bond and the yield that you will be getting.

Bond Funds: The Upside

There are exceptions to everything—and that holds true for bond funds as well. There are bonds funds of all kinds. Sometimes they can be a good place to put short-term money or even intermediate-term money, but overall, for the long haul, when you are looking for a stable

income and want control over your money, I would go with individual
bonds. Make sure they have a safe rating or stick with Treasuries. That
is my reality.

DIFFERENT KINDS OF BONDS/ BOND FUNDS: A MENU

If bonds pique your interest, you will find a bond (or bond fund) for
every need. Here's a sampling:

CONVERTIBLE BONDS AND BOND FUNDS

Convertible bonds/funds are issued by corporations originally as a
debt instrument, but the corporation retains the option to convert the
bond into actual stock in that company.

If you want growth along with some income, convertible bonds are
well worth looking into. Just know that when you buy a convertible
bond, you trade income for possible growth, so if pure income is your
goal these may not be for you. Also the conversion feature and the
quality of the corporation issuing these bonds is key here, so make
sure you understand these fully before investing. *Note:* These bonds
are usually far less liquid than others, so be careful.

GOVERNMENT AGENCY BONDS OR BOND FUNDS

As you know, when the government issues a bond, the bond is known
as a Treasury. In addition, various government agencies also issue
bonds. These bonds are known as Ginnie Maes, Fannie Maes, or Freddie Macs, and they are issued to back home mortgages and keep

money in the banking system so that there will always be a flow of mortgage money for prospective homeowners to tap into.

If you are looking for more of a cash flow for income purposes than straight Treasuries will give you, Ginnie Maes are not a bad place to look—but learn the facts, so you won't be in for a surprise. Ginnie Maes are bonds borrowed from investors in order to buy mortgages. These bonds often pay about .5 to 1 percent above what a regular Treasury will pay, and usually have maturities of 7 to 10 years; however, payment schedules show 80 to 90 percent of them paid off by the twelfth year. Unlike a Treasury, on which interest is paid every 6 months, Ginnie Maes pay interest every month.

The downside to a Ginnie Mae starts here. The reason they pay monthly is that people pay their mortgages monthly, so those payments are passed right on to the investor. Mortgage payments, however, comprise both interest and principal. So when homeowners refinance their mortgage, or pay off their loans ahead of time, then Ginnie Mae has to pass that money on to you. Thus at a time when you want to be locked into the high interest rate, let's say, of your original investment, here you are getting all your money back when interest rates are lower.

Here's how it could work. Let's say that you bought a Ginnie Mae bond for $25,000, paying 6 percent. The next month, you would get a payment for $125 in interest—but you might also get a payment of principal for $75. Now you no longer have a full $25,000 in the bond earning interest; you have only $24,925. This could continue with every payment, so that by the end of the year (depending on how quickly people are paying off their mortgages), you might have only $23,500 earning 6 percent. The year after that it could be $21,000, and so on. Your interest rate is staying the same, but the amount of money that you are earning that interest on is declining.

To put it another way, people who invest in Ginnie Maes tend to forget that they are getting back some of their principal each month, and often they spend it rather than save it. When the money finally matures, investors can be in for a shock when they get hardly any money back. Even so, given that, as of the writing of this book, interest rates are extremely low, Ginnie Maes are great bonds to look into, especially if you would like just a little higher interest rate. If you want to buy into Ginnie Mae, you could do so by buying into a Ginnie Mae fund, because the minimum investment for an individual Ginnie Mae bond is $25,000 and the minimum of funds can be much lower. Make sure, however, that it is a no-load fund with low expense ratios.

ZERO COUPON BONDS AND BOND FUNDS

Zero coupon bonds became popular in the 1980s and have retained their popularity. A *zero coupon bond,* also known as a *strip,* is a bond that does not have a coupon, or interest payment. It has a coupon rate of a certain percentage, but the income that it generates is not paid out to you—it is stripped from the bond, so to speak—so it stays in the bond, earning interest at that same coupon rate. This can be a great feature. Let's say you're in a high-interest-rate environment, you have a bond that has a coupon rate of 8 percent and you bought it 8 years ago. If every time that bond paid you your 8 percent, you were to reinvest the money, you would have to find an investment with a return of 8 percent to match the yield you were getting on the bond—which could prove difficult if not impossible for you if the current interest rate had dropped, in the meantime, to 5 percent. With a zero coupon bond, however, if the interest rate is 8 percent, the interest can be reinvested in the same vehicle at 8 percent, and your overall rate of return will be much higher.

What you have to be careful of with a zero coupon bond is that even though your interest is reinvested rather than paid out to you, you are expected to pay taxes on that money, as if it were. To get around this, all you have to do is purchase your zero coupon bonds in your tax-deferred retirement account, or else buy a municipal zero coupon that is tax-free. By nature, these bonds tend to be more volatile than conventional bonds with respect to price movements and interest rates. Also, when you buy these bonds, you ordinarily do so at a discount. For instance, if you were to buy a $50,000 zero coupon bond, the $50,000 represents not the price you paid for the bond but the maturity value, or how much you would get back if you held this bond till it matured. For instance, a $50,000 zero coupon bond maturing in the year 2008 with a coupon of 5 percent, bought in the year 2000, might cost you around $30,500 up front. When this bond matures, if you still own it, you will get $50,000 back. On a smaller scale, an individual bond would cost you $610 to buy it, and when it matured it would pay you $1000.

Zero coupon bonds can be had in many ways—such as zero coupon Treasuries, munis, and occasionally corporates. When you are dealing with a municipal zero coupon, it is essential that you get one that has some kind of insurance, which will come with the bond itself; since the interest is not being paid to you, nothing could be worse than if the bond defaulted and you got nothing at all from it, not even the interest income.

Why Zero Coupon Bonds?

♦ In a high-interest-rate environment where rates are expected to come down, and if you do not need the interest income to live on while the money is invested in the bond, zero coupons could be a great investment. This way your interest is reinvested at the coveted high rate. In fact, any decline in rates could make this investment well worth your while, since zero coupons tend to make bigger price moves than conventional bonds. However, the opposite is also true—if interest rates were to go up, zero coupons would decrease in value more rapidly than conventional bonds.

♦ You may have money in your retirement account that you want to keep safe and sound while reinvesting the interest at the same rate.

♦ You may know without a doubt how much money you are going to need by a certain date, such as with a college fund. There are very few investments besides a zero coupon bond that can give you this exact information in advance. That is because no other investments can also lock in the rate of return for the reinvestment of your interest income.

SAVINGS BONDS: SERIES E/EE AND H/HH BONDS

Many of us have what are known as savings bonds. We either bought them for ourselves or our parents gave them to us, or we have given them to our children. The problem is that many of us put them away and never look at them again. This is a big mistake, for after a certain period of time they stop earning interest. I remember an occasion just a few years ago when a client brought in tens of thousands of dollars' worth of bonds dating back to 1945, convinced they were worth a fortune. They were worth a lot, but not anywhere near what she had hoped, because the extended maturity date had long since passed, and they had not been earning any interest for a decade. Please do not let this happen to you.

You can buy a series E/EE bond at a 50 percent discount of its face value. The *face value* is simply the amount that is printed on the bond. So when you buy a $100 bond, it will cost only 50 percent of that amount, or $50.

Series HH bonds work a little differently, because they are what is known as current-income securities. The HH bond doesn't go up in value, the way the E/EE series does. When an HH bond is issued, you pay the full face value ($500, $1000, $5000, or $10,000), and then you receive interest every 6 months—"current income." The interest payments on HH bonds are deposited directly into the account you designate. How much interest? You know the day you buy the bond, because the rate is fixed. Since March 1, 1993, the rate for HH bonds has been 4 percent.

The only way you can get HH bonds, however, is by exchanging series E/EE bonds and notes for these bonds—trading up, so to speak—or by taking series H bonds that have matured and reinvesting them into the HH series.

These bonds assure you that you will receive your interest payments twice a year, and also offer an additional tax advantage: You can defer federal income taxes on the interest accrued on the EE/E bonds or savings notes until you cash in the HH bonds, or until they reach final maturity.

If you value money over things, series EE bonds are, for some, a conservative way to express that value—think of money gift certificates when you're buying presents for your children, grandchildren, or yourself. They're available in denominations of: $50, $75, $100, $200, $500, $1000, $5000, and $10,000. The maximum series EE bonds you can buy in one year is $30,000 face value, or $15,000 cost. (There is no maximum on the HH series.) Interest on the EE series is paid when the bond is redeemed, but it compounds semiannually. The interest—which is exempt from state and local tax, but not federal, inheritance, or estate taxes—is calculated on an average of 5-year Treasury securities yields. If you redeem a bond during the first five years, you will incur a 3-month interest penalty. On the other hand, if you redeem the bond to pay for qualified education expenses, you may not have to pay taxes on the interest. See your tax preparer about this. You also can call the Treasury to find out your current yield.

Original Maturity

Original maturity is the date when the series E/EE bond or savings note reaches its face value. Find the issue date on your series E/EE bonds and match it up to the issue date below, and you'll see how long it is until your bond reaches its original maturity date.

Issue Date	Original Term, in Years
1/80–10/80	11
11/80–4/81	9
5/81–10/82	8
11/82–10/86	10
11/86–2/93	12
3/93–4/95	18
5/95–present	17

Extension Periods

After your bond reaches its original maturity date, or face value, it continues to grow in value—but not forever. At this point, without your doing anything, it will enter what is known as an *extension period* (usually 10 years long).

During extension periods (and most bonds automatically go into one or more extension periods), bonds issued before May 1995 earn interest calculated by a guaranteed yield or a market-based yield. The applicable guaranteed yield is the one in effect at the time the bond enters the extension. Bonds issued after April 1995 have no such guaranteed minimum yield. They will earn interest depending on what is happening with interest rates at the time the bond enters its extension period.

Let the Buyer Beware

Here is where trouble can begin. At final maturity—or when the extension periods are up—bonds stop earning interest. This is when they begin to languish in a desk drawer somewhere, so if you've hidden away some bonds, please go find them and check the final maturity:

Series E | Final Maturity

May 1941–November 1965	40 years
December 1965–June 1980	30 years

Series H

June 1952–January 1957	29 years, 8 months
February 1957–December 1979	30 years

Savings Notes	All issues	30 years
Series EE	All issues	30 years
Series HH	All issues	20 years

What are the bonds sitting in your desk drawer earning? During their extension, series E/EE or savings notes earn these guaranteed minimum rates:

11/82–10/86	7.5%
11/86–2/93	6%
3/93–4/95	4%
5/95–present	There is no guaranteed minimum for older bonds entering an extension during this period.

Calculating Your Interest

The Savings Bond Earnings Report—http://www.publicdebt.treas.gov/savreport.htm or call (816) 881-2919—will tell you what your bond is currently earning and will give you the current value of $100 E and EE bonds. If you don't happen to have $100 bonds, you can figure out the value of your bonds, which are proportional to $100. For example, if you have a $50 bond, just divide the value of the $100 bond by 2. If you have a $500 bond, multiply the value of the $100 bond by 5.

Redeeming Savings Bonds

Series E/EE bonds and notes should be redeemed at final maturity, unless you want to trade them in for series HH bonds. If you redeem your bonds, and you have deferred reporting interest, you should report all accrued interest on your taxes in the year they reach final maturity. If you exchange your matured bonds for HH bonds within a year after they reach final maturity, you can continue to defer reporting interest earnings on the exchanged E/EE securities until the HH bonds are redeemed, are disposed of, or reach final maturity. (H/HH bond interest must be reported annually.)

SERIES I BONDS

The last bond that is important for you to know about is the *series I bond* issued by the government as a protection against inflation. These bonds differ from series E or EE bonds in that the interest rate is attached to the consumer price index. If inflation goes up, so does the interest that these bonds pay.

Series I bonds are available in denominations of $50, $75, $100, $200, $500, $1000, $5000, and $10,000. Series I bonds are issued at face value, so a $500 I bond will cost you $500. You can buy $30,000 worth of these bonds each year.

How they work is that when interest rates are announced (on May 1 and November 1), they are calculated at a fixed rate of return over and above inflation. I bonds issued up until April 1999 will earn a 3.3 percent fixed rate of return over and above inflation. At the time of this writing, the annualized rate of inflation as measured by the *CPI* (*consumer price index*) was 1.72 percent. In other words, bonds bought from November 1998 through April 1999 will earn 3.3 percent above the CPI of 1.72 percent, for a total of 5.05 percent. The 3.3 percent will be fixed for the life of this bond, though the CPI will change. The bonds increase in value every month, and interest compounds semiannually. (Interest is paid when the bond is redeemed.) If there is a period of deflation—the opposite of inflation—the bond value could remain unchanged.

All I bonds mature in 30 years. If you cash in your bond before the end of 5 years, you will be hit with that 3-month earning penalty. Again, there may be tax benefits if you redeem I bonds for qualified education expenses. Unlike series EE, I bonds cannot be exchanged for any other series of savings bonds (such as the HH series). All I bonds are exempt from state and local income taxes.

BOTTOM LINE ON BONDS

Eventually, all of us are going to need a bond somewhere in our portfolios. No one should be invested at 100 percent growth all their life, which is why it's essential to know how to make sense of the options available to you when you're looking to invest in bonds. In this situation as in every other prospective investment situation, don't just accept a broker's advice at face value. Take the time to learn the fundamentals, and carefully assess your immediate and long-term needs. You need learn it only once to own that knowledge. Trust me, it will be time well spent.

CHAPTER 20

How Does Your IRA Grow?

You've heard the phrase *Pay yourself first?* What this means is that tending to your future is the highest financial obligation there is—and the best way I know how to do this is by opening up an *IRA (individual retirement account)* or other retirement account as soon as you possibly can, and adding to it year after year, all the way through your working life. This act of self-service will reward you richly.

I have had young people tell me they can't afford to open an IRA; they don't make enough money yet. To this I say, You can't afford *not* to think about your future *now*, in your early adult years, for even the smallest contributions made during these years can grow into huge sums later on, and later on comes sooner than we expect—for all of us. I have also had people say to me that they're investing the max in their 401(k)s at work, so why bother with an IRA? Because a little less money for you to live on today will mean a lot more money later; it's that simple. People often tell me they feel too old to open an IRA—what difference will it make now? Such reasoning lacks courage, for there is no room for wealth in defeat. If you're playing catch-up, opening an IRA is the place to start. In fact, if you're over age 50, the 2001 tax law allows you to contribute even more to your IRA, to help you catch up.

Traditional IRAs Versus Roth IRAs

There is a lot of confusion between the traditional IRA and a Roth IRA, and it is important that you understand the differences between the two and how they work. Below are questions and answers to help you learn everything you need to know.

Traditional IRA

How much can I contribute to a traditional IRA?

If you are working and earning money or receive taxable compensation and you have not yet attained age 70½, you can contribute a maximum of $3000 (for 2002) to a traditional IRA. With a traditional IRA, this $3000 (or any amount up to this limit) can be deducted from your income, so that in some circumstances you do not have to pay income taxes on that money. For instance, if you make $25,000 a year and you contribute $3000 to an IRA, you would only have to pay income taxes on $22,000 minus any other deductions you may have. If you will have celebrated your 50th birthday before the end of 2002, you can contribute (and deduct, if eligible) an additional $500. The maximum contribution and the over-50 additional contribution will increase in future years. The following chart shows the maximum contribution in each year, starting with 2002.

Year	Regular	Over 50
2002	$3,000	$3,500
2003	$3,000	$3,500
2004	$3,000	$3,500
2005	$4,000	$4,500
2006	$4,000	$5,000
2007	$4,000	$5,000
2008	$5,000	$6,000

After 2008, the $5,000 regular contribution limit is indexed for inflation.

Does alimony qualify as taxable compensation?

Yes. Also falling under this category are:

- ♦ Commissions
- ♦ Bonuses
- ♦ Self-employment income
- ♦ Wages
- ♦ Tips
- ♦ Salaries
- ♦ Fees for professional services

Please note: If *all* of your income is derived from any or all of the following: Social Security, interest or dividend checks, annuity payments, pension payments, real estate, or deferred compensation, you do not qualify to put money in any IRA. In other words, only earned income and alimony can be contributed to an IRA.

If I am already covered by a retirement plan at work, such as a 401(k), can I still make a contribution to an IRA and take the full deduction on my taxes?

Because of restrictions in the tax law, if you are covered by a retirement plan such as a 401(k) at work, you may not be able to fully or even partially deduct your contribution, depending on how much money you make. In the year 2002, for example, you can fully deduct your IRA contribution only if you are either single and your *modified adjusted gross income (MAGI)* is under $34,000, or if you are married, filing jointly, and your MAGI is under $54,000 a year. You can take partial deductions if your MAGI is up to $10,000 more than these amounts, but once you reach an MAGI of $44,000 for a single and $64,000 for married, filing jointly, then you would get no deduction for your IRA contribution. In this case you would be far better off opening a Roth IRA instead. If you are covered by a company retirement plan, the income limits to determine whether you can take a deduction for your IRA are listed below.

Single

Year	Modified Adjusted Gross Income Phaseout Range
2001	$33,000–$43,000
2002	$34,000–$44,000
2003	$40,000–$50,000
2004	$45,000–$55,000
2005, etc.	$50,000–$60,000

Married Filing Jointly

Year	Modified Adjusted Gross Income Phaseout Range
2001	$53,000–$63,000
2002	$54,000–$64,000
2003	$60,000–$70,000
2004	$65,000–$75,000
2005	$70,000–$80,000
2006	$75,000–$85,000
2007	$80,000–$90,000

If I make more than the minimum for a full deduction, but less than the maximum, how do I know how much of my IRA contribution I can take as a deduction?

There is an easy formula that will determine how much you can take off your taxes for your IRA contribution. Go to the chart above and find the tax year in question. Simply subtract your MAGI from the upper limit on the chart for that year, divide that figure by $10,000 and multiply that figure by the maximum contribution you are entitled to for the year. This will tell you how much money you can deduct.

Let's say that it is 2002, you are over 50 and single with an MAGI of $40,000. Subtract $40,000 from the maximum allowed for that year, $44,000, which leaves you with $4000. Divide that by $10,000 which gives you .40; multiply .40 by $3500 which is the maximum deduction for 2002 if you are over 50. The result is $1400. You would be able to deduct $1400 of your $3500 contribution from your income. The deduction is not based on a percentage of the contribution. If in this example you only contributed $1400, you would be able to deduct the entire contribution. Also, as long as your MAGI is under the maximum, your deduction will be at least $200.

If my spouse is not working but I am covered by a pension plan, can I take the $2000 contribution for him off my taxes?

You can take a deduction for your nonworking spouse only if your MAGI (married filing jointly) is below $150,000 a year. If your income is over that amount, then there is the phaseout of the full deduction once you hit a MAGI of $160,000 a year or more. After that amount, your spouse can make an IRA contribution, but you cannot deduct it for tax purposes.

Where can I open an IRA?

You can open an IRA account at many different places: a full service or discount brokerage firm, a mutual fund company, an insurance company, a bank, or a credit union. You have until April 15 of the year after the close of the tax year to open up an IRA. In other words, for 2002, you will have until April 15 of the year 2003 to open up your IRA for the 2002 tax year. There are no exemptions from this date even if you apply for a filing extension.

Once I open up my IRA, what can I invest the money in?

You can invest it in a variety of ways. Your selection will depend on what the firm you opened your IRA with offers. Please take this into consideration before opening up an account. For instance, if you wanted to buy a particular stock with your money, and you opened an IRA at a mutual fund company that sells only its own mutual funds, you will not be able to buy that stock. For this reason, I always suggest that you open an IRA at a company that offers you a variety of investments at a good cost—such as discount brokerage firms like Charles Schwab or Waterhouse Securities.

Will I have to pay taxes on my money while it is in the IRA?

No. While the money is invested in the IRA it grows tax-deferred. This means that you do not pay any taxes on the money or earnings until you make a withdrawal from the IRA account.

What are the rules governing the money that I put into the IRA?

Here are the things you really need to know:

1. You cannot, in most circumstances, take any money out of your IRA until you are 59½ years of age. If you take money out prior to that age, you will pay a 10 percent penalty tax to the federal government, as well as a state penalty tax (which varies from state to state).

2. Whenever you take any money out of your IRA, regardless of age, you will pay regular income taxes on that money.

   So if you are 45 years of age and withdraw $30,000 to pay off your credit card debt, you will pay ordinary income tax (state and federal) on that $30,000. You will also pay a 10 percent federal tax penalty on that money, or $3000, and whatever the state penalty will be; in California, it will be around another $750. When all is said and done, of the $30,000 you just withdrew you may have only $16,000 (give or take, depending on your tax bracket) left.

3. By April 1 of the year after you turn 70½, you must begin taking money out of your IRA according to a specified formula. From this point on, all withdrawals have to be made by December 31 of the following year. If you do not withdraw at least the required specified amount, you will be charged a 50 percent penalty on the amount that you should have withdrawn but did not.

Even though you do not technically have to take the first mandatory withdrawal of your IRA until April 1 of the year after you turn 70½, you might *not* want to wait till that next calendar year to do so. Let's say that you turned 70½ in December of 2002. In any other year, you should be making your 2002 withdrawal by December 31 of that year; but on this, your first withdrawal only, the government allows you to wait until April 1 of the year following your 70½ birthday—in this case, April 1, 2003—to take the money out. The problem is that you will also have to take out 2003's minimum distribution by December 31, 2003; thus you will have two years of distributions in one calendar tax year. This could put you in a much higher tax bracket if you're not careful. Unless you are in a very high tax bracket in the year you turn 70½ and your income is expected to drop considerably the next year, I recommend that you take the minimum required distribution in the year you turn 70½, *not* in the next year.

Are there any exceptions to the 10 percent early withdrawal penalty besides being 59½ years of age or older?

Yes, there are exceptions, but please note: Even though you may not have to pay that 10 percent penalty in all of the following situations, you will still have to pay income taxes on the money that you withdraw. Also, once you take the money out, it will no longer be available for your retirement, its original purpose.

EXCEPTIONS TO THE EARLY
WITHDRAWAL PENALTY

1. *Disability*. For you to avoid the 10 percent penalty under this exception you are going to have to prove that you cannot perform any activity that would permit you to earn a living. A doctor must verify that you are seriously disabled and

expected to stay that way for a long time, possibly indefi-
nitely, for this exception to apply.

2. *Death*. When your beneficiaries inherit your IRA and start to
   take out the money, regardless of their age, they will not have
   to pay a penalty. Taxes yes, penalty no.

3. *Medical expenses.* To the extent you have unreimbursed
   medical expenses that exceed 7.5 percent of your adjusted
   gross income, you qualify for this exception.

4. *First-time home buyer*. If you are planning to build, rebuild, or
   buy a house as a primary residence, you might be able to withdraw a lifetime maximum of $10,000 from your IRA without
   incurring the 10 percent penalty. This money can be for a
   home for anyone in your family—you or your parents, grandparents, children, or grandchildren. This includes your side of
   the family and your spouse's side as well. There is a time frame
   on this withdrawal that you need to be aware of. You have to
   use the money for a viable expense within 120 days of withdrawing it from your account. The use of this money has to fall
   under the guideline of what the IRS considers a valid cost of
   buying or building a home, such as closing costs, etc. Again,
   even though you do not have to pay the 10 percent tax, you
   still will have to pay income taxes on this money. Also, please
   be aware that first-time home buyer does not mean first time
   ever. It simply means that you have not owned a home in the
   previous 2 years. So if you owned a home, you sold it, and now
   it is more than 2 years later, you can qualify for this exception.

5. *Higher-education costs*. You can use any of the money in
   your IRA to help pay for an undergraduate or graduate education. As in the example above, this applies for anyone in your
   family. The money can be used for a variety of education-
   related expenses, including room and board (for students
   matriculating half-time or more), books, supplies, tuition, or
   equipment needed for classes. Again, please note that you
   will avoid the penalty but not the taxes owed.

6. *Health insurance.* If you need money to pay for medical insurance premiums for you, your spouse, and/or your dependents and you meet *all* of the following criteria, you can take money out of your IRA and not have to pay the early-withdrawal penalty:

♦ You received unemployment compensation for at least 12 consecutive weeks;

♦ You are not employed because you lost your job;

♦ You withdraw the money from your account in the same calendar year as you received unemployment, or the year after; and

♦ Once you do get another job, you withdraw this money before 60 days on that new job have passed.

7. *Substantially Equal Periodic Payment (SEPP).* Simply put, this means you have to withdraw a certain amount of money every single year until you are 59½ or for 5 years, whichever is longer. So if you are 57 and you start to take money out of your IRA account under SEPP, you will have to do so until you are 62. If you're 52 when you start, you'll have to continue withdrawing the money until you're 59½—again, the rule is whichever time period is longer. The amount you can withdraw is calculated by one of three methods; the method you choose will determine the actual dollar amount you must take out yearly. Very few people know about this loophole, IRC section 72(t) (2) (A) (iv), Notice 89-25, but it's there if you need it. When making your calculations, make sure you are dealing with a professional who is entirely familiar with this law. I go into great detail on this subject in *You've Earned It, Don't Lose It*.

How many IRAs can I have?

You can have as many as you want. The only limitation is that you cannot put in more than the maximum amount per year total. See the chart on p. 357 for the maximum amount each year. So, for 2002, you could put $1000 in one IRA and $1500 in another and $500 in a third if you wanted. Or $100 per year in 30 different IRAs. It's up to you.

Is there an advantage to having more than one IRA account?

There could be, in certain circumstances where you have more than one beneficiary and your estate planner advises it. However, in my opinion, in most cases there is a disadvantage in having more than one account. You see, most IRA accounts charge a yearly fee. That annual fee can run anywhere from $25 to $50. That may not seem like a lot of money, but it is when you look at it in terms of percentages. If you are paying a $25 annual fee for an IRA and all you have in the account is $250, you are paying 10 percent of the account value just in the custodian fee. This means that even if you made a good investment and it went up 10 percent that year, all you did was break even. However, if you had all $3000 in one account and the fee was $25, well, that's not so bad—about .83 percent of the account value. So if your investment in the IRA went up 10 percent, after the custodian fee (assuming it is deducted from the IRA account itself) you still would have made about 9.17 percent on your money that year.

Can a 1 or 2 percent difference really add up to that much more or less in actual dollars?

Absolutely. Let's say that you put $3000 a year in an IRA that averaged 10 percent a year for the next 30 years. You would have a total of $494,000. If you had made just 9 percent a year, or 1 percent less, you would have only about $409,000, and at 8 percent a year you would have $340,000. Over time, a little less return really can make a huge difference. Obviously, as your account grows, the percentage of the fees gets proportionately smaller, but that is why it is better to have most of your money in one IRA.

Does every brokerage firm charge a fee?

No. For instance, with Charles Schwab, if you keep at least $10,000 in the account you do not have to pay fees ever again. So ask before you open your account.

Yes, but aren't fees for an IRA tax-deductible?

That will depend. If the custodian takes the money directly from your IRA account, then, no, the fees are not tax-deductible. The only way the fee from an IRA is deductible is if you choose to pay it from funds outside the IRA *and* itemize your tax return, which many people do not. Even if you do itemize your tax return, these fees may not be large enough to qualify for a deduction anyway. IRA fees fall under a category that can be written off only if they total more than 2 percent of your MAGI. Even though in theory fees can be written off if you pay them from funds outside the IRA, in reality very few people do so.

Are there any other disadvantages to having many IRA accounts?

Yes. When it comes to keeping track of all the accounts and what the investments are doing, sometimes it's easier to get just one statement with everything on it. It will also be easier for you to have a single account when it comes time to withdraw your money when you turn 70½.

How much money do I have to take out when I turn 70½?

Most of us really don't have to worry about that, for the trustee or custodian of your IRA will help you figure out the correct amount. However, for an overview, the amount of money that you are required to take out of your IRA is based on three things:

1. How much money you have in all your IRAs
2. Your life expectancy alone, or
3. The joint life expectancy of you and your spouse, if your

spouse is your only beneficiary, and is more than ten years younger than you.

You see, even though the government has allowed you to enjoy the benefits of tax deferral for all these years, Uncle Sam wants his tax money—sooner rather than later, and preferably before you are no longer here to pay it yourself. So that is why your life expectancy comes into play. The calculation is quite simple and is based on life expectancy tables obtainable from the IRS in Publication 590, Appendix E.

To give you an example, let's say you have $200,000 in your IRA and that you're 71 years of age. At age 71, the IRS, using the Uniform Distribution Table, determines that your divisor is 25.3. Divide $200,000 by 25.3, which gives you $7905. That is how much money you would have to take out that first year from all your IRAs. If, however, your spouse, age 57, is your sole beneficiary, you would look at the joint life expectancy table. Here you would see that your lives together are expected to amount to another 28.2 years. So you would divide $200,000 by 28.2, which would give you $7092 as your required distribution. Taxes on $7092 are a lot less than taxes on $7905. As you can see, the amount of money you have in your account coupled with which table you use does make a difference.

Barry Picker, CPA/PFS, CFP, has written an excellent guide containing all of the rules on taking money out of your IRA (and other retirement plans) called "Barry Picker's Guide to Retirement Distribution Planning." It costs $24.95 and can be ordered by calling (800) 809-0015. I highly recommend it.

If I name my daughter as the beneficiary of my IRA, and she is many years younger than I am, won't that make our joint life expectancy very high—and therefore I will not have to take out much money from my IRA if I do not want to?

No, I'm sorry to say it does not work this way. Regardless of the actual age of your beneficiary (with the exception of your spouse), you must use the Uniform Distribution Table. This table assumes that your beneficiary is ten years younger than you, regardless of the actual difference in age.

What happens if I have already started to take out my required distribution based on the Uniform Distribution Table and then I want to change my beneficiary?

This will not affect your distributions unless you are changing to or from a spouse who is more than ten years younger. If you are changing FROM a spouse who is more than ten years younger than you, then you must use the Uniform Distribution Table for the year of the change, rather than the joint life table. If you are changing TO a spouse who is more than ten years younger than you, then you must still use the Uniform Distribution Table for the year of the change but you can use the joint life table in the following year, provided you don't change the beneficiary in that year.

If I have left my IRA to all three of my kids, how do I figure out the amount I should be withdrawing?

Since you are using the Uniform Distribution Table, it makes no difference if you have left your IRA to one kid or three kids.

What if I do not have a designated person as my beneficiary because I have left everything to my estate? Which tables can I use to figure out my withdrawal amount?

You will still use the Uniform Distribution Table. However, you should NEVER name your estate as the beneficiary. First of all, if you name a person as your beneficiary, your IRA will not have to be probated (a court procedure) after you die. If you leave it to your estate, however, it will be probated. Second of all, if you leave your IRA to your estate, creditors can access your IRA money, where in most states IRAs are otherwise exempt from claims of creditors. Third of all, your IRA will only be allowed to use the single life expectancy table to determine mandatory withdrawals after your death.

What happens to my money in the IRA when I die?

When you die, your money goes to the designated beneficiaries that you named on your IRA application forms. *Please note:* Even if your will or trust says all your money is to go to your daughter, if you have named someone other than your daughter as your primary beneficiary on your IRA application, then that person will be the one to get all the money in your IRA. At that time he or she will have to take the money out according to rules that have already been established by the IRS. The withdrawal schedule of the money you leave in your IRA will depend on whether or not your beneficiary is your surviving spouse.

The laws that govern what happens to an IRA when a surviving spouse is the beneficiary are far different from those governing when the beneficiary is not the spouse. As the surviving spouse, you will have many options. These options depend, though, on whether your spouse had started to withdraw the minimum required distribution before he or she died.

If your spouse had already started withdrawing the minimum required distribution at the age of 70½, then you can do one of three things:

1. Continue taking the minimum distributions based upon your single life expectancy as recalculated each year;
2. Accelerate the distributions—take them faster;
3. Stop the distributions, convert your spouse's IRA to your own

name, and start the distributions in the later of the following year, or the year you are 70½ years of age.

If your spouse had not started withdrawing the minimum distributions, then you basically have three choices:

1. You can roll the IRA into your own name and treat it as if it were your money, for it now is. This means that you can continue to make contributions to it if you qualify to do so. This, in my opinion, is usually the best option, especially if your late spouse was older than you.
2. If you keep the IRA in your deceased spouse's name, you must start taking the money out of this IRA either by December 31 of the year your spouse would have turned 70½ or December 31 of the year after your spouse died, whichever is later. If your spouse was much younger than you and you wanted to defer the money for income tax purposes as long as possible, then this is the option you would choose. The other option available to you if you keep the IRA in your spouse's name is to withdraw the money over the next 5 years (not recommended), or make periodic withdrawals over your life expectancy.
3. You can withdraw the money in a lump sum. I would not suggest doing this, since depending on the amount of money in the account, the taxes could be substantial.

Most people roll over their late spouse's IRA into their own name, for this really gives you the greatest number of options. This decision is important, however, because all the money in a traditional IRA is generally money on which tax will be owed upon withdrawal, and the tax consequences must be considered. Please consult your tax advisor for help with this.

If someone other than your spouse leaves you an IRA, then your choices will also depend on whether or not he or she had begun taking the minimum distributions.

If the owner of the IRA had already begun to take withdrawals under the minimum-distribution rules, you have no choice. You must continue making withdrawals based upon your own life expectancy. Of course, you can also take out more than the minimum, but then you might have quite a tax bill on your hands.

If the owner of the IRA had not started taking minimum distributions, then you have two choices:

1. By December 31 of the fifth year after the owner's death, the entire IRA account must be swept clean. You must take all the money out of the account by that date. This option is NOT recommended.
2. You can take out a minimum amount of money each year, calculated to your life expectancy, beginning no later than one year after the IRA owner's death.

ROTH IRA

Starting in 1998 a new IRA, called a *Roth IRA*, was introduced. In my opinion, if you qualify for one, get it. There is more confusion on how the Roth IRA works than on almost any other savings vehicle I have ever seen, and it does operate quite differently from the traditional IRA. Below is all the important information that you will need to know about the Roth IRA.

What is the major difference between a Roth IRA and a traditional IRA?

With a traditional IRA (if you qualify), you are permitted to deduct your yearly contribution from your taxes. With a Roth IRA, you are not. However, forgoing the tax write-off gives the Roth IRA a tremendous advantage over the traditional IRA. With a traditional IRA, your money grows tax-deferred until you take it out, at which time you have to pay ordinary income taxes on the money. In a

Roth IRA, the money grows tax-free, meaning when you take it out, in most circumstances you will not pay a penny of tax on that money. Ever. In my opinion, that is a huge advantage.

Do all the withdrawal rules of a traditional IRA apply to the Roth IRA?

No—big no—which is another reason a Roth is so good. Everything is different. For instance, let's say you were to put $3000 a year for the next 3 years into your Roth IRA, for a total of $9000. Then something happened, and you needed the money. Guess what? Regardless of your age or how long the money has been in there, you could withdraw, tax-free and penalty-free, any or all of your $9000 contribution. You read that right. Even if you were 35 years of age and you needed that money, you could take out your original contributions anytime you wanted, without any taxes or penalties for early withdrawal. Very few people understand this. What you do have to leave in the Roth IRA for more than 5 years *and* until you are 59½, are the *earnings* that your original contributions have generated. Let's say that over the past 3 years you have put $2000 a year in the Roth, and now that money has grown to be worth $6500. You can take out your original $6000 anytime you want, without facing taxes or penalties, while the $500 that your contributions have earned must be kept in there for more than 5 years *and* until you are 59½ years of age to avoid taxes and penalties. The 5 years start ticking for the earnings portion of the account from the first day of the year that you open the account and put in your first contribution. If you take out those earnings prior to meeting those two conditions, you will have to pay taxes on the money you withdraw, plus a 10 percent federal early-withdrawal penalty tax if you are under 59½ years of age, and possibly a state penalty tax as well.

What does "more than 5 years" mean?

When it comes to Roth IRAs, 5 years does not necessarily mean 5 years! The 5 years starts from the first day of the year that you make a contribution for. Suppose that you make your first contribution to a Roth IRA on April 15, 2002, and this contribution is for the 2001 year. The 5 years will start from January 1, 2001. You already have counted more than 1¼ years, and your money hasn't even been in the Roth IRA for one day! In this case, 2002 is the SECOND year, 2005 will be the FIFTH year. So "more than 5 years" will occur in the beginning of 2006, which is less than 3¾ years after your first contribution.

Is there a way to avoid the 10 percent penalty on a Roth if I need to take out money before I am 59½ years of age?

Please note that in most cases you will not have to worry about this 10 percent penalty, since most of your money will be coming from your contributions, which you can take out penalty- and tax-free at any time, regardless of age. However, if you want to access your earnings before the age of 59½, the exceptions to this early-withdrawal penalty for a Roth are the same as those for a traditional IRA, as noted earlier (see pages 362–64). This holds true for withdrawing money from a Roth conversion as well.

I am 54 years of age and I want to put money in a Roth IRA every year for the next 5 years, but I want to take it all out when I am 60. Will I be penalized because not all of the money has been in the IRA for 5 years?

No. Remember, you can take your original yearly contributions anytime you want, without worrying about taxes or penalties. As to earnings, the time clock starts with the very first year you make a contribution, or the year, really, that you opened up your Roth. So if you open a Roth IRA and put money in every year when you are 55, 56, 57, 58, and 59, all of your yearly earnings, even though they have not physically been in the account for 5 years, will be dated as if they were in there from the time you opened the account. In this case, all the money in your account will be considered to have been in there for the 5 required years, and you will not have to pay taxes or a penalty if you take out all your money when you turn 60.

If I am covered by a pension plan at work, can I contribute money to a Roth IRA?

Absolutely. Even if you have maxed out on your 401(k), if you meet the income qualifications for a Roth IRA, you can contribute the full amount—and if you're smart, that is exactly what you will do. With a traditional IRA, if you are covered by a pension plan, you can contribute, but you may not be able to deduct the contribution from your taxes. This does not apply with a Roth, since you don't take a deduction under any circumstances. Technically, having a pension at work has nothing to do with being able to have a Roth IRA. But contributing to a 401(k) can actually help you meet the income limits mentioned below, since contributions to a 401(k) reduce your MAGI.

Can anyone have a Roth?

There are income limits and phaseout limits, just as with the traditional IRA, but the MAGI amounts are different. If you are single and your MAGI is under $95,000 a year, you can contribute the full amount to a Roth IRA. The limit starts to phase out as your income increases, until it is gone completely once you have an MAGI of $110,000 or more. For a married couple filing jointly, the starting MAGI is $150,000, phasing out at $160,000.

What is the limit that I can contribute to a Roth IRA?

The limit is the same as a traditional IRA, including the additional amount that a person over the age of 50 can contribute. The limit is $3000 for 2002 for most people. It is $3500 for those who have celebrated their 50th birthday before the end of the year. See the chart on page 357 for the limits for other years.

Can I contribute to all three of these retirement accounts in the same year: a 401(k), a Roth IRA, and a traditional IRA?

Yes. The only thing you have to remember is that the total money that you can put into IRAs, regardless of the kind, is the IRA limit for that year. So, for 2002, you could max out your 401(k) and put $1000 in a traditional IRA and $2000, in a Roth IRA—or any dollar combination you want, as long as the total amount contributed for 2002 is not more than $3000 for that year.

I am covered by a pension plan at work and make too much money to qualify for a deductible IRA. I also make too much to qualify for a Roth. Is there a retirement account for someone like me?

Lucky you! You have the option of opening a *nondeductible IRA*. Basically, a nondeductible IRA is identical to a traditional IRA except that you cannot deduct your contribution. I would encourage you to do this, even without the benefit of the immediate deduction, since you'll still enjoy the benefits of tax-deferred growth and the ability to buy and sell funds without worrying about year-end capital gains distribution tax.

Can I have as many Roth IRAs as I want?

Yes, just as you can have as many traditional IRAs as you want. In the same way, you have to watch out for the custodial fees. The more Roths you have, the more expensive it could be.

I have three different Roth IRAs at three different custodians into which I've contributed a total of $6000. One has $3000 in it, one has $2300, and the third $2100. I am only 42 years of age, and I need to take $3000 to pay for an unexpected bill. What is the best way to withdraw my money without paying taxes or penalties?

The simplest way is to withdraw the $3000 from the account that has $3000 in it. Even though this account has $1000 of earnings in it and theoretically you are not allowed to touch that part of the money for 5 years and until you are 59½, it does not work quite that way when you have more than one Roth IRA. You see, the IRS knows that you have contributed $6000, in different Roth IRAs. That $6000 is considered your contributions. The way the actual law reads is that the first money coming out of a Roth IRA will be considered your contributions, and contributions are never taxed or subjected to penalty. The next money that comes out of a Roth IRA after all contributions are withdrawn is considered your earnings. For you to withdraw earnings penalty and tax-free, you have to be 59½ or older, and the account has had to be active for more than 5 years. Since the IRS aggregates all your Roth IRA accounts and considers them one for tax purposes, in your situation if you were to take all $3000 from one account, they would consider that withdrawal part of your $6000 contribution and therefore not charge you taxes or penalties.

Do I have to start making distributions from my Roth when I am 70½, the way I do with a traditional IRA?

No. This is another feature that makes a Roth so attractive: You never ever have to take distributions from your Roth if you do not need or want the money. You can enjoy watching your money grow tax-free for the rest of your life if you want. You can also continue to make contributions to your Roth after the age of 70½ if you have earned income or taxable compensation, which you cannot do with a traditional IRA.

When I die, will my beneficiaries owe income tax on the money that I leave them in the Roth IRA?

No. Regardless of who your beneficiaries are, if the 5-year holding period is met, the Roth will pass down to them tax-free, very different from the traditional IRA, from which your beneficiaries will sooner or later have to withdraw the money and pay taxes on it.

Let's say that you have $200,000 in your Roth IRA and you are leaving it to your daughter. You make a deal with her that when you die, you want her to withdraw that money immediately and pay off the mortgage on her home so you know that she will always have a roof over her head. When you die, she does just as you wished and cashes in your Roth. Since no income taxes are owed on this money, she takes all $200,000 and pays off her mortgage per your wishes. If this had been a traditional IRA and she had withdrawn all the money at once, depending on her tax bracket, she most likely would have owed around $75,000 in state and federal income taxes, leaving her with only $125,000. Do you see why a Roth can make a huge difference to your beneficiaries?

Since the money in the Roth IRA is not income taxable to my beneficiaries, can I give them the IRA now to get the growth out of my estate for estate tax purposes?

Nice try, but the IRS says no, you cannot do this.

Will my beneficiaries have to pay estate tax on the amount they receive from my Roth IRA?

That will depend. Under current IRS law, a married person can leave as much money as he/she likes to the surviving spouse without incurring any estate tax, as long as the surviving spouse is a United States citizen. Even if you have one billion dollars in your Roth IRA, if your beneficiary on that account is your spouse, when you die, he/she will not have to pay any estate tax whatsoever on it.

If, however, your beneficiary is anyone other than your spouse, and you have an estate that is over the current estate tax exemption (please see chart below), then your beneficiaries may very well owe estate tax on the money in your Roth IRA. Estate tax rates start at 37 percent and go as high as 50 percent. This is true for the traditional IRA as well.

Estate tax combined with income tax can eat up a huge percentage of an IRA that you are leaving to your beneficiaries. With a traditional IRA, your beneficiaries are going to have to pay not only income tax on this money but also, if your estate is large enough, estate tax.

Please note: If the value of your estate is greater than the amount indicated on the chart below, please see an estate lawyer to investigate any options that you can put into place while you are alive to help alleviate the estate tax burden.

Estate Tax Exemption

If the value of your entire estate is greater than the amount indicated below (and you do not have any estate tax planning trust set up), then your beneficiaries (other than your spouse) will owe estate taxes on the money that they are inheriting. Estate taxes are due 9 months after the date of death.

2001	$675,000
2002	$1,000,000
2003	$1,000,000
2004	$1,500,000
2005	$1,500,000
2006	$2,000,000
2007	$2,000,000
2008	$2,000,000
2009	$3,500,000

Is there any way to avoid huge estate taxes?

Digressing from the subject of IRAs for a minute, there is a way, if you are married, to save your beneficiaries lots of money in estate taxes. The way to do this is by taking the time, while you and your spouse are alive and still married, to set up what is known as a *tax planning, credit shelter, AB, or marital trust*. All four of these names pertain to the same kind of trust. When a credit shelter trust, let's call it, is set up, you can in effect shelter *double* the estate tax exemption amounts that are listed in the chart above. In 2002, for instance, with this trust you could leave your beneficiaries $2,000,000 before they would have to pay any estate taxes. In the year 2004 you could leave them $3,000,000 and in the year 2009 you could leave them $7,000,000. As you can see, over the next few years the estate tax exemption is rising, and so, therefore, is the amount that you can leave estate-tax-free with one of these trusts.

If you had an estate worth about $2,000,000, which you were leaving to beneficiaries other than your spouse, and you did not have a credit shelter trust set up, your beneficiaries would owe about $435,000 in estate tax. With a credit shelter trust, they would owe nothing.

If your estate warrants it and you set this trust up now, your beneficiaries may not have to pay estate taxes on the money they inherit from you. I urge you to look into this kind of trust if you have $1,000,000 or more in assets in 2002. If you are reading this book in later years, use the dollar amounts listed for the appropriate year as guidelines.

Please remember, credit shelter trusts are available only for married couples, and the cost of creating one should be anywhere from $1000 to $2500. If you would like to learn more about them, please see *You've Earned It, Don't Lose It* or books from Nolo Press, which cover the subject at length.

Be careful not to make the assumption that a credit shelter trust will automatically shelter your Roth IRA or your traditional IRA from estate taxes, because it may not. If your IRA makes up the majority of your assets and you have $1,000,000 or more in 2002, please see a tax-planning attorney as soon as possible.

CONVERSIONS

Even though many people have written about conversions, there still seems to be a tremendous amount of confusion about whether you should convert from a traditional IRA to a Roth and how conversions really work.

How do I know if I can convert my traditional IRA to a Roth IRA?

Anyone can convert a traditional IRA to a Roth IRA, as long as your MAGI is $100,000 a year or under in the year the funds are paid from the traditional IRA.

If I am married, and my spouse and I file joint tax returns, is that a MAGI of $100,000 a year for each of us?

No. The IRS does not care whether you are married or single; your *joint* MAGI must be $100,000 or under. This is one tax instance where it does not help to be married, because a single person makes out better here.

I have just turned 70½ and I want to convert my IRA to a Roth. My only problem is that if I take my mandatory contribution out this year, it will put me over the MAGI of $100,000. Since by law I can wait till April 1 of the year after I turn 70½ to withdraw that first contribution, would you advise doing that so my MAGI would be $100,000 or under?

Definitely not. First of all, remember, if you do that, you will be double-taxed the next year on your withdrawals, since you will also have to take out that year's mandatory withdrawal by December 31. More important, the IRS has stated that if you decide to convert your traditional IRA to a Roth IRA in the year you turn 70½, then *you cannot wait until April 1 of the following year*. You have lost that opportunity, and you must take your distribution by December 31 of the year you turn 70½. After you have taken your distribution, then you can convert for that year if your MAGI is still $100,000 or under. *Distribution has to come before conversion.*

If I convert to a Roth, when are the taxes due?
They will be due when you file your tax return for the year in which you converted.

Do I have until April 15 to convert to a Roth?
No. You have to take your money out of your traditional IRA by December 31 of the year you are converting, but you then have 60 days from December 31 to get those funds into a Roth.

What are the rules that govern a converted Roth IRA?
They differ from the rules that govern a contributory Roth IRA in just one way. The amount of money that you converted must stay in the account for a full 5 years before you can withdraw it without paying any taxes or penalties. This is a very important fact to know. Let's say that it is 2002, you are 35, and you convert $10,000, paying the income taxes on it in that tax year. As long as that $10,000 stays in the Roth for a full 5 years, you can take out any or all of it without any penalties or additional taxes. So even though you will be just 40 years of age at that time, in 2007, you will not have to pay any early-withdrawal penalty tax to get that money out, and you will not have to pay taxes on that money. The earnings, however, have to stay in the account for more than 5 years *and* until you are 59½ before you can take them out without taxes or penalties.

Let's say you converted $10,000 from your traditional IRA into a Roth IRA, and 5 years later your Roth account is worth $14,700. At the beginning of the 6th year, you could withdraw that $10,000 without taxes or penalties, regardless of age; it's the $4700 that you have to leave in the account until you are 59½ *and* for more than 5 years. If you take the earnings of $4700 out before these two conditions are met, you will pay a 10 percent federal early-withdrawal tax penalty and a state tax penalty, if applicable.

Do I have to convert all of my money, or can I convert just some of it?

You can convert as little or as much as you want. For some reason, many people think that it has to be an all-or-none situation, but it's not. If you have $100,000 in your traditional IRA and you feel the taxes on that would be too much to convert all at once, then you could convert any amount of that $100,000 that you wanted, as long as you met the MAGI requirements of $100,000 or under for that year.

If I want to convert my traditional IRA to a Roth, what's the easiest way to do it?

The best way is simply to open a Roth account at the same place you have your current IRA (assuming you are happy there) and have them convert your account from a traditional IRA to a Roth. Before you do this, make sure that they allow converted Roth accounts to be recharacterized and reconverted, in case you need to do so for tax purposes. If they do not, you might want to think twice about doing business with this firm. If that were the case, I would convert my IRA to a Roth with that firm and then I would transfer my Roth to a firm that allowed me to recharacterize and reconvert.

If I want to convert my IRA to a Roth but I have only a little time before the end of the year to do it and I do not want to use the firm I have my traditional IRA with, what is the fastest way to get my money transferred so I can make sure I meet the deadline?

Probably the best way to handle this would be to do the conversion at the firm where the account is now, and then move the new Roth IRA to the new firm. Alternatively, you can move the traditional IRA first and then convert it, but you may not have enough time.

Most firms will do broker-to-broker or trustee-to-trustee transfers quickly. You can also, just to be sure, go down to your old firm and withdraw your money from your traditional IRA. You have 60 days from that point to put the money into a Roth IRA conversion account (or, for that matter, even into another traditional IRA) before you will owe taxes and a possible early-withdrawal penalty on it. If you hold stocks or mutual funds within the traditional IRA, and you need to do this quickly, you might have to sell your investments so you can simply get a check to transfer. You do not have to worry about income taxes when you sell your investments, since the money is in an IRA and sheltered from capital gains, but you might get hit with a surrender charge or interest penalties, or have to give up a sales load that you already paid on a mutual fund, so please check all the financial ramifications carefully before you do this. It would be far wiser not to get yourself into this situation. Also, be aware that sometimes a firm will charge you a fee to close an account. Make sure you ask.

Please note that money taken out of an IRA is not required to have the 20 percent tax withheld, as is the case with 401(k) and other qualified pension plans at your place of employment, so do not let them withhold any money.

Can I convert my IRA to a Roth and then use that same account to make yearly Roth IRA contributions?

Absolutely, provided you still meet the MAGI requirements for the yearly contributions.

Can I convert my 401(k) to a Roth IRA?

Not directly. You first have to roll over your 401(k) into a traditional IRA, usually after you leave the job with the 401(k), and then you can convert from a traditional IRA to a Roth.

If I am self-employed, can I convert a SEP-IRA (simplified employee pension plan) to a Roth?

Yes, and this is something you might really want to think about. By using your SEP-IRA, you could get far more than $3000 a year into a Roth. Let's say you are single, your MAGI is just under $95,000 a year, and your computed SEP-IRA contribution is about $12,400, which you fund with pretax dollars. Now let's say, too, that before the end of the year you convert your SEP-IRA to a Roth IRA. Can you do this? Yes, because your MAGI is under $100,000 a year. Let's see what we have just accomplished. You now have $12,400 in a Roth IRA account. Yes, you will owe taxes on that $12,400 after you convert to a Roth, but that will be offset by the fact that in the same year you will take that $12,400 off your income as a SEP-IRA deduction. In effect, we have just found a way for self-employed people to put more than 4 times the allowable $3000 yearly limit for most people, or $12,400, into a Roth IRA, to grow tax-free rather than tax-deferred. Please note that the amount one can contribute to a SEP-IRA is directly related to how much money you make, so see a tax advisor to determine your allowable contributions.

My MAGI is under $100,000 a year, but because I received an inheritance from my parents I have a substantial net worth, about $5,700,000, including $700,000 in my IRA. Most of my inheritance money is tied up in real estate and is not liquid. I don't want my kids to have to pay as much in estate taxes as I had to pay. Does it make sense for me to convert to a Roth?

Yes. If you are in a situation where you know that your beneficiaries will be paying estate taxes and you qualify as far as the MAGI requirements are concerned, then I have to tell you that I think converting to a Roth is a great thing to do. If you convert to a Roth, the money that you will pay in income taxes will essentially be money on which your children will not have to pay income or estate taxes. Think about this: If you convert the

$700,000, most likely you will owe about $250,000 in income tax and, depending on your state, maybe another $75,000 in state income taxes. That is a total of $325,000 that you will have to pay out in taxes to convert, which means you've just reduced your estate by $325,000, to $4,675,000 ($5,000,000 minus $325,000). Now, for illustration purposes, let's assume you die right after you do this. Because you paid the taxes and your kids did not inherit that $325,000, they would owe, in 2002, $2,113,300 in estate taxes.

If you had not converted to a Roth, all $5,000,000 would have been left to them and the kids would have owed $2,113,300—or $2,275,800 more—in estate taxes. Now, at first glance that seems like a good deal, but remember, in order to save that $162,500, the kids inherited $325,000 less. That doesn't look so great, but keep watching.

The big difference is this: In a Roth IRA, all the money—or in this case $700,000—is income-tax-free to the kids. Since most likely they will need all $700,000 to help pay the estate taxes, that money can be withdrawn from the Roth, tax-free.

If the money had been left in a traditional IRA and they had to withdraw the funds in one lump sum, they would owe income taxes on that money to the tune of about $325,000. What do you know—it's the same amount Dad had to pay! The only difference is that since Dad paid the $325,000 in income taxes, the kids didn't have to pay estate taxes on that money. So when all is said and done, Dad truly saved his kids $162,500.

You happen to be lucky, for most people who have this kind of money also have a MAGI of more than $100,000 a year, so they cannot take advantage of this planning tool. However, please have a tax professional run the numbers for you to make sure a decision like this makes sense for you.

RECHARACTERIZATIONS
AND RECONVERSIONS

I converted my IRA to a Roth, and since doing so the value of
the Roth has gone down considerably. Is there anything that I
can do to reduce my tax liability to the IRS?

Yes. You have until October 15th of the year after the year of
the original conversion to *recharacterize* your conversion.
When you recharacterize, you move your money from a Roth
back to a traditional IRA. Then you can *reconvert* back to the
Roth at the later of the year after the year of the original conversion, or more than 30 days after the recharacterization. For
example, in 2002 you converted your traditional IRA to a Roth
when its value was $50,000. Therefore, you owed taxes on that
$50,000. Let's say you are in the 28 percent tax bracket. That
means that you'll owe $14,000 in taxes on that conversion by
April 15, 2003. A few months later, your portfolio in your Roth
IRA decreases in value to $30,000. You can take advantage of
this decrease by recharacterizing the Roth and moving the
money back into a traditional IRA. If you recharacterize on or
before December 1, 2002, you can reconvert any time in 2003,
assuming your MAGI in 2003 is $100,000 or under. If you
recharacterize after December 1, 2002, you cannot reconvert
until the 31st day after the recharacterization.

It is almost the deadline for recharacterization, and I want to
recharacterize a Roth IRA. Can I take the money out of the
Roth myself and put it back into a traditional IRA to make
sure I meet the deadline?

No. Recharacterizations must be done by a transfer from trustee
to trustee. You cannot take the money out yourself and put it
back into a traditional IRA.

What if I converted to a Roth for this year, and then I find out

that I have made over the $100,000 MAGI limit, but it is
already the year after I converted—now what?

As long as you are within the time frame allotted to do so, there
will be no problem. You have until October 15th, as long as you
timely file your taxes (including extensions) to recharacterize your
account back to a traditional IRA. So if in 2002 you converted your
traditional IRA to a Roth IRA, and then you find you have more
than $100,000 in MAGI for the year, you can recharacterize the
account back to a traditional IRA up to October 15, 2003.

Let's say I recharacterize my Roth back to a traditional IRA
because the value has gone down, with the intent of reconvert-
ing back when I am permitted to do so. By the time I am able to
reconvert back, the value is even higher than it was when I
originally converted. Can I use the older value?

No. Once you recharacterize your Roth, in order to reconvert
you have no choice but to use the new value of the account the
day you convert back to a Roth. Be careful when you do this,
because you could end up paying more in taxes. For instance,
let's say that when you converted your traditional IRA to a Roth
IRA, your account was worth $100,000. A few months later, it is
worth $85,000. Rather than paying taxes on $100,000, you
decide to recharacterize your Roth, or change it back to a traditional IRA with the intent of converting back at the lower value
of $85,000 when you are permitted to do so. So you undo your
Roth, transfer the money back to your traditional IRA, and then
reconvert back to the Roth at a later date. When you are ready to
reconvert, your IRA is now worth $110,000. Guess what? You
will now owe taxes on $110,000, and there is nothing you can
do about it, unless you want to recharacterize again, and wait
until the next year to reconvert.

If the value of my account has gone down even more since I
reconverted to a Roth, is there anything else I can do?

You can always, if you want, recharacterize back to your traditional IRA again. It may be worth doing this if the decline has been dramatic. But be careful here, for you do not want to find that you've recharacterized your Roth and waited till the next year to reconvert again only to find that the value of your account is even higher than when you did all this in the first place, and it will cost you more to now convert the account to a Roth IRA.

So here it is 2002. You have reconverted your IRA to a Roth, an account worth $30,000, which is the amount you will owe taxes on. A few months later, your Roth is worth only $20,000. Yikes! If you wanted, you could recharacterize the account, but you could not reconvert back that same year. You might want to do this and wait until the next calendar year to convert back to a Roth, for it could save you lots of money in taxes if the value of your account stayed for a time at that lower value. But if the account has grown $40,000 by the time you are permitted to reconvert, you will owe more taxes on the reconversion.

What happens if I converted to a Roth, made more than the $100,000 of MAGI, and am not able to meet the deadline to recharacterize the account because the trustee of my account took too long to transfer it back?

You have the problem, not the trustee. The IRS will charge you a 6 percent *excess tax* on the amount of money that you put into the converted Roth. That 6 percent penalty will be charged every year that the money stays in the Roth IRA, so get it out of there as soon as possible. They will also charge you ordinary income tax on this money in the year you converted, as well as the 10 percent early-withdrawal tax if you are not 59½ or older. This is not something that you want to take lightly. So please make sure you give yourself lots of time to do this if you think your MAGI might be over the limit. The trustees or custodians of your Roth may not work as quickly as you want, so don't wait till the last minute to do any of these recharacterizations.

Summary

What are some of the guidelines I can use to decide if I should convert or not? Is there a Web site that can help me with this?

This is not always an easy decision to make. There are financial calculators available on the Internet to help you. Among these, my favorite site is www.rothira.com. This site is the best up-to-date site bar none when it comes to the rules and decisions that have to be made about Roth IRAs. That said, here are some guidelines to help you make your decision, assuming that you meet the MAGI limitations:

1. If you were planning to draw upon the funds in your IRA account to pay the taxes you would owe the IRS upon converting to a Roth, do not convert. Convert only if you have an alternate means of paying that tax bill.

2. If the money that you are thinking about using to pay the taxes on the conversion is currently in an investment that you will need to sell, and that sale will cause you to incur capital gains, it may not make sense to convert.

3. If you are currently getting Social Security and you convert, will the additional income make your Social Security taxable for that year? Do you care?

4. If you have only a few years before you retire and you know that you are going to need to live off the money that is in the IRA, then most likely it does not pay to convert.

5. If you have many years before you retire and you have the money outside the IRA to pay the taxes for the conversion, then most likely it makes sense to convert.

6. If you think that you will never need to use the money that is in your IRA as you get older and would like to pass it down tax-free to your beneficiaries, and you have the tax money to pay for the conversion, then you should most likely convert.

7. If you have a lot of money and you know that your beneficiaries are going to pay a huge estate tax, then you should convert if you can meet the MAGI limitations.

8. If you have just a few years till retirement, or you have retired and are under 65 years of age, but you have no need for any of the money that is in the IRA, then you should most likely convert.

9. If you have money in a nondeductible IRA that hasn't seen great earnings, you are actually a better candidate for conversion than someone with a traditional IRA. In this case, you've *already* paid taxes on your contributions, so your taxable income (in the year of conversion) will be increased only by the amount of your earnings. If your earnings have been substantial, however, do the tax calculation before you convert.

10. If you are currently in a low tax bracket and know that you will be in a higher one in retirement, then you should most likely convert.

11. If you have named a nonprofit organization or a charity as the beneficiary of your traditional IRA, then you should think twice before you convert. Your estate's beneficiary will not have to pay taxes on this money when you die, so it may not be worth it for you to do so. Make sure you have someone run the numbers on this before you do anything.

Bottom line: Which do you think is better, a Roth IRA or a traditional IRA?

I have run the numbers every which way: high tax bracket in your earning years and lower bracket when you retire; lower bracket in your earning years, higher when you retire; and last, the same tax bracket during your earning years and your retirement years. In all cases, I have assumed low, medium, and high rates of return on the money in the IRA. I have assumed you invested your tax savings from your traditional IRA and I have assumed you didn't; I assumed different lengths of time the money was in the account; and I assumed different ways of withdrawing the money. Sometimes the winner was the Roth IRA and sometimes the winner was the traditional IRA, but then I realized how crazy this all was and that really, in my mind, there is only one way to go if you can, and that is with the Roth. Let me tell you why. In life we can make as many assumptions or plans as we want, calculate everything to the nth degree, but in the end none of us knows what is going to happen to us in the next five seconds, let alone thirty years from now.

So for my money I decided why not go with the few things that I do know are for certain in our lifetime: taxes, death, and uncertainty.

1. The fact that you can take out your contributions to a Roth IRA at any time, without taxes or penalties, regardless of your age and of how long the money has been in the account—important factors not true with the traditional IRA—makes the Roth the winner here, because the Roth removes some of the uncertainty from the what-ifs of life. For instance, let's say you are 45 years of age, something happened that you were not planning for, and you desperately needed to get your hands on some money. If you had money in a Roth IRA, you could access some of the money, maybe even all of it, without having to pay taxes or a penalty. This would not be true with a traditional IRA. A lot of advisors will read this, and say, yes, that is one of the downfalls of Roths—it's *too* easy to get the money out. I have to disagree. When people are in financial trouble, if they have any money in their traditional IRA they will take it out regardless of the taxes and penalties. What a pity that people in financial difficulty have to give up so much in taxes and penalties when there's a way to avoid them in the first place, by having a Roth.

2. There is no way to predict what tax bracket you will be in when you start withdrawing some of this money. I remember a

time not so very long ago when many people were paying 50 percent and higher when it came to taxes. Why not take the uncertainty out of this situation and know that no matter what happens, the money in your Roth will never be subjected to income taxes? The traditional IRA cannot do this for you.

3. There is also no way for us to know whether we will actually need the money from our IRA as we get older. With a traditional IRA, you have no choice. You have to take it whether you want to or not when you reach 70½. What a shame to have to withdraw money from your IRA, pay taxes on this money—which could possibly put you in a higher tax bracket and subject your Social Security to taxes—and give up the privilege of letting your money compound without tax consequences. With the Roth, if you don't need the money, you never have to take it, but if you do, no harm done; you still don't have to pay income taxes on it at the time of withdrawal.

4. Again, many advisors as they read this will say yes, yes, but if you were to use a Roth instead of a traditional IRA, you would be giving up the current tax deduction and the growth on that money over all those years. To this I have to say, it is true you will be giving up the tax deduction, but I just don't buy the second part of that assumption. I don't know one person (that does not mean they are not out there, however) who has ever taken the money they saved on their taxes from their IRA deduction and invested it. It doesn't work like that in real life. When most people put money in an IRA, they just pay less in taxes. They do not get this amount refunded, so it is not as if they see the money. For those who do get a tax refund, usually that refund money is spent on a vacation, on a credit card bill, or on something fun; people rarely invest it. If you are reading this and are a diligent exception, I still say that the other reasons I have cited override this one. *Bottom line:* I would much rather know that I was never going to have to pay taxes on the earnings of the money in my retire-

ment account than get a deduction now and have total uncertainty as to what the future taxation of that money will look like.

5. Even though we do not know for sure that our destiny will be one that allows us to enjoy our older years, there is a good chance that many of us will. What is uncertain, however, is what our financial situation will be like twenty or more years from now. Will we suffer an illness that requires special care, thereby costing more money? Will one of our children need extra financial help? Will we be the victim of a con game and lose all our money? Or will Mother Nature take away our home in a flood, mudslide, earthquake, fire, hurricane, or tornado? There is no way for us to know these things. Why not take some of the uncertainty out of the future and know that you can access some of the money in your Roth IRA without having to worry about taxes and penalties? Know that no matter what happens later on in your life, what you see in your Roth is yours.

6. When you're just starting out in a career is the hardest time to invest—yet the most important. If you are just out of college, working at an entry-level salary, and can manage—somehow, anyhow—to invest $3000 a year in a Roth, then it could change your future big time. Remember, you may be earning more money later and be ineligible for a Roth, so here's why you should do it now. Let's say that beginning at age 22 you invest $3000 in a Roth for the next 15 years, a total investment of $45,000. And let's say that after that, you are making too much money to qualify for a Roth, so you just let the money sit there until you turn 65. At age 31, at the end of the 15 years that you put money into your Roth, if your money earns 9 percent, you will have $88,000 in this account. *Tax-free money*. By the time you turn 65, if your money continues to earn an average return of 9 percent, you will have $983,000. All this money was created from investing $3000 a year starting at age 22, for just 15 years. No matter how much

you make later on, this will be a wonderful nest egg—and all tax-free. I urge you to start now.

If you had done the exact same thing using a traditional IRA, you would have paid about $450 less a year in income taxes for those 15 years because of the tax deduction, and you would have the same amount of money in the end in your account, but it would all be 100 percent taxable when you withdrew it. Big difference. And you wouldn't be able to withdraw it without incurring penalties until you were 59½.

Just for those skeptics out there, if I were to assume that you took your tax savings of $450 a year and invested it for those original 15 years at an average return of 9 percent and then, assuming the same rate of return (and ignoring taxes over all those years), you kept that money invested until you were 65, you would have $148,000. Let's say you cashed in everything at the age of 65. In the Roth, assuming that 9 percent return, you would have a total of $983,000. In the traditional IRA, including the deduction money you had been investing after taxes, you would have a total—after state and federal taxes (at, say, 38 percent)—of about $757,000. That is a $226,000 difference. The skeptics might be saying that they would never cash in everything at once! And that is most likely true. However, if you are going to compare apples to apples, since we could cash in the Roth IRA all at once (and not suffer any tax consequences), we have to assume we could do the same with the traditional IRA. The above shows the advantage of a Roth IRA based upon $3000 per year being contributed. Now that the limits are increased, the Roth IRA is an even better deal!

7. Since death is a certainty, I would want to know that my beneficiaries are going to be able to get some or all of the money in my IRA tax-free. There is no way of knowing for sure whether your beneficiaries will be in a high tax bracket or a low one when you die. Let's say they are in a high one and

that this distribution comes at a time that's disastrous for them with respect to taxes. There goes a nice chunk of your money to Uncle Sam. Or what if they are in horrible financial shape, and they need to get their money right away? With a Roth, they will be able to do so and not worry about income taxes—not true with the traditional IRA.

The one element about the Roth IRA that has always bothered me is that people with an MAGI of more than $110,000 if they are single and a combined MAGI of $160,000 if they are married cannot contribute to one at all. This is not true with a traditional IRA. You can make oodles of money and still contribute to a traditional IRA, and deduct the contributions from your taxes if you are not covered by a company pension plan. Even if you are covered by a company pension plan and make oodles of money, you can still contribute to a traditional IRA; you just cannot deduct your contribution from your taxes. If you look at the rules that allow someone to convert a traditional IRA to a Roth without penalties, you will see that only people who have an MAGI of $100,000 a year or under are allowed to do so.

Have you ever wondered why the rules were set up like this? I have. What this says to me is that on some very strange level Congress does not want people who have a lot of money to be able to utilize these accounts, since the Treasury can get more money out of them in the long run if they force them to use a traditional IRA. If this in fact is true—and there really is no way of knowing for sure, since it is just my assumption—I would march myself out and get a Roth as fast as I could. You see, one day you may be one of those people who can no longer qualify for the Roth. If that becomes the case, you will be thrilled about whatever money you were able to put into one, accumulating tax-free.

There are not many politicians that I can say truly changed our financial lives for the better while they were in office, but I can tell you this—Senator William V. Roth, Jr., for whom the Roth was named, did just that. Thank you, Senator.

PART VI

THE COURAGE TO BE RICH

THE COURAGE TO CONNECT TO THE WORLD

Do you remember being taken on family outings as a child and coming home hours after you were usually tucked in bed? Do you remember how it felt to curl up on the backseat of the family car, marveling at the way the moon followed you and seemed close enough to touch through the car window? Now try to remember your first visits to the zoo, and how the wild animals paced up and down, never meeting your eyes. Did you wonder what the animals were looking at, or did you know, instinctively, that their gaze was locked on the bars that formed their cages—bars that shut them in and cut them off, and that, after years of pacing, were all that they could see? The world outside was nothing but a blur.

This second memory has a bearing on how many of us live with our finances now. For the most part, what we focus on is the money we don't have. We lock our gazes on the things that we don't own, can't buy, can't afford to do. We feel caged by what we lack. We feel trapped by our debts, if we have them, particularly by credit card debt, which clings to us like the stale, clammy air of the animals' cages. And we peek out at the world as if we were looking through the bars of a bad deal.

If there's one message I want to convey to you, it's this: Your debts may be real, but the cage they seem to create is not. It's imaginary. The bars are made of thoughts, feelings, and actions; and new thoughts, feelings, and actions can dismantle them. Your childhood perception that the moon was yours for the grabbing was remarkably close to the truth. There's more to the sky than can be seen through a cage or a window. To find out how much more, all you have to do is step outside.

It's amazing to discover how powerful you become as the prison of unconscious, self-defeating thoughts, words, and actions dissolve. I've seen the results again and again. As soon as people begin to view their resources in a new way, their energy increases. The future appears brighter. Their faith in themselves gets surer and stronger. Waking up in the morning feels more joyful, and so does looking in the mirror. So does looking at the world outside.

Once the clouds of folklore, misconception, and fear are dispelled, you're free to take action on your own behalf. Little by little, you will find that you can repair your mistakes, enjoy your blessings and opportunities, plan for the future, and protect loved ones in an almost instinctively apt way. You can meet the material challenges of the different stages of life—and discover the pleasure of doing so. And although you may simply be taking small, obvious steps to look after your own well-being and that of those you love, a marvelous thing will be happening along the way. Whether you realize it or not, with each right-minded action you'll be bringing yourself more directly in line with the nature and energy of money.

The nature of money is to be put to work. Once you've freed yourself from the constraints of self-defeating thoughts and actions, it's time to draw upon your growing strength and send your money into the world. This is not exactly like sending a child to college, but it's close: When you contribute money to a cause you believe in, you extend your resources for the world's betterment. Why is this important? When you achieve a clear awareness of your own financial power and potential and put that awareness into careful practice, the day arrives when the only debts you carry are debts of gratitude. Everyone knows what gratitude is. It is a conscious combination of thankfulness, joy, and humility, a pronounced sense that you've been lucky, been blessed—and been aided. Haven't you ever wanted to say to someone who has done you an important favor—a person who has seen you through a time of intense emotional trouble, for example, "Thank you. I'm indebted to you"? Didn't you want to extend yourself to that person in return? When we're grateful, most of us are eager to give something back, something valuable. It's no different when it comes to your money. The key is to be grateful all the time.

Having the courage to be rich means counting your blessings as well as your pennies, and sharing your wealth with the world.

THE SPIRIT OF GIVING

In the last few years, one of my greatest joys has been helping to raise money for PBS, the American Public Broadcasting System. My work with PBS came about unexpectedly but very naturally. For years before I wrote my first book, *You've Earned It, Don't Lose It*, I'd been explaining to clients how I discovered the importance of giving—by writing a check to PBS. In *The 9 Steps to Financial Freedom*, I told the story in print. Shortly after the book came out, a PBS executive called and asked if I'd be willing to take a more active role. I was happy to agree. Before I knew it, I was traveling around the country, helping public TV stations—large and small, rural and urban—meet their operating budgets for the year by asking for contributions on the air. It was an incredible experience. The stations got the money they needed (in what turned out to be among the most lucrative PBS fund-raisers ever held) and I got the chance to watch firsthand the whole intricate, fascinating process of people giving and receiving money.

I'd be the last person in the world to deny that money is a tangible, practical commodity. You can touch it and trade it, accumulate it and waste it, just as you can with any of earth's natural resources. But money is also energy. Like electricity, it is attracted, harnessed, and repelled by the conditions it encounters, especially by the way people treat it. That fact was brought home to me hundreds of times during my PBS tour.

Here's an example. Before every broadcast, I'd find the person in charge of fund-raising for that particular station and—no matter how large or small the station, or what part of the country it was in—I'd ask an identical, single question: "What amount of money would you like to raise tonight—what amount would make your heart sing?" You'll notice I didn't ask how much we had to raise, and I didn't ask for a figure out of the wild blue; I have learned to be very careful about the language I use. In every instance, the amount named was exactly the amount we raised. It was uncanny. And instructive.

I particularly remember one station in a large eastern city. The first year, we broke every record. Our team of volunteers raised $200,000. Instead of behaving like paupers begging for a handout, we acted, and felt, as if we were creating that amount of money together—the pledge drive manager, the local volunteers, the viewers, and I. The experience was breathtaking. The next year, I went back to the same manager and put the same question to her—"What amount of money would make your heart sing?" But this time, she was afraid to ask for what she really wanted; that last year was just fluke. To my amazement, she asked for less than a third of what we had raised the year before. I tried to reason with her. "Don't you understand?" I asked. "People out there aren't giving you money. You are drawing it to you. If you can remain open, you'll receive everything the station needs." But I could tell that I wasn't getting through to her—in spite of the evidence of the previous year, she thought she wasn't powerful enough to affect the outcome of such a big, impersonal event. She asked for very little—and that little was exactly what we raised.

What is your relationship with giving and receiving? Is it possible that you, too, are standing as an obstacle in your own path?

EXERCISE

Over the course of the next two weeks, make a list—as complete as possible—of everything in life you're grateful for. Then pick a day and make a secret resolution to say yes to every single reasonable request that comes your way—including, if you live in a city, giving a quarter to everyone on the street who asks you for money, saying yes to a colleague who requests help on a project that's not your responsibility (and for which you'll get no pay or credit); contributing time and merchandise to a rummage sale at your children's school; and performing any other good deed that is within your power to do. (By the way, this doesn't include buying the latest Barbie or PlayStation for your kids.) Finally, at the end of the day, sit down and write out at least one small check—in an amount you think is suitable, even if it's tiny—to a charity that seems worthwhile and that has solicited your help through the mail.

During this one day, please pay very strict attention to the feelings you have as you work to help others in whatever way they feel they need. Is it hard for you to suspend judgment—do you find yourself thinking, Why can't that homeless person find a job, and, Why can't Jimmy's school ask someone else to volunteer? Do you feel embarrassed, inadequate, resentful, or overwhelmed? If you do, take note: Here are the old feelings of fear ("They're taking advantage of me"; "If I give away money, I'll never be able to retire"), shame ("I'm not sure I can come up with a good idea for that project"), and anger ("*I've* never asked anyone for help!") that lie to us, isolate us, and keep us from being everything we can be in the world. When those feelings come up, take out your gratitude list. Look at it. Say a silent prayer of thanks, and then just do it.

WHOSE WORLD IS IT, ANYWAY?

Every action you take is an offering to the world. When you litter, you make an offering of unsightliness and clutter; when you hold a door open for a stranger, you offer goodwill and an unobstructed path to future acts of kindness. Courtesy in daily affairs is a cumulative offering of good faith and goodwill. Curtness is an offering of discord, impatience, and aggression.

You tell the world who you are a thousand times a day. But that's not all. The world receives your gifts, whatever they may be, and sends them right back to you. Your thoughts become words. Your words become actions, and your actions have an effect from one person to another. Thoughts and actions become habits, often bad ones. The problem with negative thoughts and heedless actions isn't simply that they can result in a bad outcome—a traffic accident because you're anxiously speeding through a yellow light, say. In a sense, each of us creates the world over and over again, a thousand times a day.

In this respect, you can live a rich life or a poor one, and it won't make one bit of difference whether you have a lot of money or none at all.

Or, as someone I know once said, As long as you're creating your world, why don't you make it a great one?

LAW OF MONEY

When you open your hands to make an offering, your hands will always draw the goodness of the world back to you.

CULTIVATING ABUNDANCE

What does money give you? In many ways, it gives you your place in the world. It gives you your home, your work, the chance to travel and have new experiences, your ability to live a healthy life.

I urge you give some of the money you bring in back to the

world—freely, out of gratitude, with no expectations or ulterior motives. Something wonderful happens when you do this. You allow the richness and abundance of the world at large to find a place within yourself.

I ask you to consider giving money away every month. Whenever there is a flow of money into your life, even if it's only a trickle, send a proportionate amount of money out.

There's a very good reason why you should do this—and it's not simply that you want to aid the causes you believe in, although that's important. You will never become rich if poverty consciousness governs your actions. If you dread paying bills and feel depressed and inadequate when you face financial obligations, you are cultivating a poor demeanor. And that's what the world will see and reflect back to you. You cannot feel poor or powerless when you are writing a check to charity. If you do this consistently every month as you pay your bills, you will be cultivating a frame of mind that is expansive, decisive, and ready to receive. You will feel more powerful as you mail your checks, and you will find yourself thinking richer thoughts. You are able to do something to help.

The world will take note and, as a result, more will come your way. This phenomenon is like breathing in and out. If try to hold on to the air you take in, saying, "This air is mine!" the body will force you to exhale—or die. Money is energy. Energy, like breath, has to move in two directions. Please don't give in order to receive, but know that, in one way or another, a gift will always be returned.

HOW MUCH SHOULD I GIVE?

Donations are the lifeblood of every religious and charitable organization. Our offerings keep goodness circulating in many concrete forms. In fact, the world would be unrecognizable, unimaginable, without the tangible benefits that charitable contributions create and convey.

Most people realize this. Just about everyone participates in some form of giving, if only on special occasions. But how many of us do it regularly? How many take a good look at what we have and, feeling obliged to give something back, seriously contemplate how much we should give? Not many, I have found. Fewer than you might imagine.

Statistics show that America is not a nation of openhanded givers—certainly not a nation that gives away the traditional 10 percent of income that most religions suggest. In 1995, 69 percent of the households in America did give money to charity—clearly a majority. But take a closer look. The rate of giving was highest in households with incomes of less than $10,000 a year: they gave 4.3 percent of their income. Among households with incomes in the range of $40,000 to $50,000 a year, the level dropped to 1.3 percent. Giving rose again in households whose income is $100,000 or more; but, at 3.4 percent, the proportion of income these folks gave away was still significantly less—almost a whole percentage point lower—than that of people making less than $10,000.

These numbers confirm an old truism of philanthropy, which is that people who have less give more. But the numbers do little to help you and me decide how much to give. Even knowing what middle-class households give isn't much help. Each of those households is unique, with its own set of resources, concerns, values, and obligations. Personally, I don't believe there is a formula that works. After all my years of helping people with their money, I have concluded that fixing the amount of our giving is something each of us must do alone. Yet it must be a respectful amount—respectful to ourselves and to our sense of gratitude. I am all for giving as much as you can—not a penny less and not a penny more.

JULIA'S STORY

I always knew I wanted to be an attorney. I was lucky when I went to law school, because back then, when women first began gaining ground in the legal profession, there weren't so many of us, and everybody wanted (or had) to hire female attorneys. I was the first woman to make partner at my firm. I've always been pretty hard-driving, a workaholic, but to a great extent I've had to be. I travel a lot and I'm hardly ever at home, but I don't feel deprived, because I love my work. And how could I complain, when I'm so well compensated? I make two hundred thousand dollars a year and don't spend a lot of it. I have money invested in the market and in retirement accounts.

Recently, when I went to see a new accountant to prepare my taxes, she asked me about charitable deductions. I had given very little. I felt so embarrassed. She didn't say anything directly; she simply explained that charitable donations make a great deduction and said I ought to look into finding some organizations to give to. But I knew what she was thinking. Here I was, making all this money, and I hadn't given more than the five hundred dollars I donated in honor of my uncle when he died. I don't think that I'm greedy or selfish; it's just that I'm so busy that I never stop to think about giving in any organized way. It was never an issue in my life.

GIVING TOO LITTLE

In spite of her salary, her savings, and her high-powered career, Julia is anything but rich. By her own admission, she has a single-track life. She's lucky that she loves her work and is well paid for it. But notice how easily she was embarrassed by her accountant's reaction to her stingy giving. What that tells me is that beneath her assured exterior is a person living uncomfortably with herself.

If you hold on too tightly to what you have, if you hoard, then money is not all you're accumulating. You're building a wall between you and the world and limiting your own ability to expand in new directions and receive new gifts.

L E S L I E ' S   S T O R Y

We weren't doing all that well before, but once I lost Sam, my husband, three years ago, things went from bad to worse. After the medical bills and the funeral expenses, I never caught up. I make thirty thousand dollars a year, but the thing is that I also have twenty-five thousand dollars in credit card debt. I've always been a spender, but now I've stopped that and am spending only on necessities—and still, I'm just trying to stay afloat. Sam and I bought a new car shortly before he got sick, and it's been repossessed. I put our house on the market, and once it sells, I'll move in with my daughter to save money, but I'll be lucky if I get enough money out of it to pay off the mortgage.

In desperation, I made an appointment with an attorney I found in the phone book to ask about declaring bankruptcy, but that's as far as I got; I ended up canceling the appointment. It's such a small town, you know. I'd be mortified if anyone found out.

I don't know what I'm going to do. I look at my bills, and I can't figure out how I can live any more cheaply. I shut off the lights every time I leave a room, and sometimes I build a fire in the fireplace to heat the house so I can save on my gas bill. I never eat out or go to the movies. The only good thing is that I still manage to give two hundred fifty dollars a month to my church. I haven't missed a payment yet!

GIVING TOO MUCH

I can't tell you the number of letters I've received telling stories like Leslie's, from people who haven't a penny to their names, are close to declaring bankruptcy, and yet are still giving ten percent a month, month in and month out. Is this pleasing to God? Is it what God wants from His congregation? I have to tell you, I don't think so.

I have not traveled the world as widely as some, but wherever I have gone I have been struck by one thing. God's dwellings—the churches, temples, synagogues, mosques—exist everywhere and, more often than not, they are magnificent structures. Even in the poorest regions of our world, God dwells in splendor, or at least in relative splendor compared to the conditions ordinary people live in. Now, I know that many of these temples and mosques were built by the wealthy, as expressions of gratitude, and that is inspiring.

Yet when I see these beautiful structures standing amid squalor and deprivation, I can't help thinking about people like Leslie, and it makes me wonder. How can it please God for you to give more than you can afford? Do you really believe that God wants you to live with the anxiety that comes from being unable to pay your bills? For your children to live in need while His own house is gilded? Does it ever occur to you that, in a way, you are obliging God to work twice as hard to take care of you? And that it is not only a deity who sees your suffering, but your family and everyone who loves you? Also, frankly—and as painful as it may be to admit—when you are in debt and give more than a small, respectful amount every month, you aren't giving your own money. You're giving your creditors' money.

Hearing stories like Leslie's, I think back to the difficult time in my life when I, too, went into debt to put up a front for my friends and colleagues. And again, I start to wonder. Are people in this position giving away money they so desperately need out of a religious spirit? Or are they giving to save face in the community? I want to ask them straight out, "Are you afraid to admit that you're not making it? And with all your hard work and worry and struggle, don't you sometimes wake up in the middle of the night so angry that your bones ache?"

So here we are again, nose to nose with fear, shame, anger, and guilt, those corrosive emotions that the spiritual traditions of India call "the thieves of the heart." Chances are that these are very old feelings, as we discussed earlier. It takes time, patience, and courage to work through them. But I think you are probably selling your fellow parishioners short. They would probably honor and support your efforts to get your affairs in order.

When giving has been your pride and joy, it takes courage to give less than you usually do, and less than you would like to. But try looking at the situation in a new way. Think of the extra money you now will have to pay your debts as a gift from God, to help you when you need it most. With God's help, you may be able to pay one additional bill each month and so, instead of feeling burdened, will have one more reason to feel grateful. As a matter of fact, consider that the answer to your prayers may come in this form; seen this way, the offering you don't make this month may actually be a divine helping hand.

LAW OF MONEY

*You must give to feel richer,
never to become poorer.*

Nowhere is it written that you must be poor in order to be spiritual. Too many people struggle with the notion that there is something intrinsically wrong with wanting or pursuing money. I believe the opposite is true. The more you have, the more good you can do—for your loved ones, for your community, for the causes you hold dear, and for the world at large.

What is a respectful amount of money to give every month? The answer is different for each of us. If you are in a situation of financial stress and strain, the right amount may be five or ten dollars a month. If you have more than you need to pay your bills, build for your future, and support and protect your family, the amount may be much, much more.

Whatever the amount you decide to give, make your contributions from the heart. Choose a meaningful sum.

GIVING THE RIGHT AMOUNT

When you don't have a lot of money, writing a check to a charity or a cause that you believe in can require strength and courage, and the gift you may get in return is a new sense of freedom and personal control. As your income grows, though, it can be hard to write commensurately larger checks—to keep adding the right number of zeros to the amount you give and stick resolutely to the principle of giving away the same generous percentage of your income every month. For instance, if you are making $60,000 a year, it can be a feat to write a check for $500 every month, but it can be done, and you will feel enhanced by your action in ways you cannot predict. It may be even harder to write a monthly check for $2,000 when you are making $250,000 a year, or to give away $20,000 a month if you are making $2,500,000 a year. Suddenly, 10 percent can seem enormous.

WHAT MY CLIENTS TAUGHT ME

A few years ago, I had a client who had suddenly become very successful in television. His face was famous. People loved him. After a decade of odd jobs and shabby apartments, he was earning enough money each year to last him a lifetime. He was a nice guy and close enough to the years of struggle to feel grateful, effortlessly. He wanted to give something back. So he found a cause that meant something him personally, because of an incident of illness in his family; and he began to host benefits for a research foundation that specialized in that disease. One day, I asked him if he also gave money to the foundation. He said no. "You ought to," I told him. "You can afford to now." He didn't agree. "I'm giving my time. Time is money. And my name— that's worth a lot. That's enough. I don't have to give dollars." There it was, however faintly: the sour note of trying to hold on too tightly. In the midst of good fortune, he felt more fear than gratitude. He couldn't bring himself to part with his money. In the course of time, that same reluctance began to creep into his professional life. He played it safe on screen and hit a ceiling in the kinds of roles he was offered. He couldn't move on.

It was shortly after I had that conversation with my actor friend and client that I received this letter from a young artist named Pamela.

PAMELA'S STORY

I have to say, I'm the last person who ever expected to make any money. I'm an artist, and I always thought that being an artist meant being poor. And it did for a long time. All through my twenties and thirties, I was poor. But after an influential critic singled out my work in a group show, it began to sell—then really sell. After two decades of toiling away in virtual obscurity, I was picked up by an important gallery and given my own show. It was incredibly exciting— living out the dream I'd nurtured back in art school. A lot of the pieces sold even before the opening! At that point, the money started rolling in.

At first, I just spent it. I bought a house, a car, clothes, until that started feeling pretty empty. It actually felt kind of weird, having so much more money than I ever expected I would. I didn't like this "art star" thing. It came with a sort of heavy feeling, like being off balance, and I didn't like the work I was producing. My gallery started getting anxious; I was feeling all this pressure, and nothing seemed to make me happy. I began to think that the money was really getting in the way of my life. I had to restore the balance.

One day I was leafing through a financial magazine in my dentist's office and I came across an article about giving money, and for some reason it felt as if it had been written just for me. I've always supported certain causes, fifty dollars here, fifty dollars there, but now I began to think that since I had more, I should give more. I began giving money away every month. Don't misunderstand—I wasn't reckless. I kept plenty and invested plenty. But I decided I could do more. The first check I wrote was for five hundred dollars; that felt scary, but I sent it. Not long after, I sold a painting for more money than I ever had before; so I sent a check for a thousand dollars. I really felt exhilarated about that, but also, in a funny way, more in control. I know it sounds odd, but I really began to feel better about my work, and my work got better—other people could see it, too.

Last year for Christmas I opened college funds for my two nephews, which gave me an incredible feeling of power, and then I began to understand something. It's true that money is power but, as with any kind of power, you have to use it the right way. That's where the balance comes in, for me anyway. Keep too much, and you weigh down your side of the scale. Let go of some, and you will feel released.

Do you see the lesson here? Every charitable act enhances you, without diminishing what you have. What happened after Pamela's first big donation? She sold a painting for more than she ever had before. She did not give in order to get something back. If she had, it would have been a business transaction, and succeeded or failed in those terms. (This happens all the time. Lobbyists make donations to political campaigns and businessmen donate wings to hospitals or universities, and they want something specific in return. They may want influence, fame, or immortality. It does not matter; they're looking for a specific return on their money, and the benefits they receive will be limited, bound by their expectations.)

A pure offering of gratitude comes back to you in unpredictable, often invisible ways. Pamela's second contribution restored her sense of inner harmony, which appeared in her work, her family life, and her finances. She found the courage to be rich.

Even if you find it difficult to give, your duty is to overcome your internal resistance and give as much as you can without harming yourself financially. If your offering has been thought through, shows reverence for the world, and expresses an appreciation for all that you have, you have chosen the right amount. You have joined in the flow of abundance. You have offered a gift sincerely and will be rewarded a thousand times over in the quality of your life. Rich thoughts, rich words, rich actions, rich offerings. With those elements in place, you are living a rich life indeed.

CHAPTER 22

THE COURAGE TO BE RICH

If you are a professional athlete, your achievements are apparent in your numbers—the number of goals you scored in today's game, compared to yesterday's; how long it took you to run your last mile; whether you were over or under par; and, bottom line in today's world, what you are paid for your achievements. If you manage other people's money for a living, you measure your professional worth by the return you earn for your clients and how much those returns net for you. If you remain in a single job or profession, year after year, you measure your performance by the money you earn, by how quickly your practice or division is growing, and by how profitable your products or services are. It's very tempting to let such numbers define success or failure for us, both in our own minds and in the eyes of the world. There are other achievements that we all respect and cannot quantify in numbers. We admire the inspired teacher and the caring doctor. We value the spirit and generous heart of a vital human being, wherever we encounter them—in a coworker or a corner grocer, in a salesperson or a neighbor. At least, we try to. On the whole, though, if we're not careful, our self-worth and our net worth become bound together so tightly that we can barely tell them apart. This is what I make and have, therefore this is who I am. I can buy everything I want—I am a success. I can't make ends meet—I am a failure. This one is richer than I am, that one isn't doing as well as I am . . . and on and on. We know that there is something wrong with this thinking and something missing from our lives, but we don't know what.

S U Z E ' S   S T O R Y

The courage to be rich: I have it, but where did it come from? I think about my mom and my dad, and everything they tried to do—succeeding in some ways, failing in others. Their example is a great part of my strength. Even though they often didn't have much hope, they had courage; and like most parents, they always did the best they could for my brothers and me.

Like most parents, too, they sent us all kinds of mixed messages. And like most kids, my brothers and I ultimately had to find our own way in this world. And we have.

I have written before about working for many years after college at the Buttercup Bakery, how comfortable I was there, and how unimaginable a better life seemed. But then, through a combination of circumstance and timing and blind chance, a better life (or so I imagined) presented itself to me. I was offered a job at Merrill Lynch and later, an even better job at Prudential-Bache, and I said yes both times. What is harder to remember and write about is how terrifying those moves were. How petrified I was to walk through those doors. I was afraid to be found out—I was little Suze Orman, without a standard credential to her name.

I have to tell you, I have always been much more afraid when I was trying for more than when I was settling for less.

From Wall Street I moved on to trying to set up my own financial firm and was nearly destroyed—and I was scared all the way. For the longest time, every expansive action I took made me feel not richer but poorer, smaller, more vulnerable. I felt like retreating so many times—but I never did. I kept going.

I have often wondered what gave me the courage to keep moving on. The answer, I think, is that I was also pursuing a spiritual journey, and that is how I learned that I am stronger than my fear. Like all of us, I was trying to earn money, as much money as I could; but I also wanted to find meaning, to make the money I earned for myself and others matter.

There are those who will say that there is no emotional or spiritual content to money, that the point of money is only to make it, invest it, and spend it, and that it is foolish to ask more of money than that. This view is what I believe is foolish. It is much too limited. When I became an investment adviser, the way I saw people dealing with money was infinitely more complicated than that. So I studied the ancient scriptures of different traditions and attended classes, seminars, and retreats; and I began to thread what I was learning into my work.

Finally, I began to understand the spiritual principles of abundance and how they apply to money. I saw that in order for money to bring true wealth, it cannot simply pass in and out of your hands; it must also pass through your heart. Let the financial naysayers scoff as they will. I have met plenty of people with lots of money who could never be called anything other than poor; I have also met people with far less money who lead lives that can only be described as rich. I don't mean to suggest—not for a moment—that I don't think money is important. It is. I believe money is so important, in fact, that, if you can get your financial house in order, many other kinds of wealth will follow you right inside.

There are certain principles, both subtle and concrete, that can help you do this. I have called them the Laws of Money and they are the backbone of this book: valuing people over money and money over things; putting money in the right

*place—in your heart and in your investments; turning toward
your money, not away from it, and then turning a part of your
money toward righteous causes, regularly and in appropriate
amounts. I truly believe that if you adhere to these principles,
you will get the most out of your money. But will that be
enough to make you feel rich? And if it isn't, what will?*

YOUR EXERCISE

Find a time when you won't be disturbed and settle yourself in a place
you like, a place where you feel completely comfortable and will not be
reminded of the chores and other issues clamoring for your attention.
Go to a park, if you like. Or sit on the sofa. Take the phone off the hook
and turn off your cell phone. And have a pencil and a pad of paper with
you.

Now, when you're settled, think of a moment in your life during
which you were really happy, when you felt full, whole, totally content.
What moment was it? Sift through all your memories until you find one
that's special, one that you love. Relive it for a while. Let the experience wash through you and, when it is really vivid, ask yourself this:
Where did it come from? How did you get there?

Go a little further now. Ask yourself why you didn't remain in that
state of happiness. What was it that took you out of the moment, and
why? Why do we have these feelings for only moments at a time? Why
aren't there days, years, lifetimes when we feel this way? What makes
them happen? And why do they go?

SPIRITUAL ABUNDANCE

The answer may not be apparent at first. Without knowing your particular circumstances, however, I bet I can give you a clue. All I have to
do is ask, What thoughts were you thinking? What words ran through

your mind that broke the spell? Was there something that someone said, or something you wanted to say? Did whatever it was make you feel angry? Small? Frightened?

Abundance is not only a matter of what you have or how well you manage what you have. Abundance is also an inner condition. Abundance is spiritual wealth, and to be rich inside yourself also takes courage.

A few years ago, I was visiting with a friend whose father had recently died. She told me that at the end of his life her father had often spoken about a certain day when, for a moment or two, he had felt completely contented. He was a man who loved to play golf and, on that day, he was on his way home from an afternoon on the links. The sun was setting. He knew his wife and daughters were at home, that dinner would be ready when he got there, and that they would all sit down together. And it happened—pure, uncomplicated, indescribable happiness. He never forgot that afternoon, and when he talked about it at the end of his life, my friend said, the sweetest and most wistful expression came over his face. That drive home was one of the best memories of his whole life. Why? Because, for a moment, he was thinking only rich thoughts. Nothing was missing for him. Nothing interrupted or suppressed his enjoyment. He was rich. If only he had turned that moment into a lifetime! If only he had known how!

Once you begin to understand, really understand, how your thoughts create your inner reality, and how that reality spills into your world through your words and your deeds, then you are on your way to transforming them, and yourself. In order to live a life of material and spiritual abundance, everything about you must be in harmony. It's funny—I used to think that spiritual pursuits took place in private, removed from the hubbub of the larger world. But now I believe that's not so. Our souls are on display every day. Rich or poor, we all make our daily offerings. We leave a much deeper imprint on the world than we know.

Just as there are laws of money that apply to the creation of material riches, there are other laws—laws of life—that, if you follow them, can—and will—fill your life with spiritual wealth. These laws are like signposts, little Post-it notes that help you to remember what you can so easily forget. They are important: I've learned that the hardest thing to do in life is to remember, and the easiest thing to do is to forget. We forget how to treat people well, and we forget to think great thoughts about ourselves. The laws of life are there to remind us of who we are, were, and always will be—rich beyond our wildest dreams.

I ask you to take the laws of life, as well as the laws of money, with you on your journey as you create a life of material and spiritual abundance. Always hold them close.

THE FIVE LAWS OF LIFE

1. *May every thought that you think be etched in fire in the sky for the whole world to see, for in fact it is.*
2. *May every word that you say be spoken as if everyone in the world can hear it, for in fact they can.*
3. *May every deed that you do recoil on top of your head, for in fact it will.*
4. *May every wish that you wish another be a wish that you wish for yourself, because in fact it is.*
5. *May everything you do be done as if God Himself is doing it, for in fact He is.*

Life is a journey. If you open yourself up to the journey's possibilities, it can take you to places you've never dreamed of. A rich life doesn't necessarily drape you in cashmere and cover you with gold.

You may not travel first class, but that doesn't mean that you won't arrive at a first-class destination. You need never measure yourself against anyone else. Your journey is your own.

May you always have the courage to think great thoughts and relish small treasures.

Suze Orman

VALUABLE RESOURCES

◆

Here are some excellent additional sources of information on some of the subjects covered in this book.

> *The Overspent American: Upscaling, Downshifting, and the New Consumer* by Juliet B. Schor (Basic Books, 1998)
> *Legal Affairs: Essential Advice for Same-Sex Couples* by Frederick Hertz (Owl Books/Henry Holt, 1998)
> *100 Questions Every First-time Home Buyer Should Ask: With Answers from Top Brokers Around the Country* by Ilyce R. Glink (Times Books, 1994)
> *Maximize Your IRA* by Neil Downing (Dearborn Trade, 1998)

And let's not forget my favorite Web sites!

http://www.wallstreetcity.com offers free stock quotes as well as research on stocks—almost any information you need regarding stocks you can find here. For instance, you can even ask the site to select stocks that meet your specific criteria and it will generate information and create charts based on your request.

http://www.investorama.com is run by financial journalist Douglas Gerlach, author of *The Investor's Web Guide: Tools & Strategies for Building Your Portfolio* (Ziff Davis, 1997). This site lists information on eight thousand on-line financial sites.

As I also mentioned in the book, I love to listen to Bob Brinker, whose show on ABC radio airs from 4–7 P.M. EST on Saturdays and Sundays, and I also love to visit his Web site, http://www. bobbrinker.com, which includes active on-line discussions and investment advice. Bob Brinker's knowledge is encyclopedic, and as of the writing of this book, his predictions about the current market have been right on the money. This is the man who will take the theories you find in financial books and show you how to put them into play. In my opinion, Bob is one of the greats.

Finally, I'm also a fan of http://www.quicken.com. Like their personal finance software, this company's Web site features on-line calculators and interactive financial formulas to help you crunch your numbers.

INDEX

◆

ABOUT THE AUTHOR

♦

Suze Orman is the author of the *New York Times* bestsellers *The 9 Steps to Financial Freedom, The Courage to Be Rich,* and *The Road to Wealth,* and the national bestseller *You've Earned It, Don't Lose It.* The personal finance editor for CNBC and a financial contributor to NBC's *Today,* she is also a contributing editor to *O: The Oprah Magazine.* The three PBS specials that she wrote, co-produced, and hosted are among the network's most successful fund-raisers ever. A Certified Financial Planner® professional, Orman directed the Suze Orman Financial Group from 1987 to 1997, and before that was vice president of investments for Prudential-Bache Securities and an account executive at Merrill Lynch. A sought-after speaker who has lectured widely throughout the United States and South Africa, Suze Orman has been featured in *Newsweek, The New Yorker, The New Republic, USA Today,* and other publications, and has appeared numerous times on *Larry King Live* and *The Oprah Winfrey Show.* She lives in California.